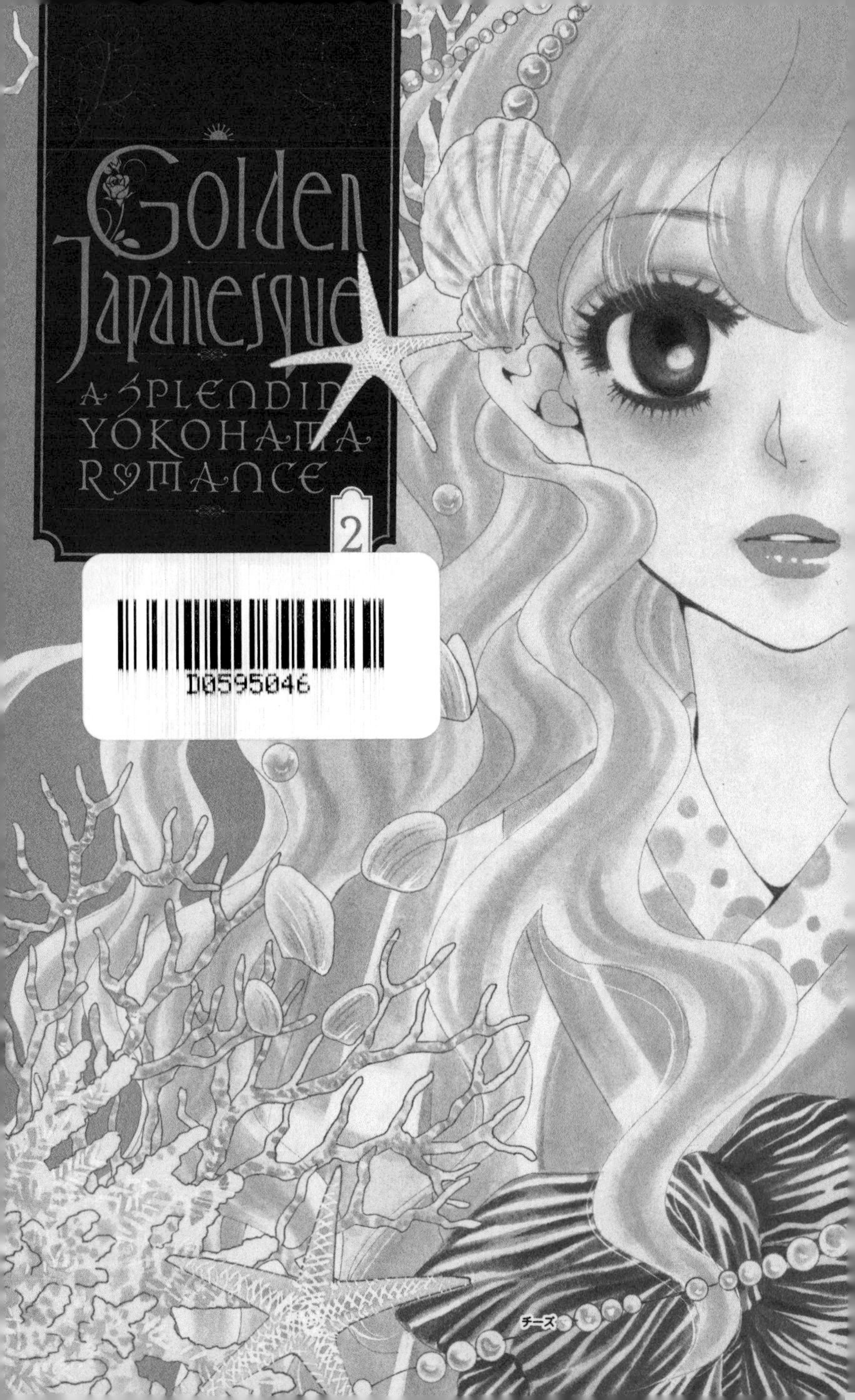
Golden Japanesque
A Splendid Yokohama Romance
2
チーズ

Golden Japanesque
A Splendid Yokohama Romance

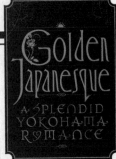

Characters

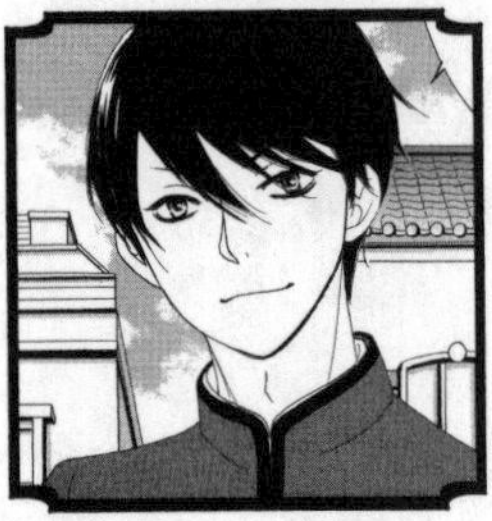

Rintarou Mayuzumi
Age 15
The son of the wealthy family that lives in the Western-style mansion where Maria's mother works. He saw Maria's true hair and eyes but didn't make fun of them.

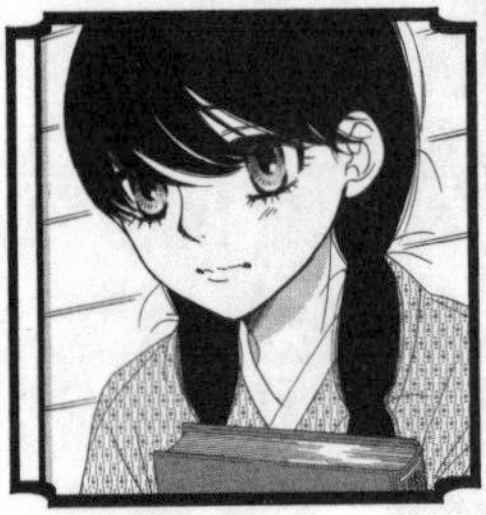

Maria Natsume
Age 16
Her father was foreign, and she doesn't even know his name. She hides the fact that she doesn't look like other people, always keeping her head down. She's particularly good at handicrafts.

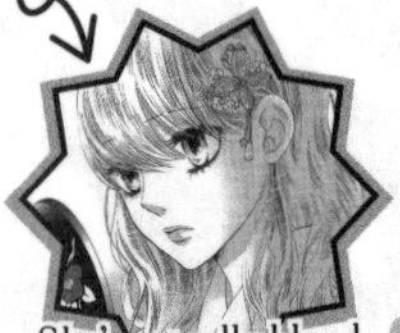

She's actually blond with blue eyes.

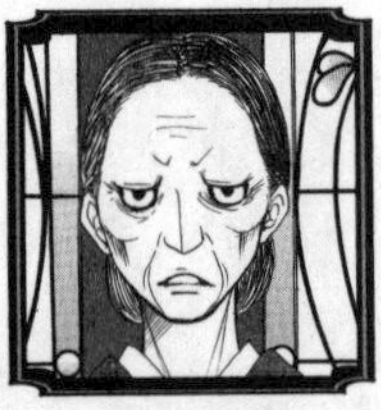

Kisaragi
The Mayuzumi family housekeeper. She's quietly protecting Rintarou and Maria.

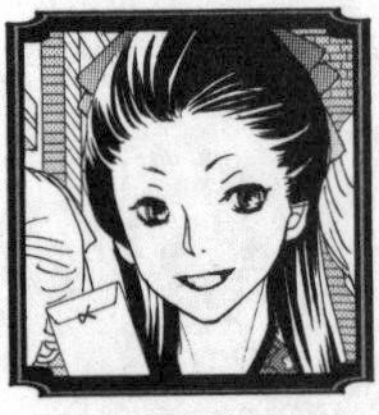

Yuriko Hatakeyama
The daughter of a good family. She's attracted to Rintarou, and gave Maria a letter for him.

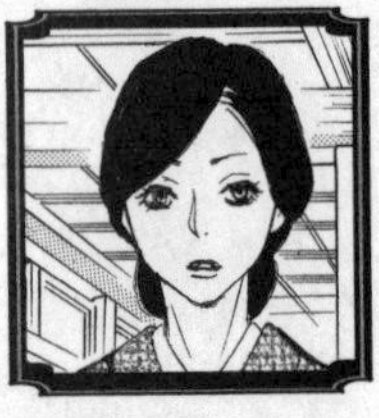

Sachie Natsume
Maria's mother. She's suffered discrimination along with Maria.

Story

◆ Maria always hid the blond hair and blue eyes she inherited from her father. Her mother had strictly trained her not to stand out so she wouldn't be targeted for discrimination, and she got through her days by keeping her head down.

◆ One day, she met Rintarou, the son of the distinguished family that employed her mother. Every time they met, Rintarou pranked and teased her. Not only that, but when it started raining while they were together, he ended up seeing what Maria really looked like. But then he said "You're like the Little Mermaid..."

◆ Rintarou gave Maria a beautiful imported hair ornament shaped like a butterfly because he said it matched the color of her eyes. However, Maria's mother thought she'd gotten it through indecent means, and she told her to return it.

◆ When Maria tried to give the hair ornament back, Rintarou told her not to hold herself in contempt, and he refused to take it. On top of that, when Maria's mother came to pick her up, he explained that he was the one who'd given her the hair ornament and that he wanted her to accompany him to a party held by his family.

◆ Maria went home with her mother. However, she couldn't seem to get Rintarou—who was spiteful, yet kind, and always true to himself—out of her mind...

Golden
Japanesque

A SPLENDID
YOKOHAMA
ROMANCE

2

Contents

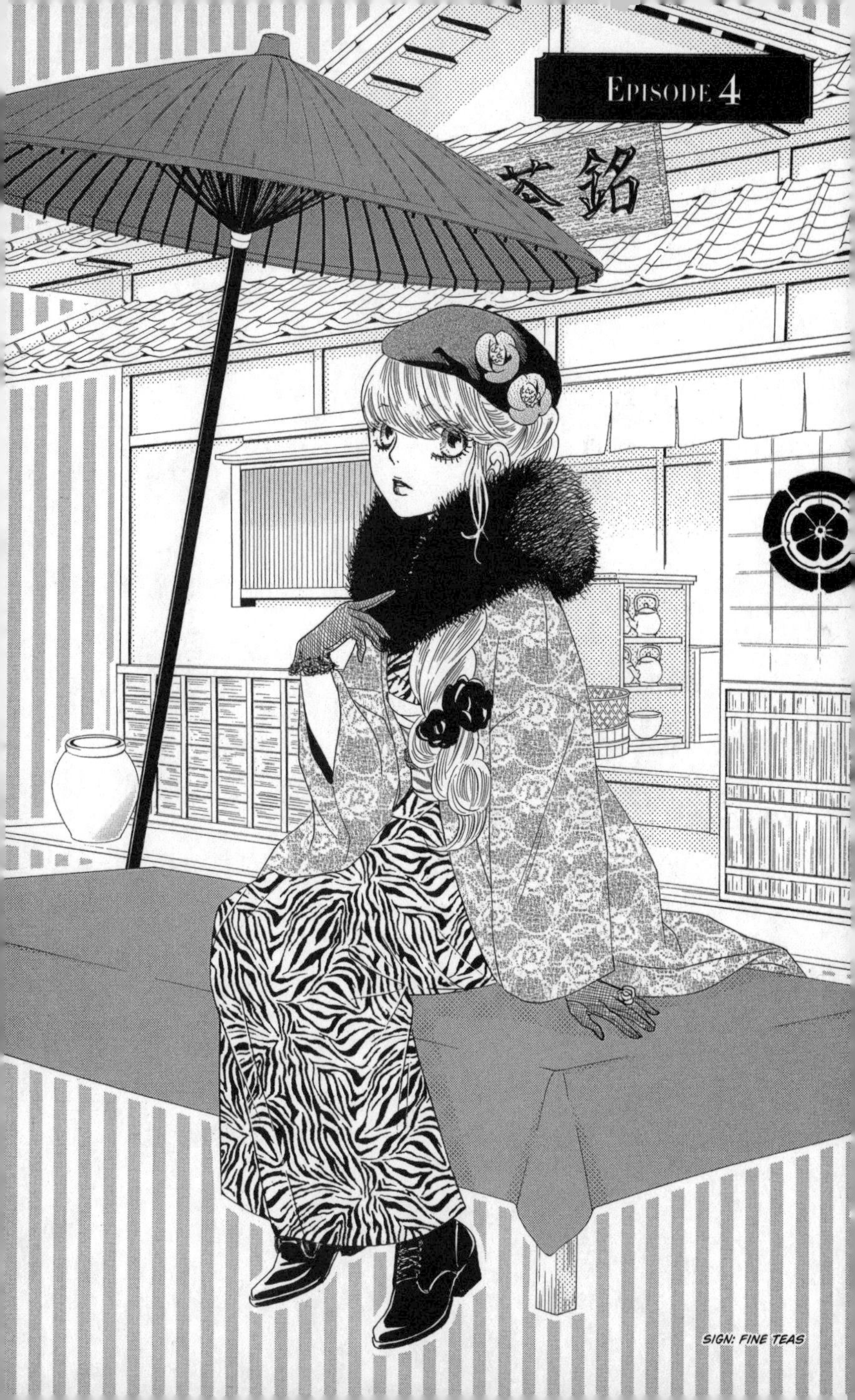
Episode 4
銘茶
Sign: Fine Teas

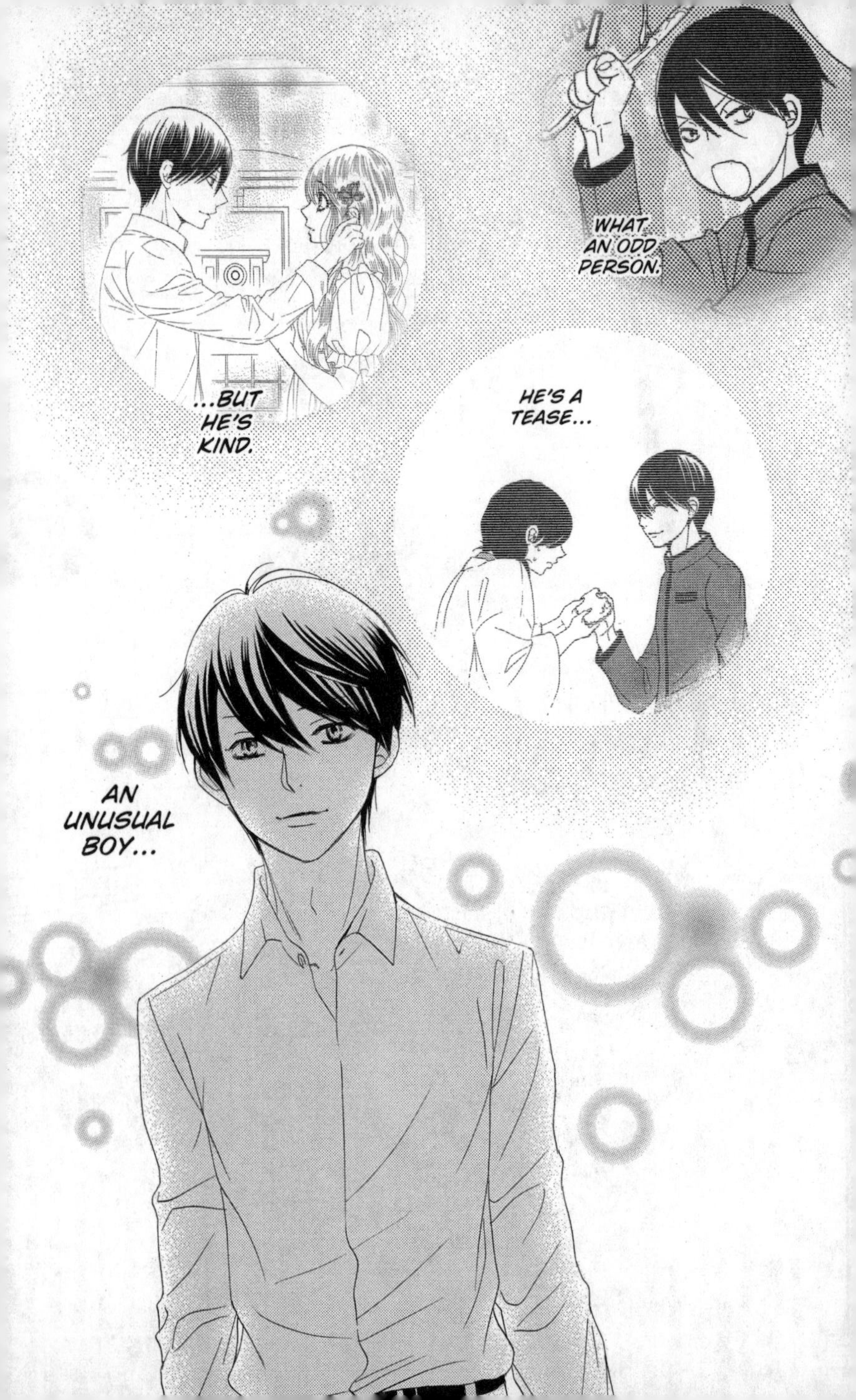
WHAT AN ODD PERSON.
HE'S A TEASE...
...BUT HE'S KIND.
AN UNUSUAL BOY...

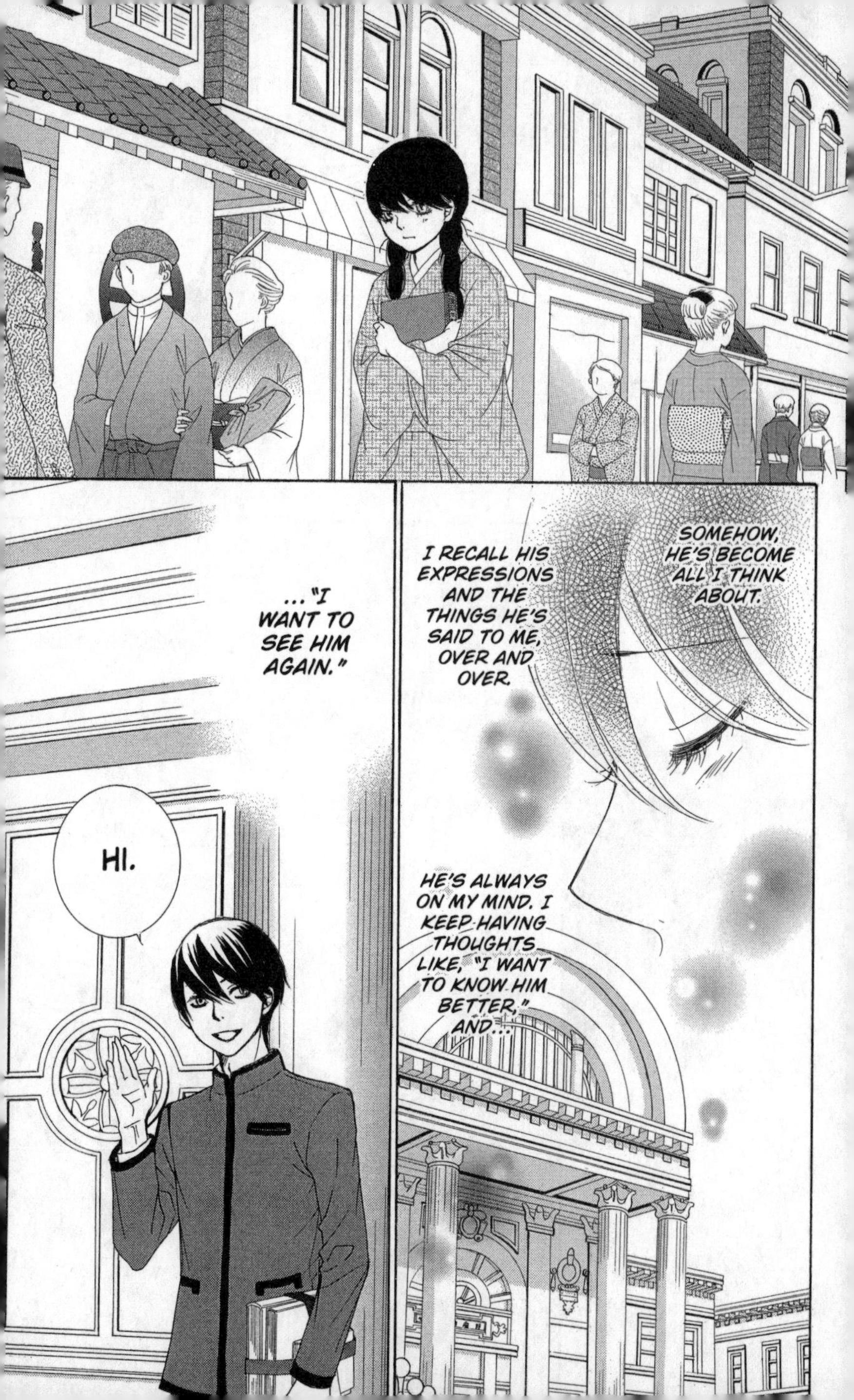
SOMEHOW, HE'S BECOME ALL I THINK ABOUT.
I RECALL HIS EXPRESSIONS AND THE THINGS HE'S SAID TO ME, OVER AND OVER.
HE'S ALWAYS ON MY MIND. I KEEP HAVING THOUGHTS LIKE, "I WANT TO KNOW HIM BETTER," AND...
..."I WANT TO SEE HIM AGAIN."
HI.

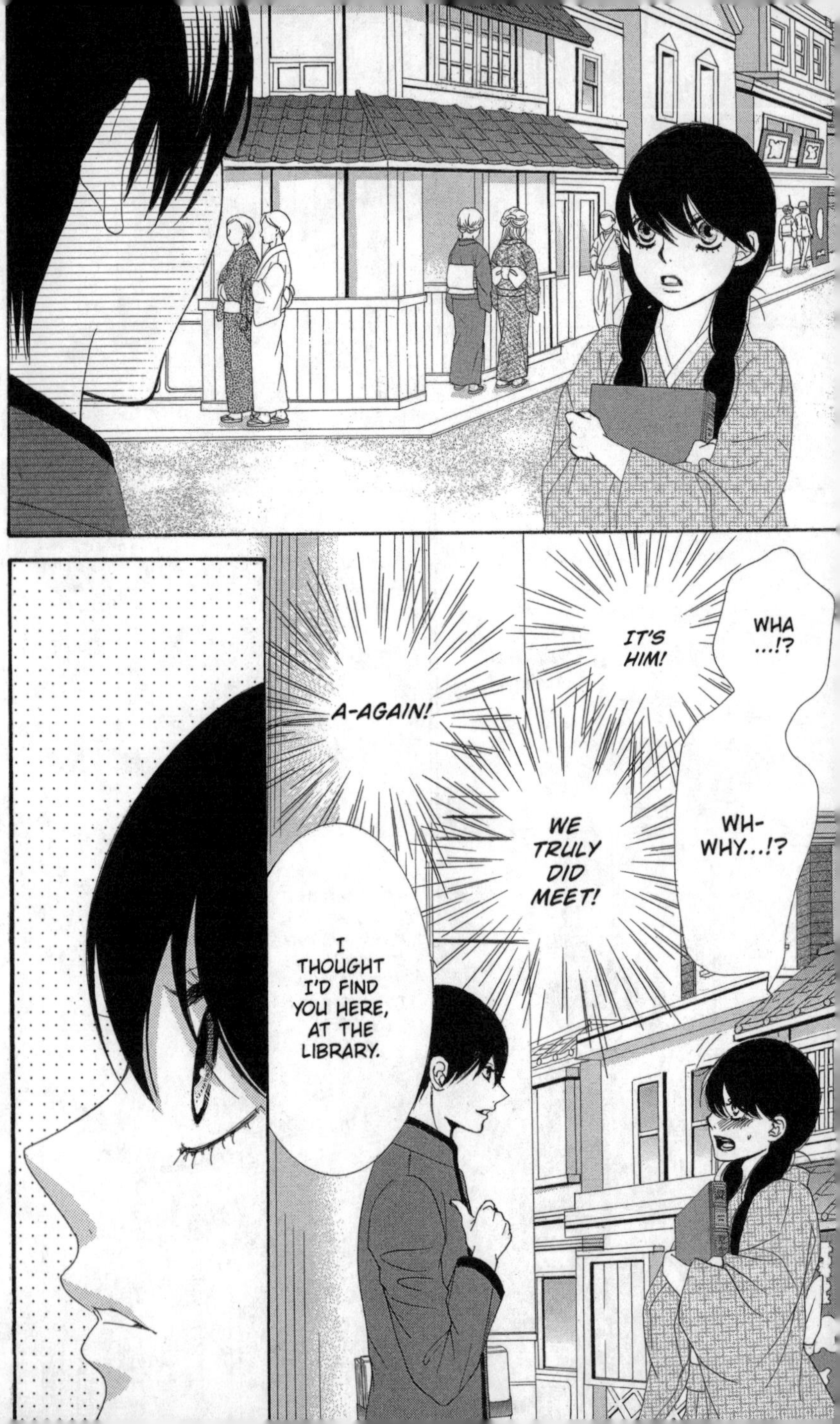
WHA...!?
IT'S HIM!
A-AGAIN!
WH-WHY...!?
WE TRULY DID MEET!
I THOUGHT I'D FIND YOU HERE, AT THE LIBRARY.

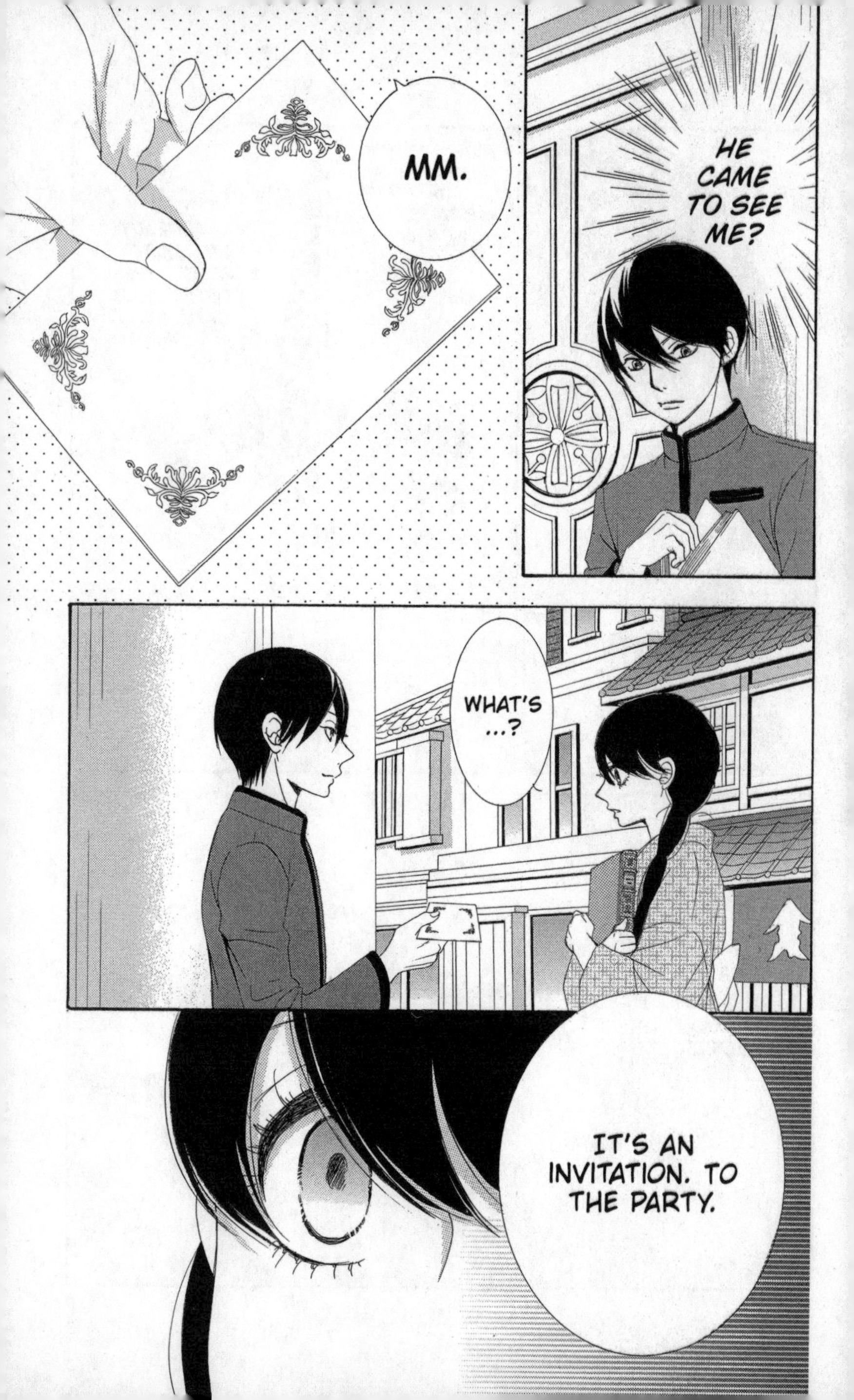
HE CAME TO SEE ME?
MM.
WHAT'S ...?
IT'S AN INVITATION. TO THE PARTY.

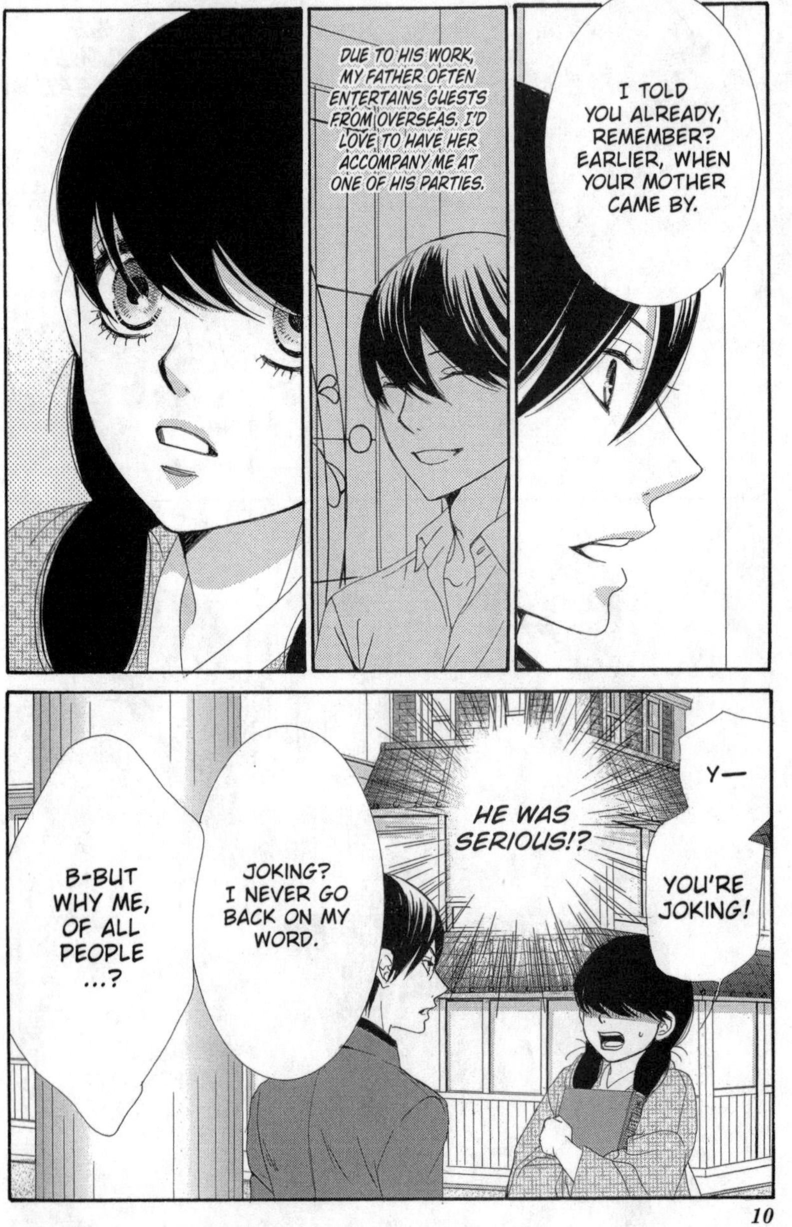
I TOLD YOU ALREADY, REMEMBER? EARLIER, WHEN YOUR MOTHER CAME BY.
DUE TO HIS WORK, MY FATHER OFTEN ENTERTAINS GUESTS FROM OVERSEAS. I'D LOVE TO HAVE HER ACCOMPANY ME AT ONE OF HIS PARTIES.
Y—
YOU'RE JOKING!
HE WAS SERIOUS!?
JOKING? I NEVER GO BACK ON MY WORD.
B-BUT WHY ME, OF ALL PEOPLE ...?

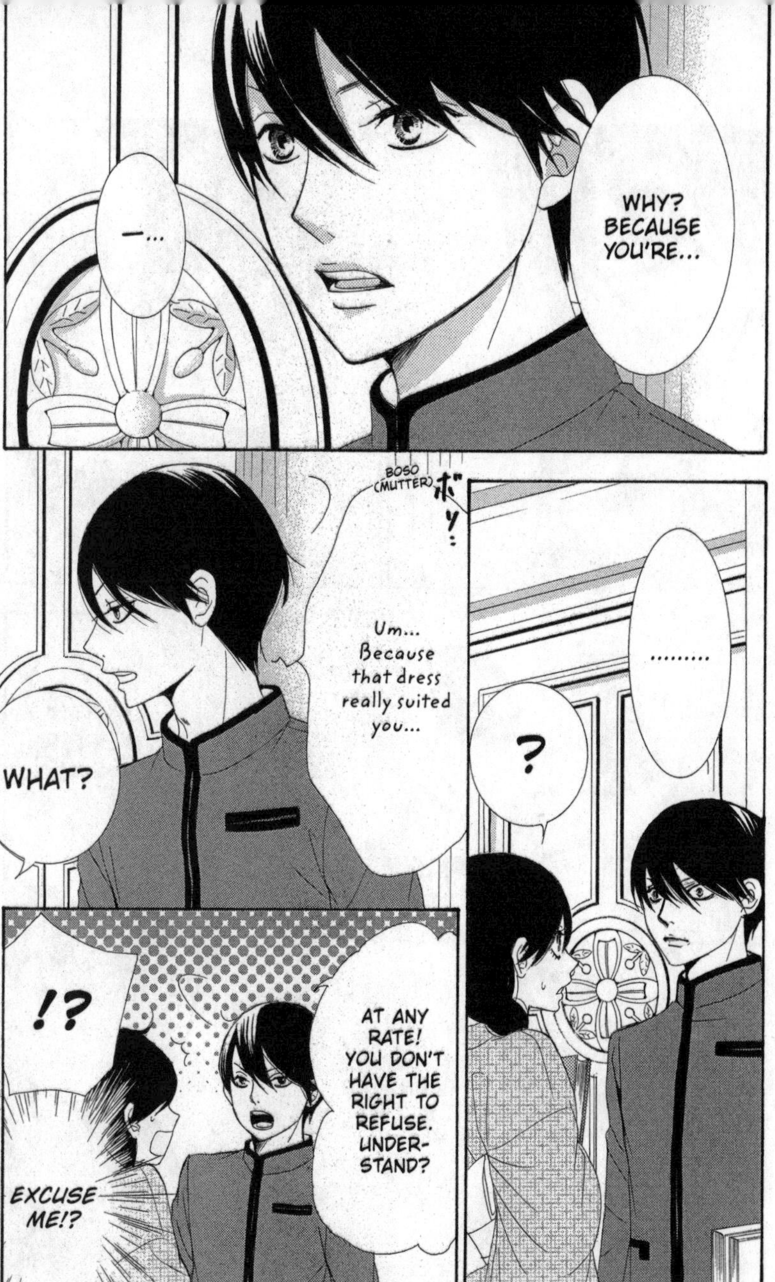
WHY? BECAUSE YOU'RE...
—...
....
?
BOSO (MUTTER)
Um... Because that dress really suited you...
WHAT?
AT ANY RATE! YOU DON'T HAVE THE RIGHT TO REFUSE. UNDER-STAND?
!?
EXCUSE ME!?

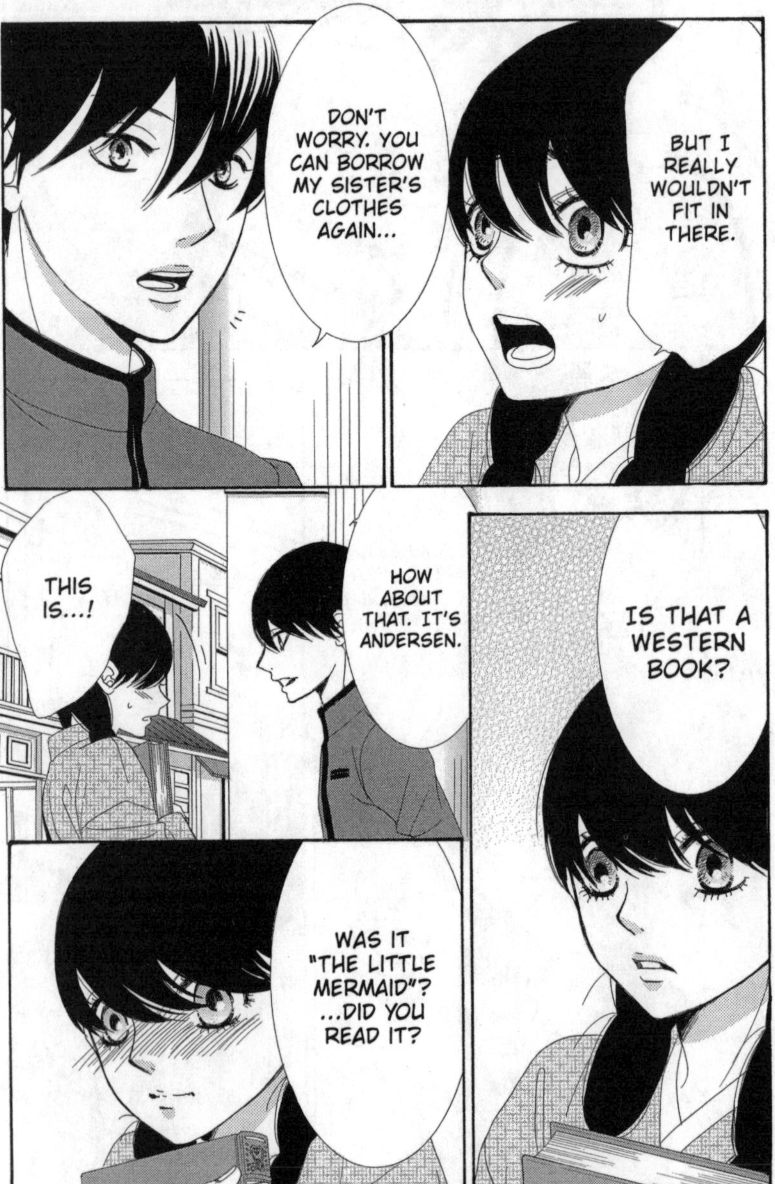
BUT I REALLY WOULDN'T FIT IN THERE.
DON'T WORRY. YOU CAN BORROW MY SISTER'S CLOTHES AGAIN...
IS THAT A WESTERN BOOK?
HOW ABOUT THAT. IT'S ANDERSEN.
THIS IS...!
WAS IT "THE LITTLE MERMAID"? ...DID YOU READ IT?

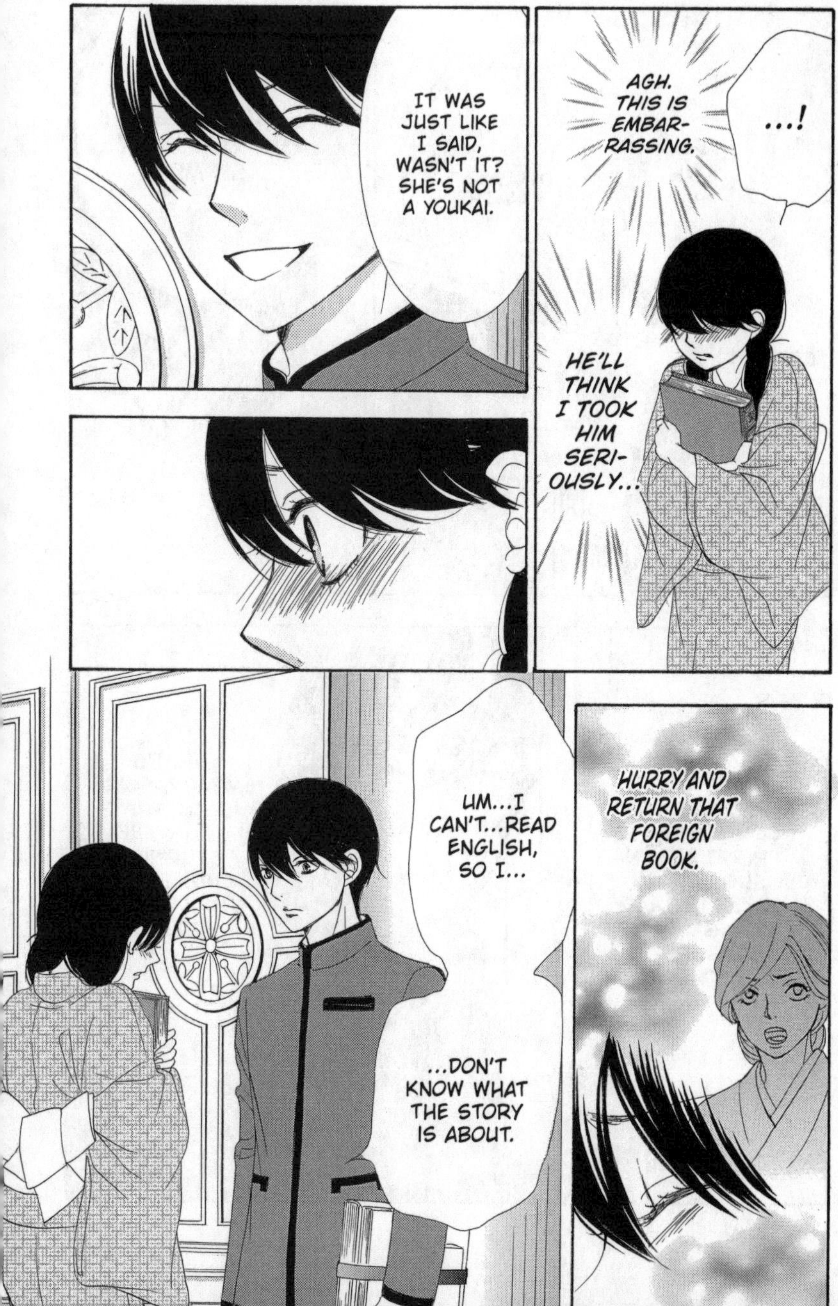
...!
AGH. THIS IS EMBARRASSING.
HE'LL THINK I TOOK HIM SERIOUSLY...
IT WAS JUST LIKE I SAID, WASN'T IT? SHE'S NOT A YOUKAI.
HURRY AND RETURN THAT FOREIGN BOOK.
UM...I CAN'T...READ ENGLISH, SO I...
...DON'T KNOW WHAT THE STORY IS ABOUT.

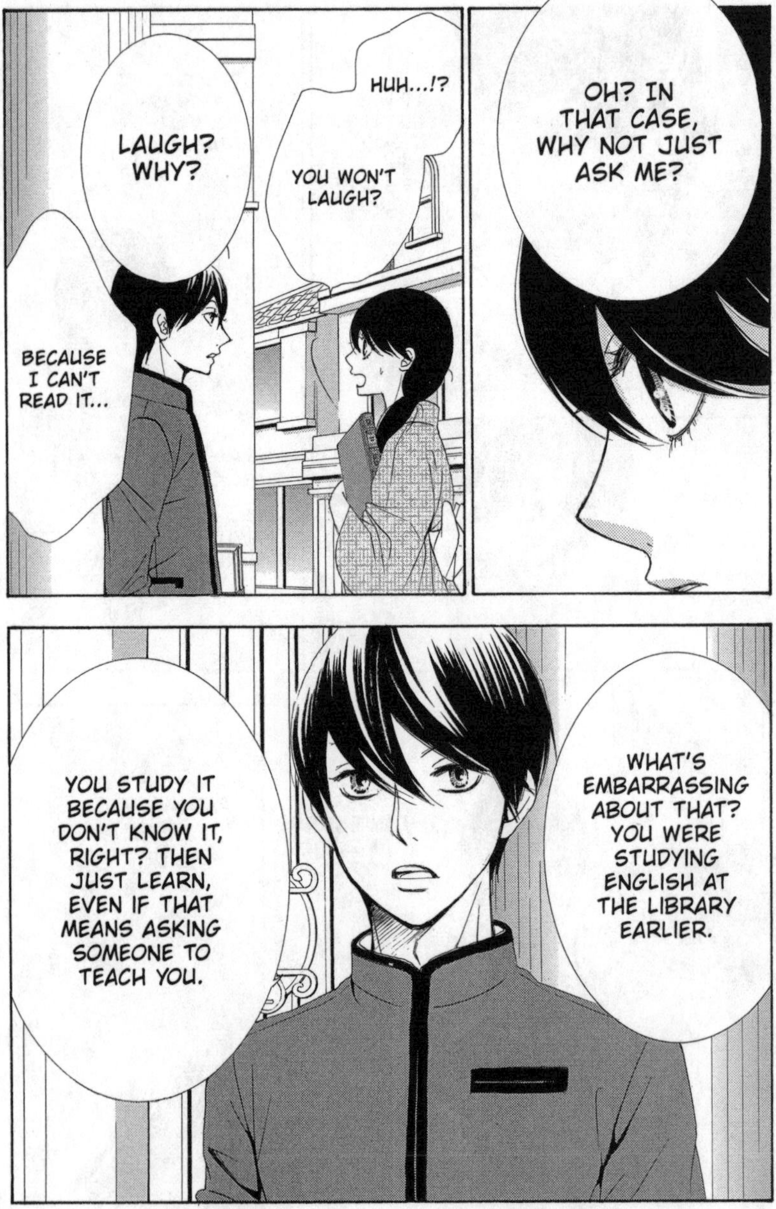
OH? IN THAT CASE, WHY NOT JUST ASK ME?
HUH...!?
YOU WON'T LAUGH?
LAUGH? WHY?
BECAUSE I CAN'T READ IT...
WHAT'S EMBARRASSING ABOUT THAT? YOU WERE STUDYING ENGLISH AT THE LIBRARY EARLIER.
YOU STUDY IT BECAUSE YOU DON'T KNOW IT, RIGHT? THEN JUST LEARN, EVEN IF THAT MEANS ASKING SOMEONE TO TEACH YOU.

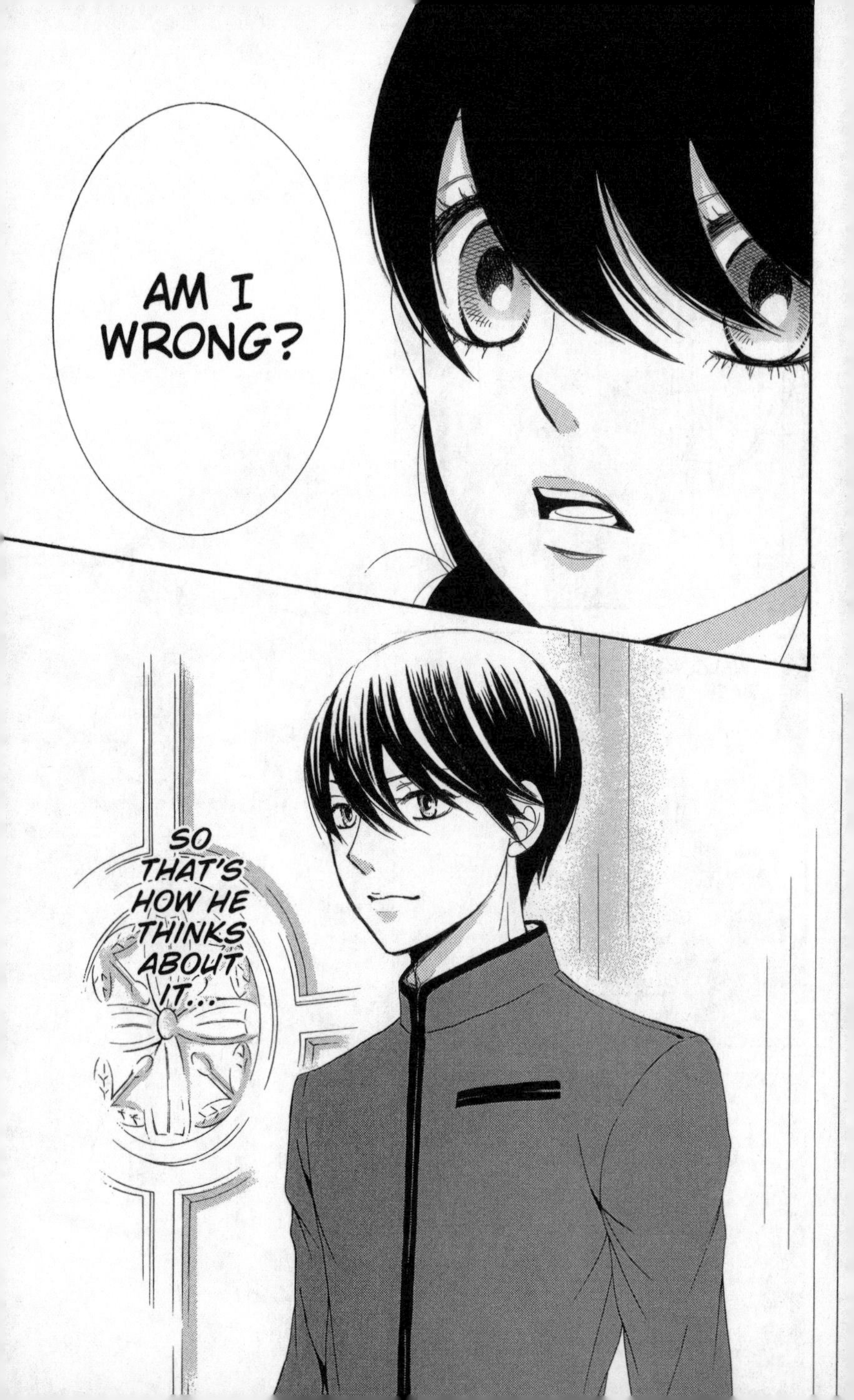
AM I WRONG?
SO THAT'S HOW HE THINKS ABOUT IT...

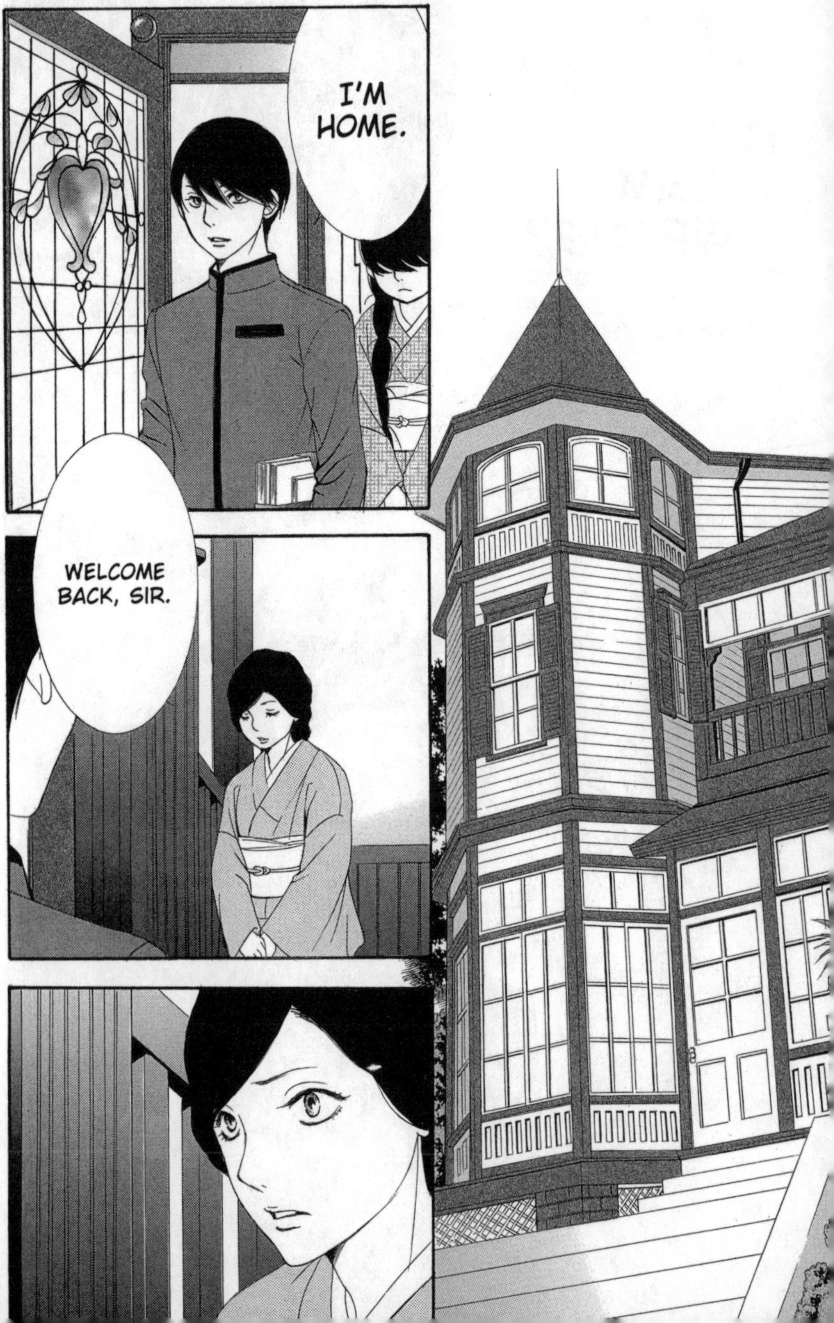
I'M HOME.
WELCOME BACK, SIR.

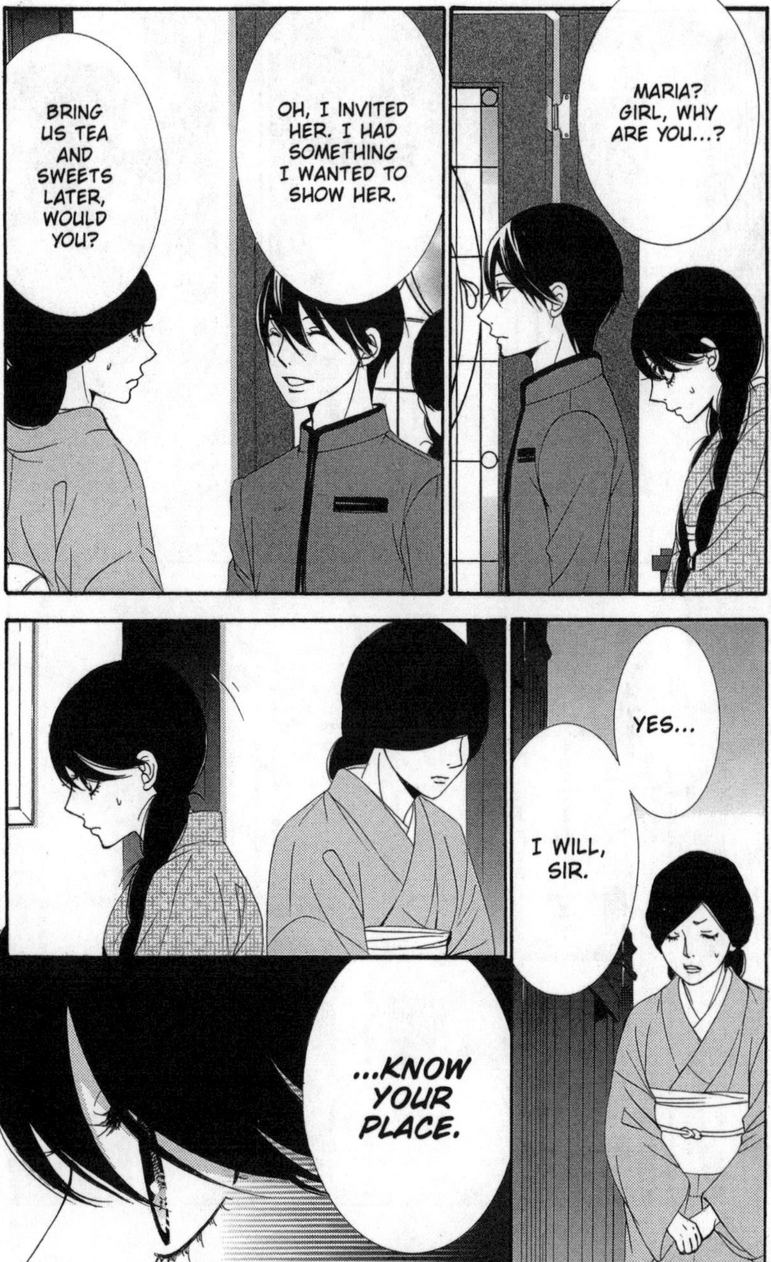
MARIA? GIRL, WHY ARE YOU...?
OH, I INVITED HER. I HAD SOMETHING I WANTED TO SHOW HER.
BRING US TEA AND SWEETS LATER, WOULD YOU?
YES...
I WILL, SIR.
...KNOW YOUR PLACE.

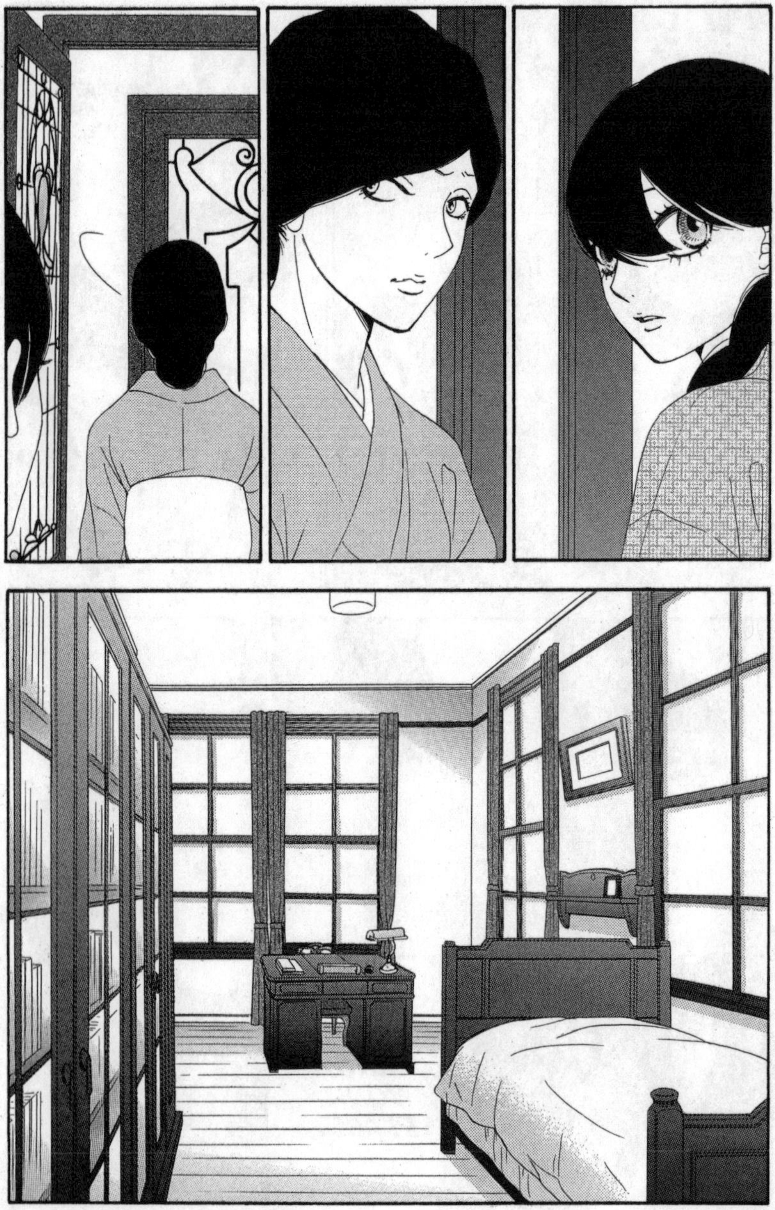

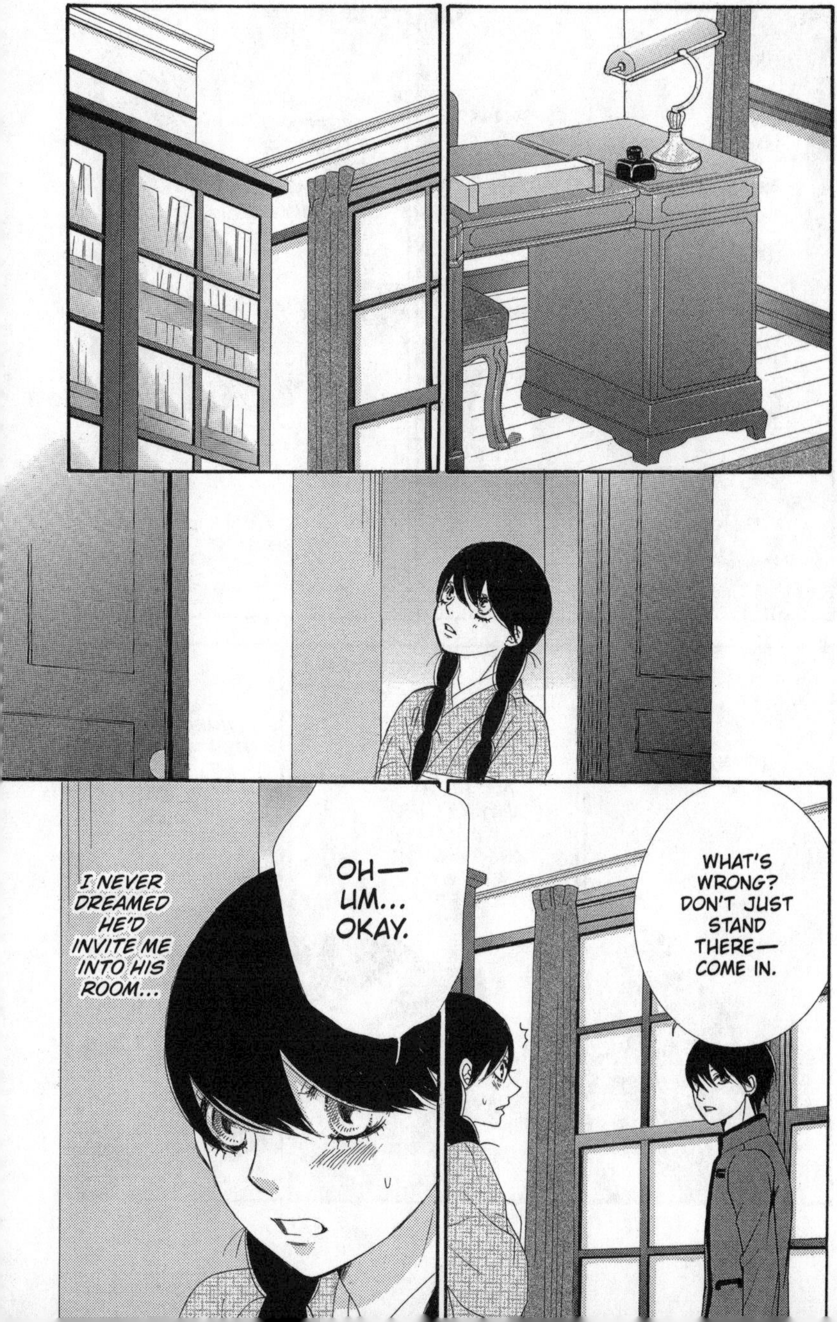
WHAT'S WRONG? DON'T JUST STAND THERE— COME IN.
OH— UM... OKAY.
I NEVER DREAMED HE'D INVITE ME INTO HIS ROOM...

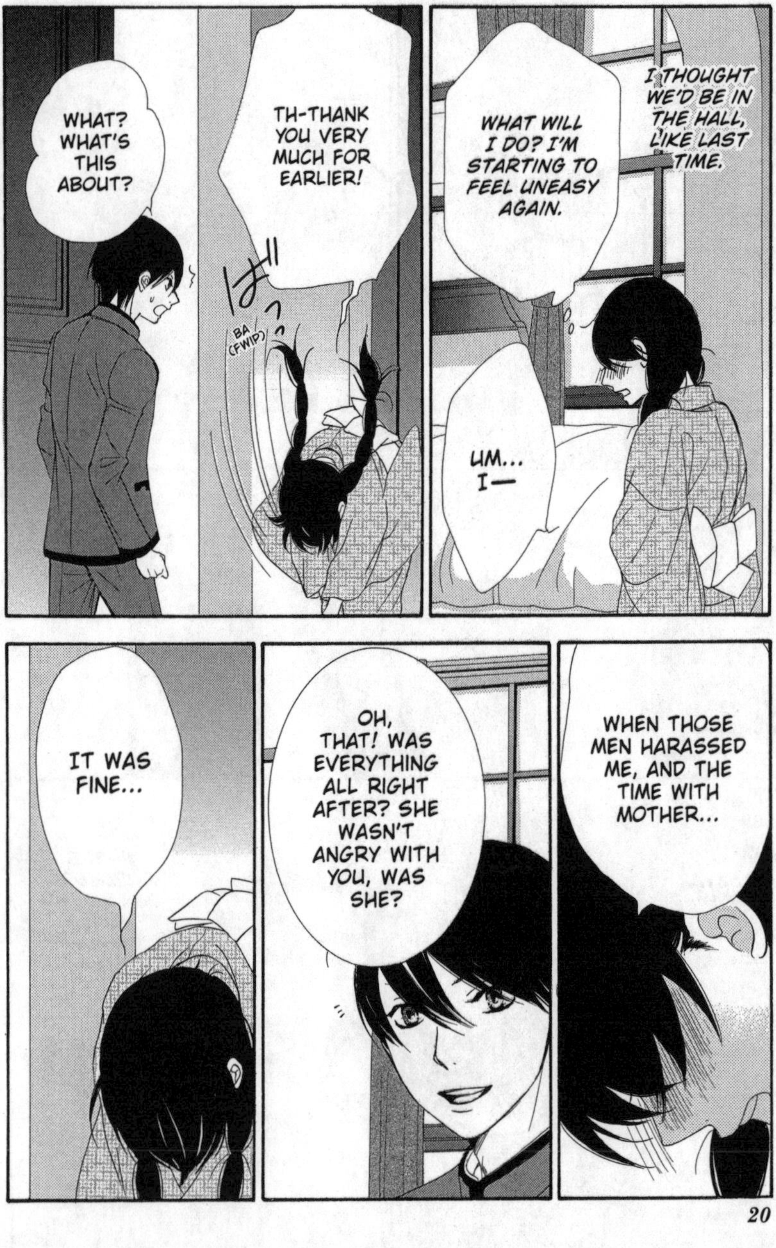
I THOUGHT WE'D BE IN THE HALL, LIKE LAST TIME.
WHAT WILL I DO? I'M STARTING TO FEEL UNEASY AGAIN.
UM... I—
TH-THANK YOU VERY MUCH FOR EARLIER!
ばっ
BA (FWIP)
WHAT? WHAT'S THIS ABOUT?
WHEN THOSE MEN HARASSED ME, AND THE TIME WITH MOTHER...
OH, THAT! WAS EVERYTHING ALL RIGHT AFTER? SHE WASN'T ANGRY WITH YOU, WAS SHE?
IT WAS FINE...

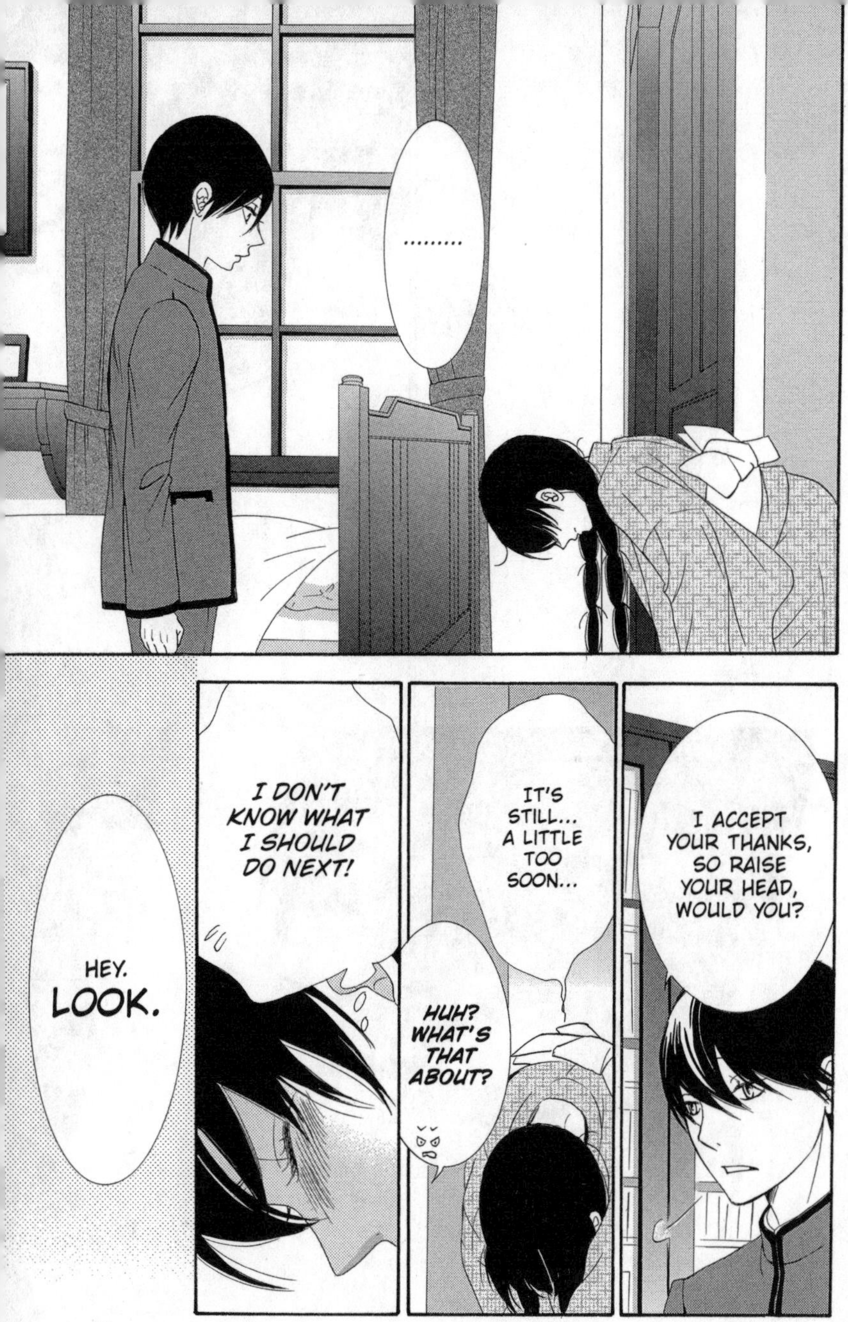
....
I ACCEPT YOUR THANKS, SO RAISE YOUR HEAD, WOULD YOU?
IT'S STILL... A LITTLE TOO SOON...
HUH? WHAT'S THAT ABOUT?
I DON'T KNOW WHAT I SHOULD DO NEXT!
HEY. LOOK.

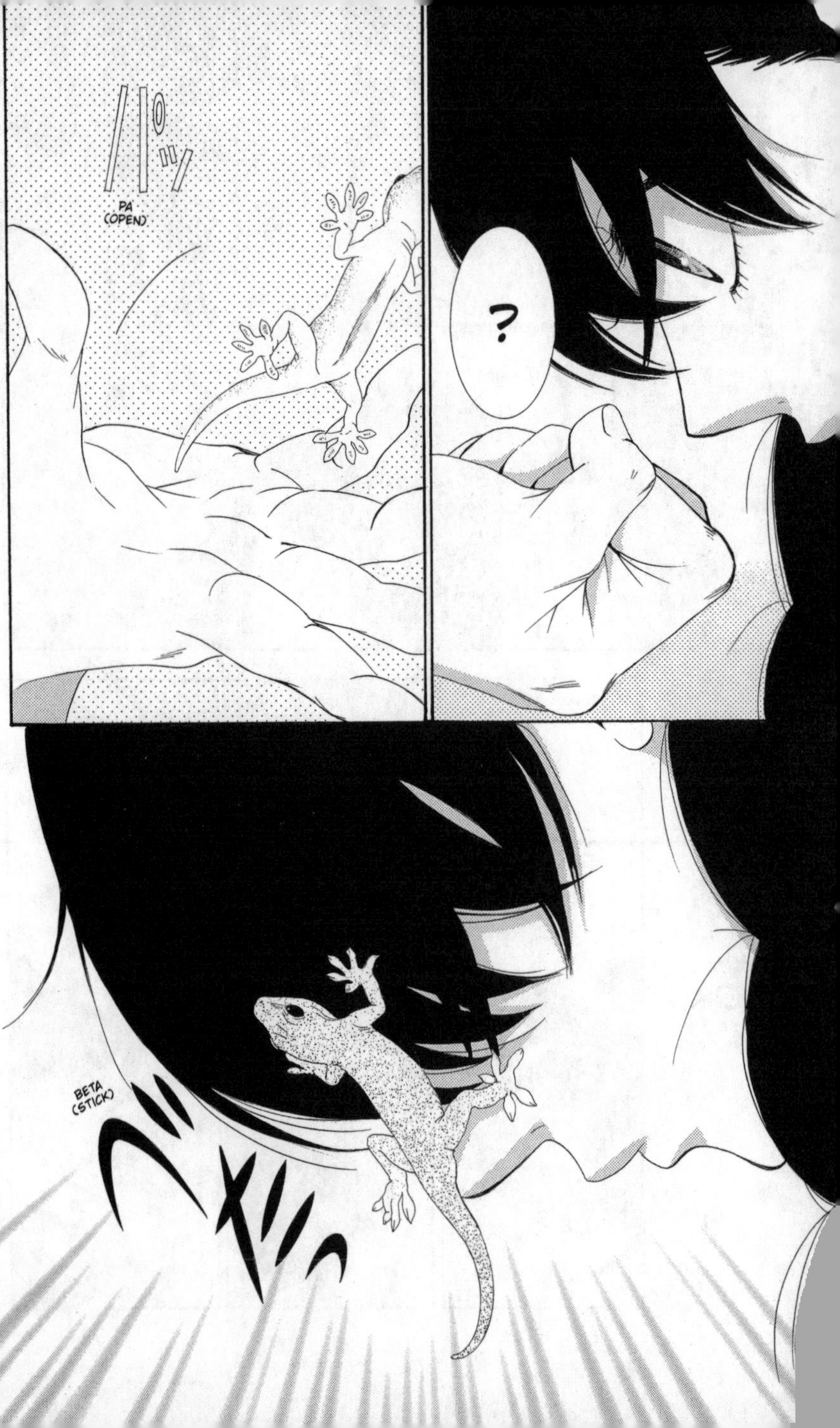
?
PA (OPEN)
BETA (STICK)

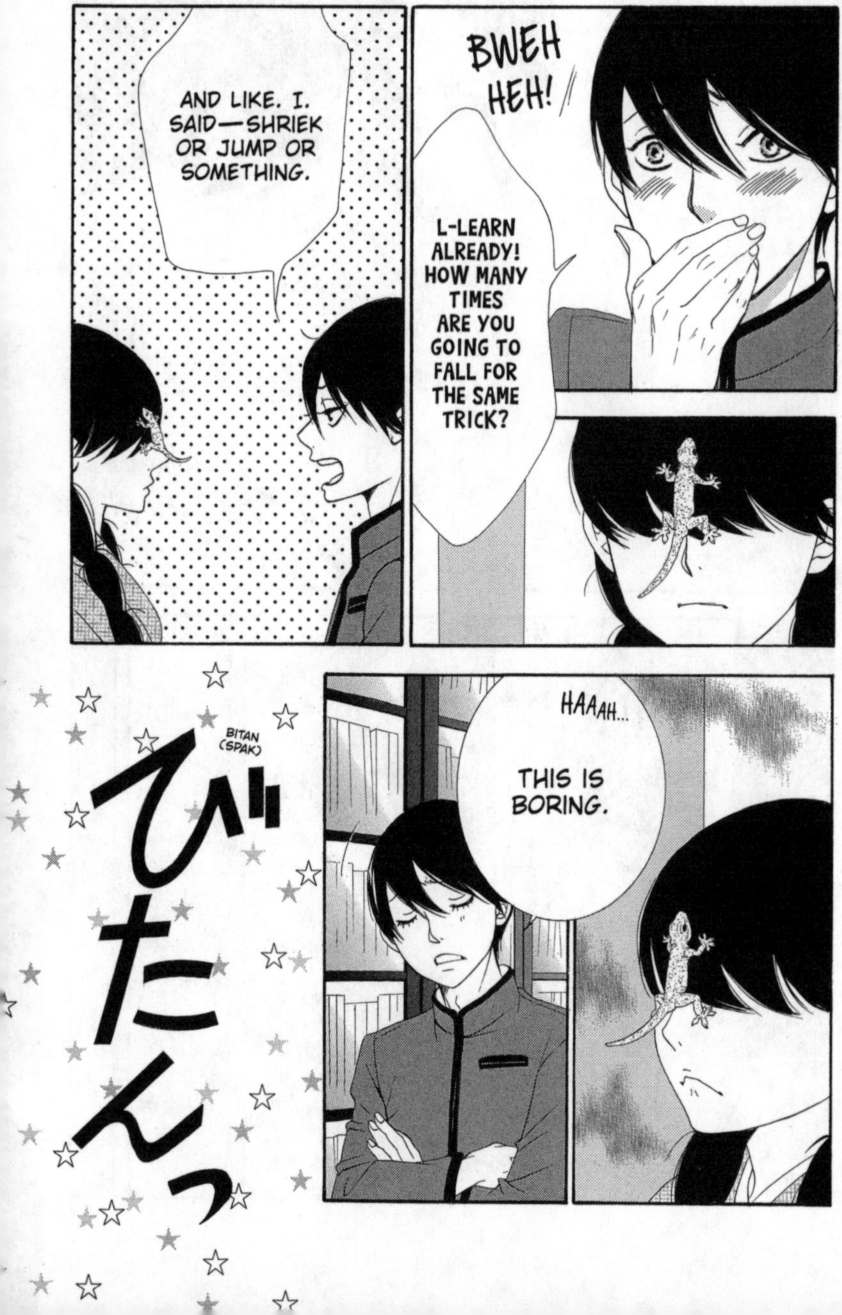
BWEH HEH!
L-LEARN ALREADY! HOW MANY TIMES ARE YOU GOING TO FALL FOR THE SAME TRICK?
AND LIKE. I. SAID—SHRIEK OR JUMP OR SOMETHING.
HAAAH...
THIS IS BORING.
BITAN (SPAK)
びたんっ

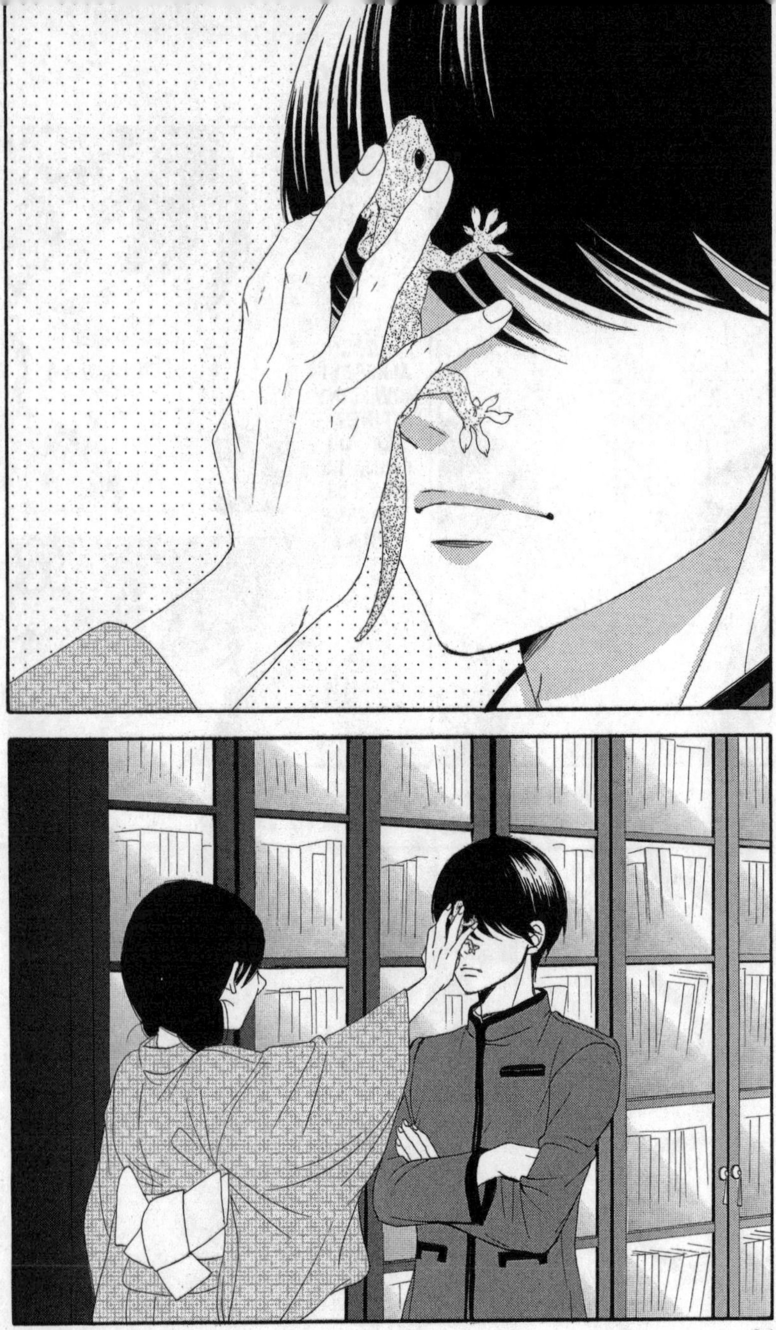

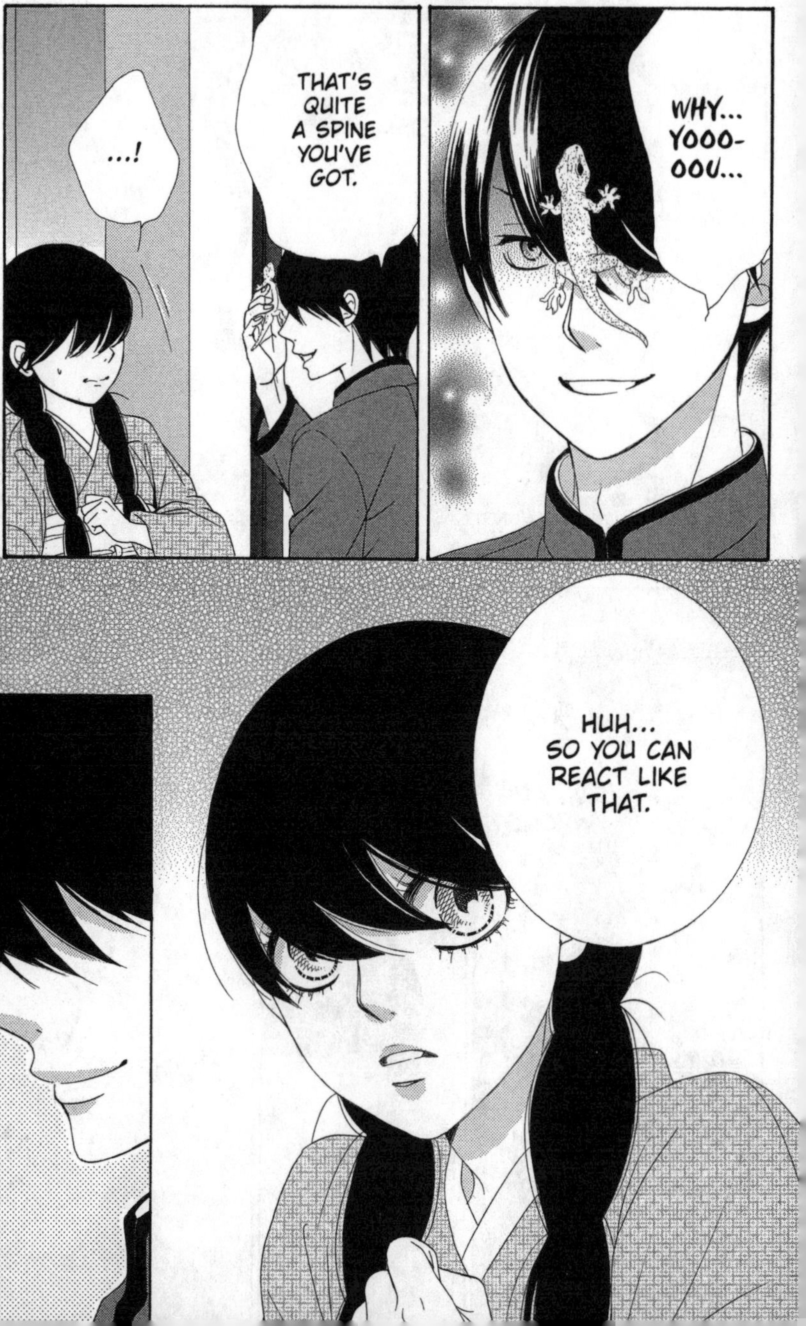
WHY... YOOO-OOU...
THAT'S QUITE A SPINE YOU'VE GOT.
...!
HUH... SO YOU CAN REACT LIKE THAT.

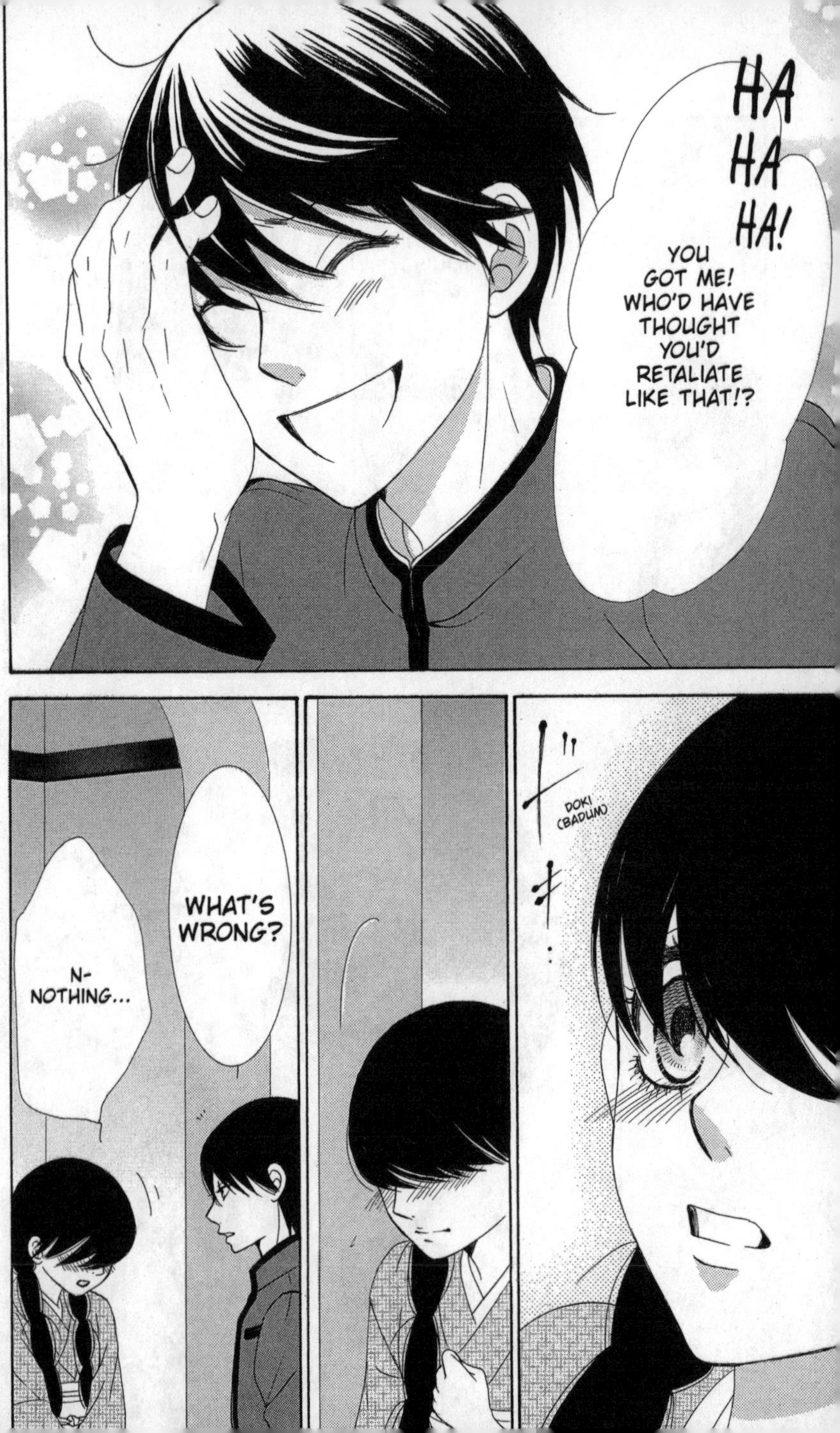
HA HA HA!
YOU GOT ME! WHO'D HAVE THOUGHT YOU'D RETALIATE LIKE THAT!?
DOKI (BADUM)
WHAT'S WRONG?
N- NOTHING...

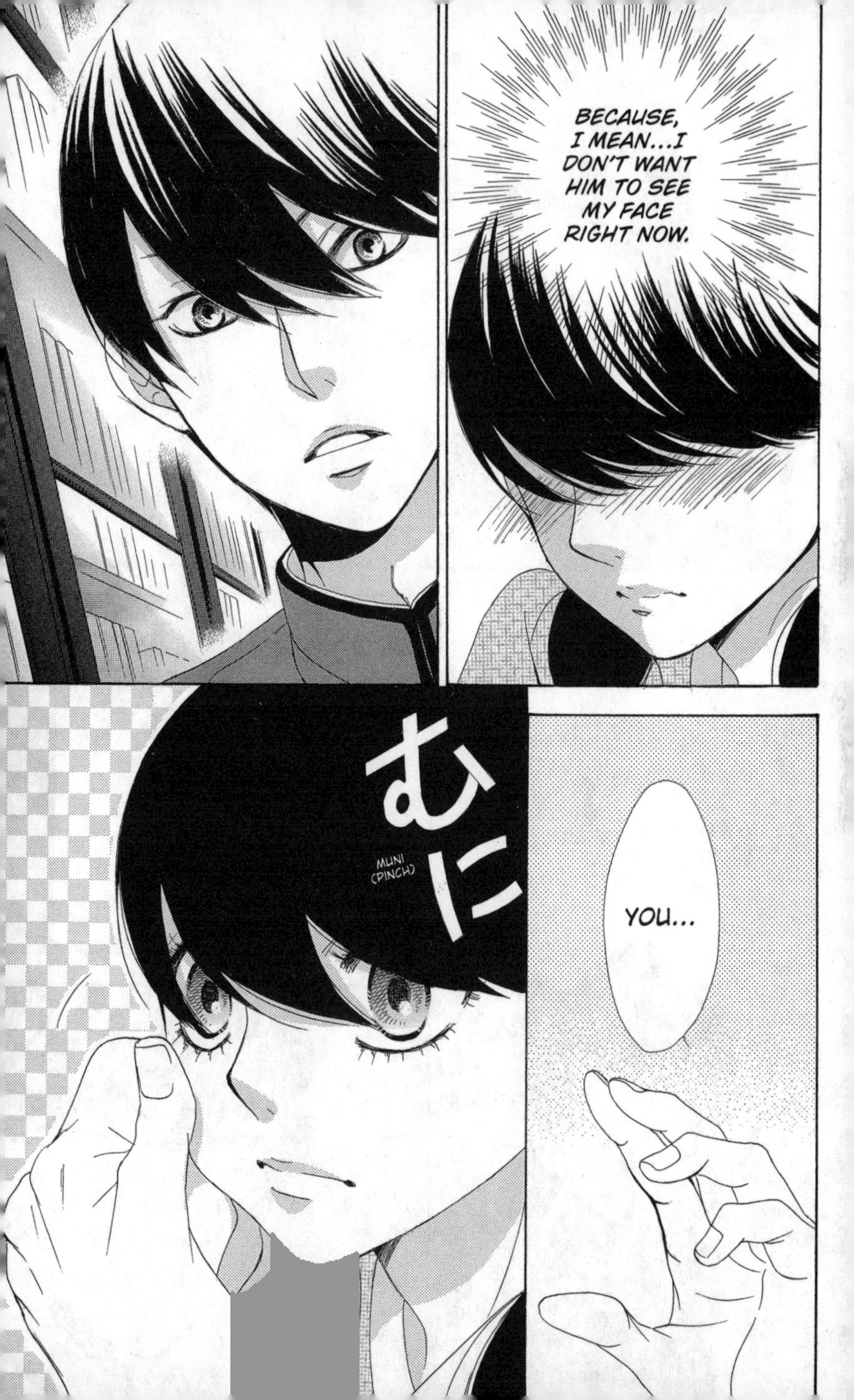
BECAUSE, I MEAN...I DON'T WANT HIM TO SEE MY FACE RIGHT NOW.
YOU...
むに
MUNI (PINCH)

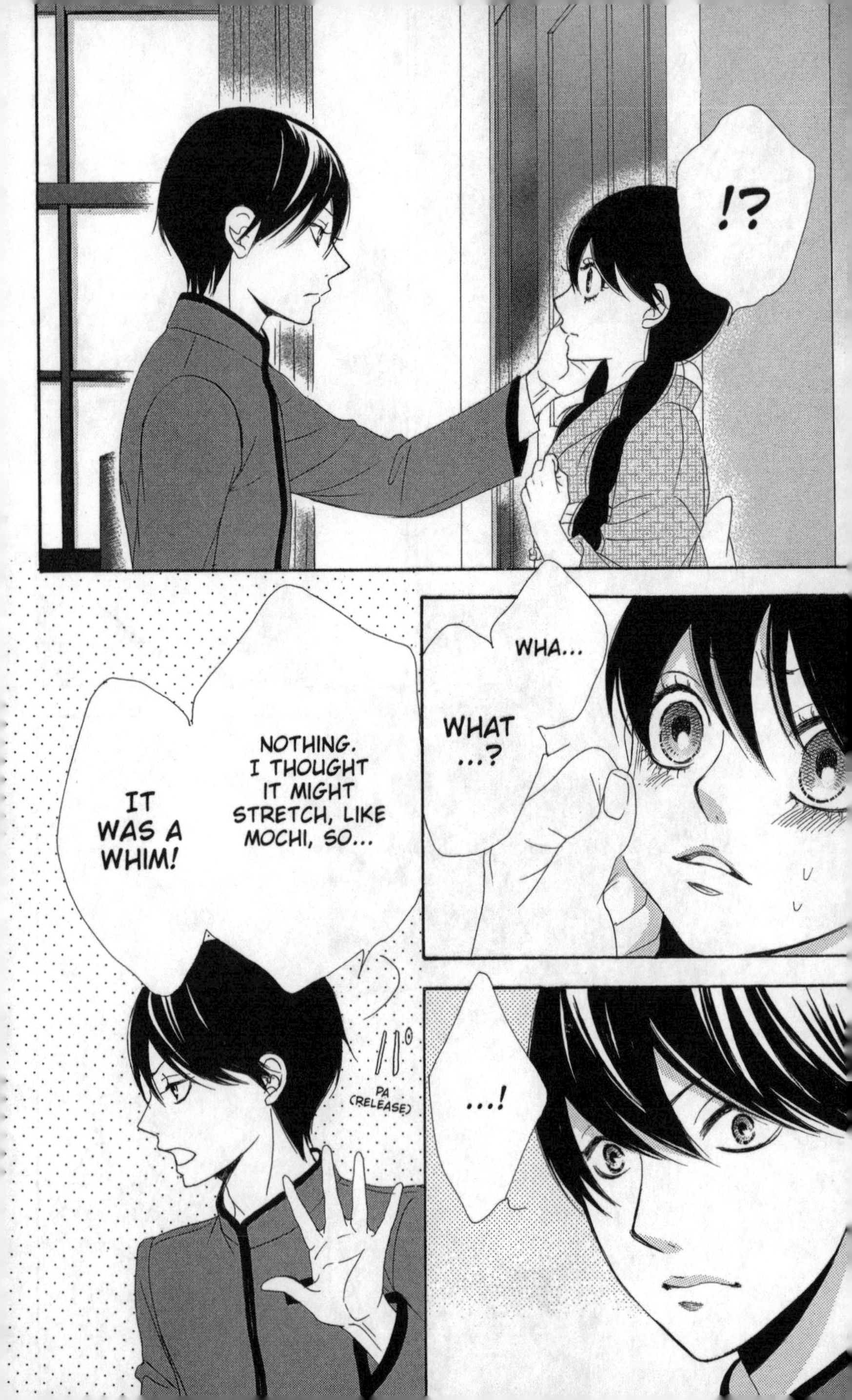
!?
WHA...
WHAT ...?
...!
NOTHING. I THOUGHT IT MIGHT STRETCH, LIKE MOCHI, SO...
IT WAS A WHIM!
PA (RELEASE)

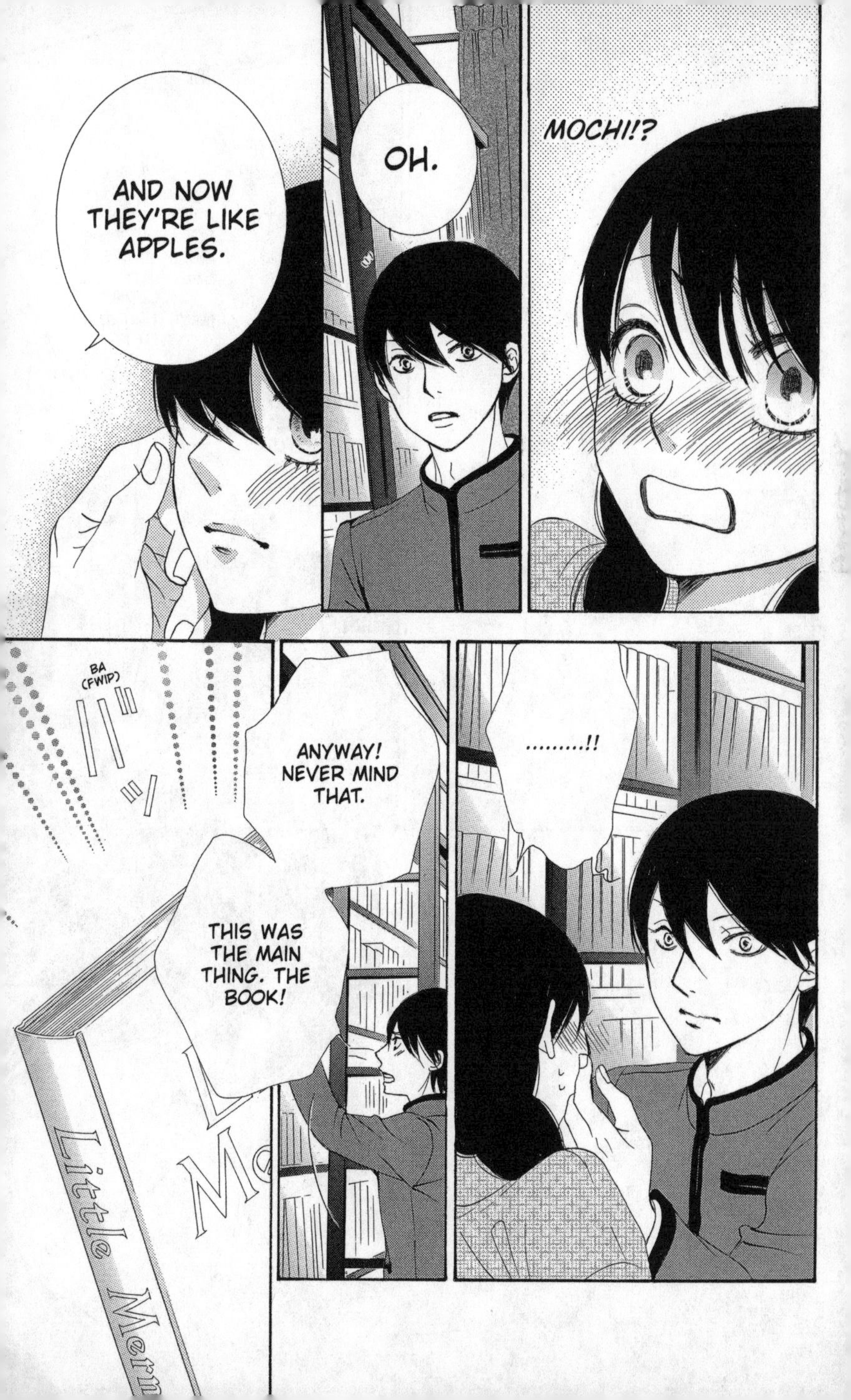
MOCHI!?
OH.
AND NOW THEY'RE LIKE APPLES.
.........!!
ANYWAY! NEVER MIND THAT.
THIS WAS THE MAIN THING. THE BOOK!
BA (FWIP)

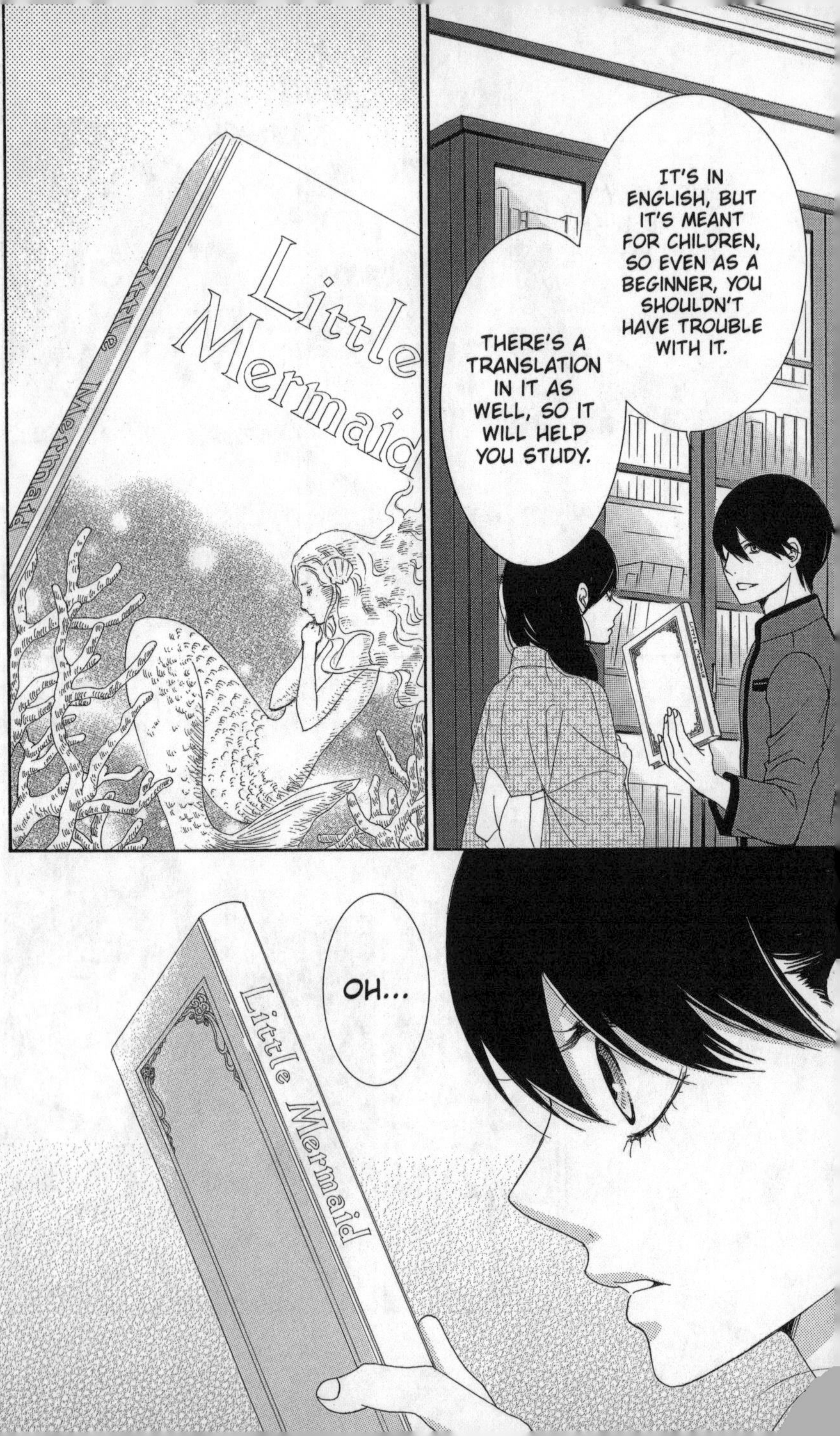
IT'S IN ENGLISH, BUT IT'S MEANT FOR CHILDREN, SO EVEN AS A BEGINNER, YOU SHOULDN'T HAVE TROUBLE WITH IT.
THERE'S A TRANSLATION IN IT AS WELL, SO IT WILL HELP YOU STUDY.
Little Mermaid
Little Mermaid
OH...
Little Mermaid

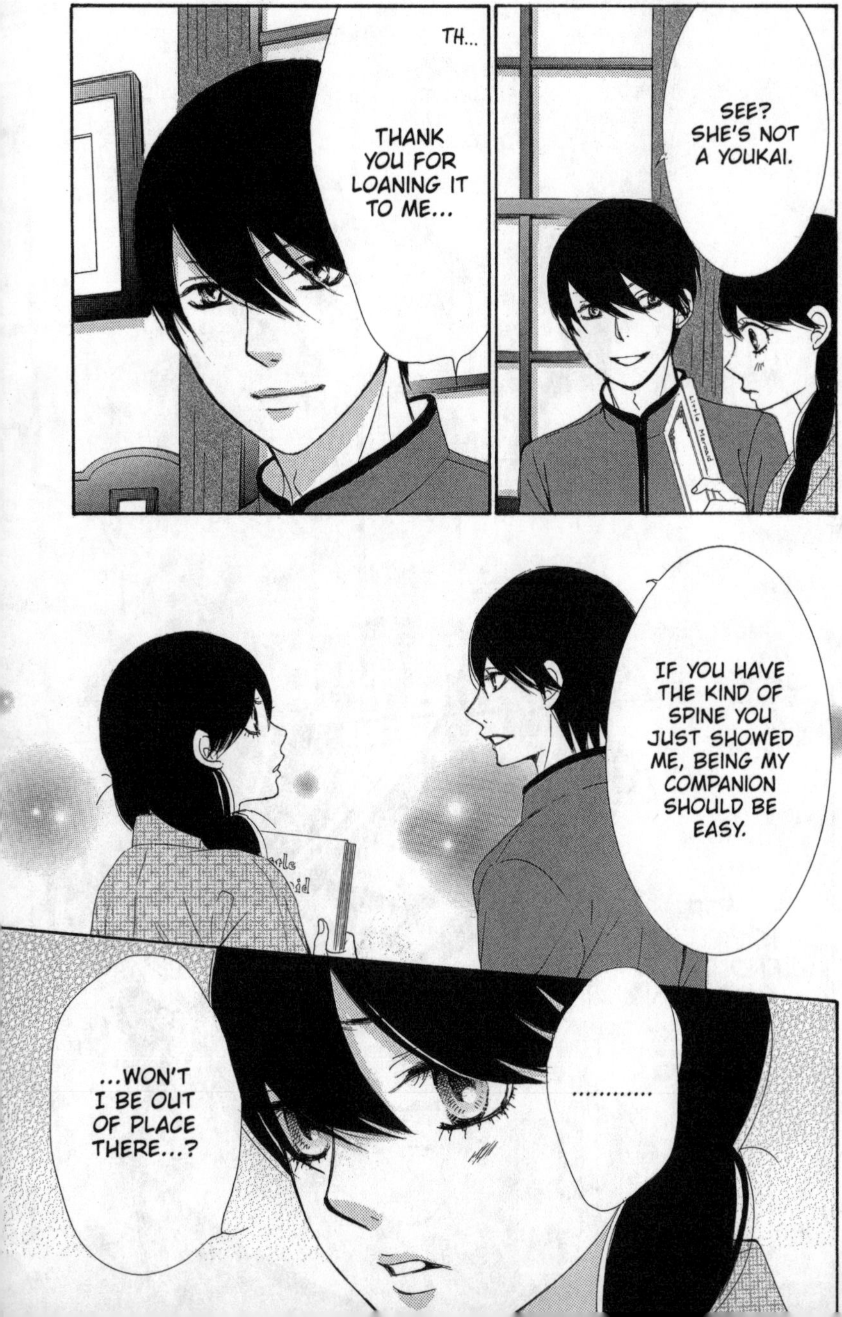
SEE? SHE'S NOT A YOUKAI.
TH...
THANK YOU FOR LOANING IT TO ME...
IF YOU HAVE THE KIND OF SPINE YOU JUST SHOWED ME, BEING MY COMPANION SHOULD BE EASY.
....
...WON'T I BE OUT OF PLACE THERE...?

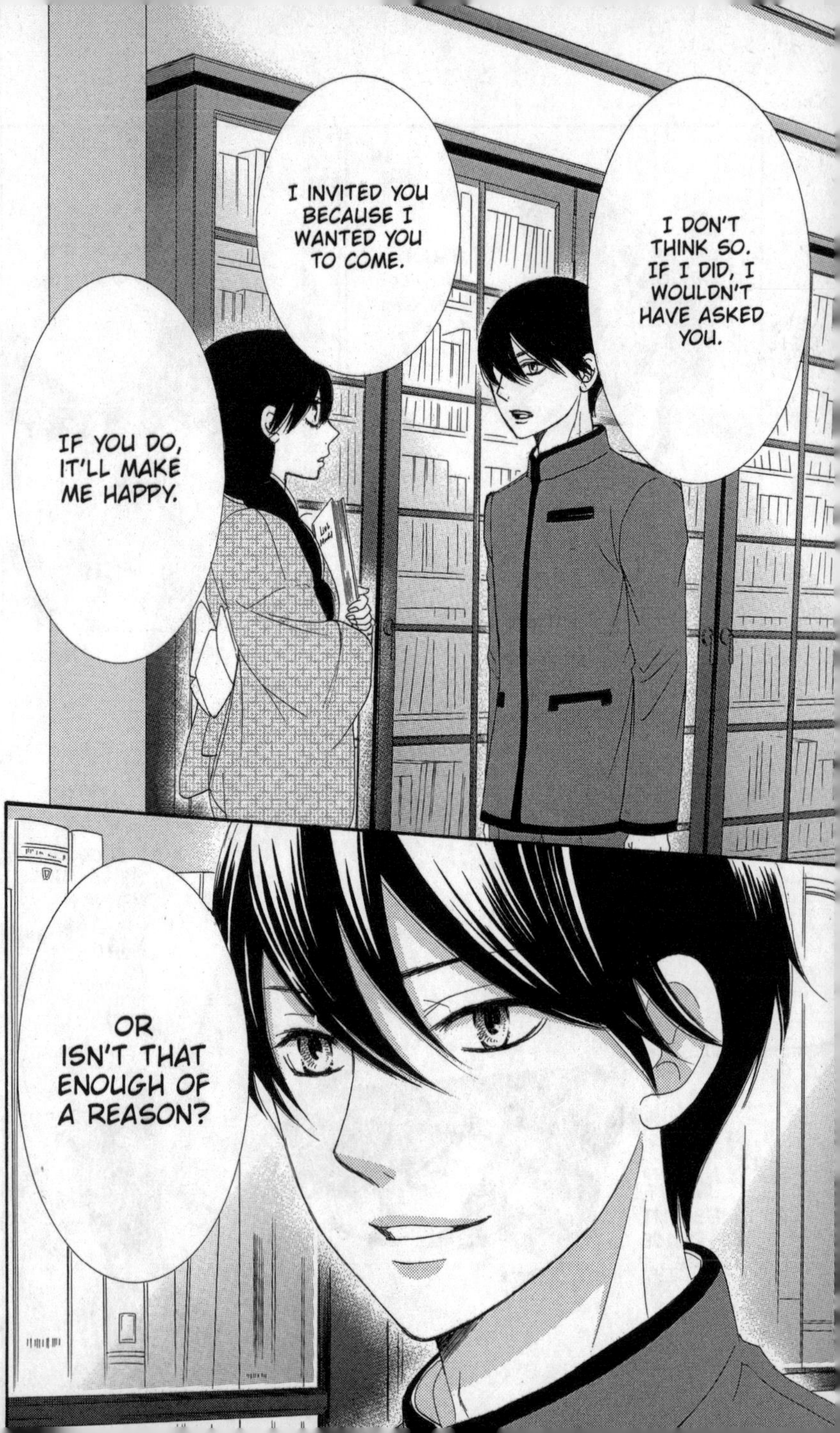
I DON'T THINK SO. IF I DID, I WOULDN'T HAVE ASKED YOU.
I INVITED YOU BECAUSE I WANTED YOU TO COME.
IF YOU DO, IT'LL MAKE ME HAPPY.
OR ISN'T THAT ENOUGH OF A REASON?

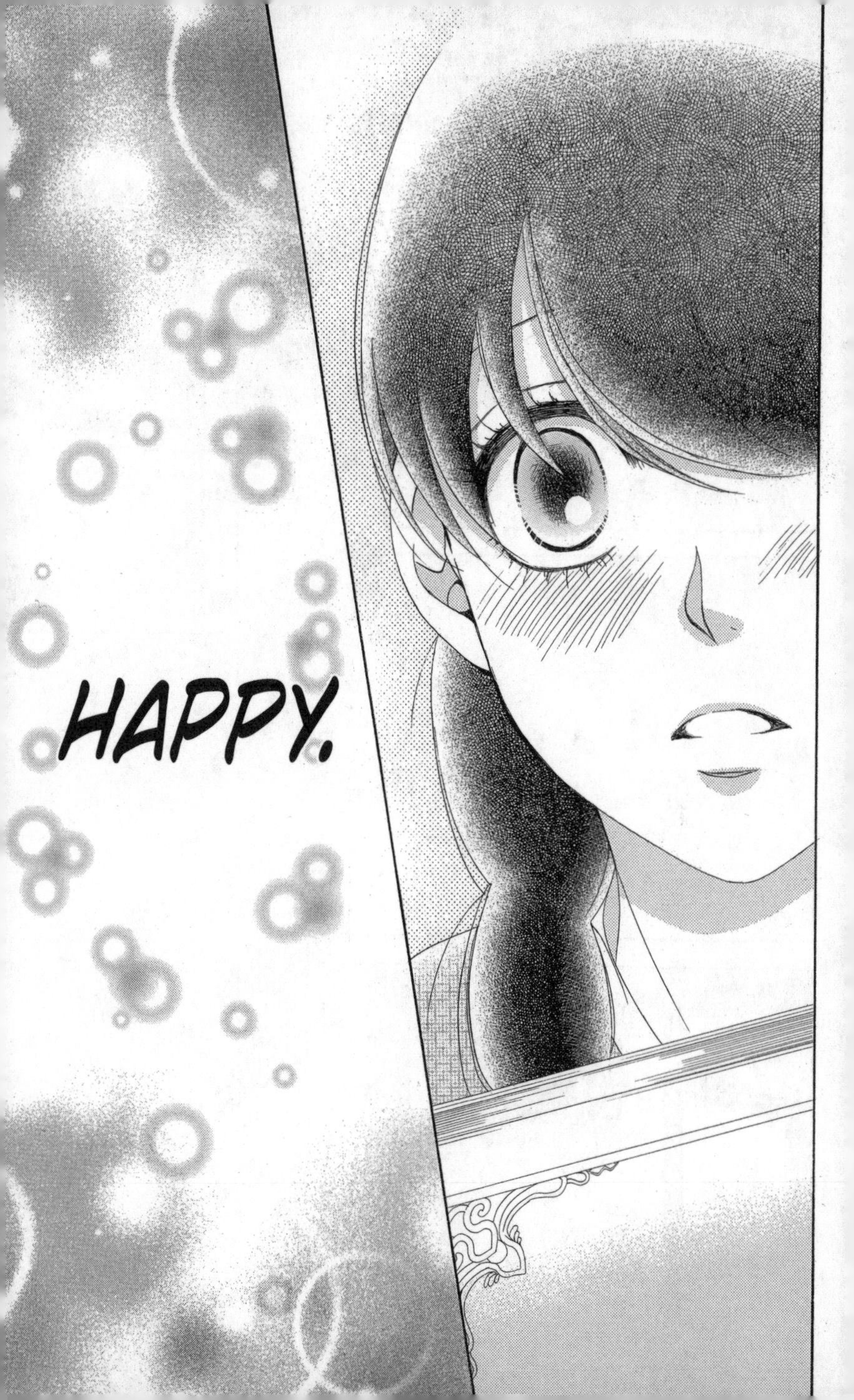
HAPPY.

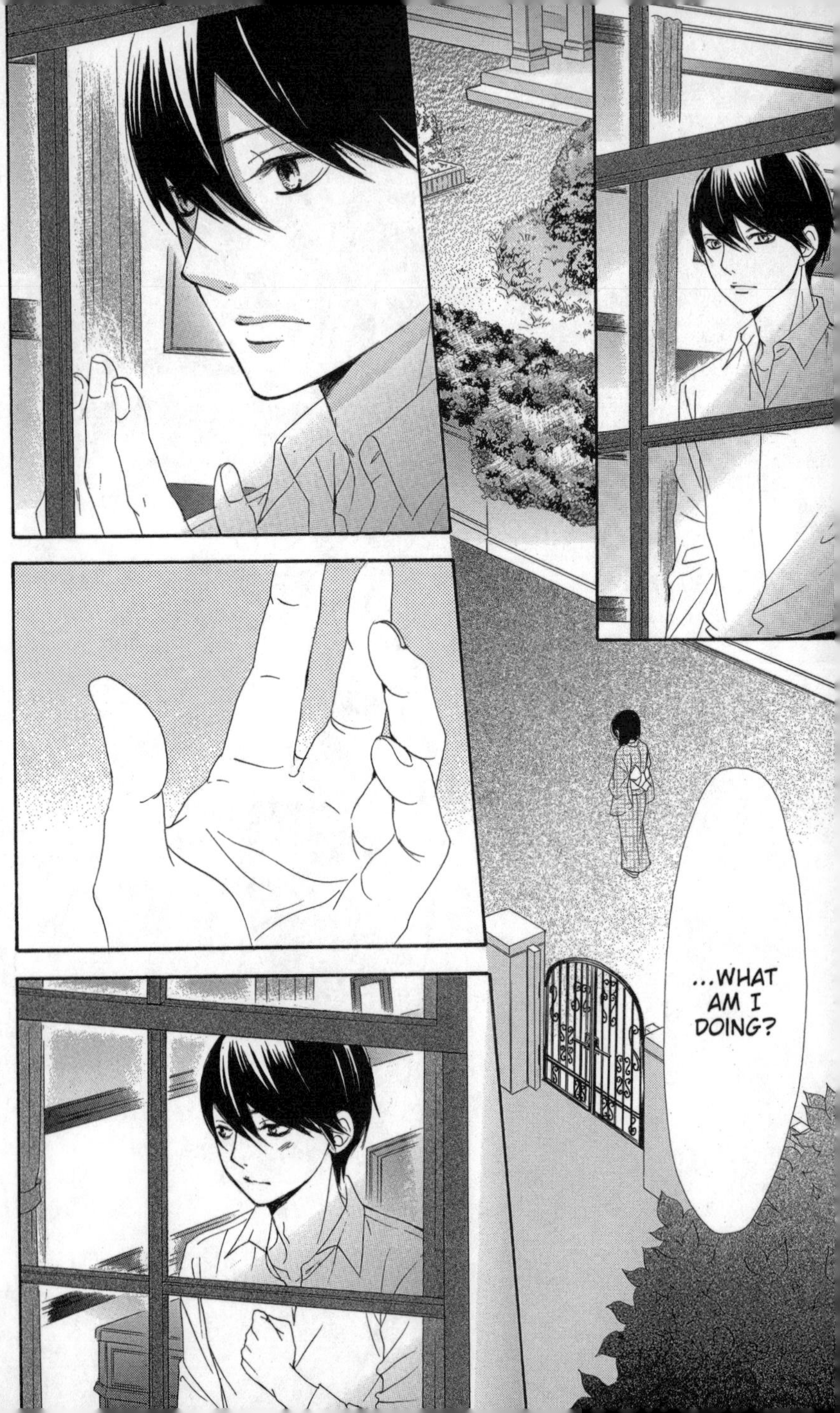
...WHAT AM I DOING?

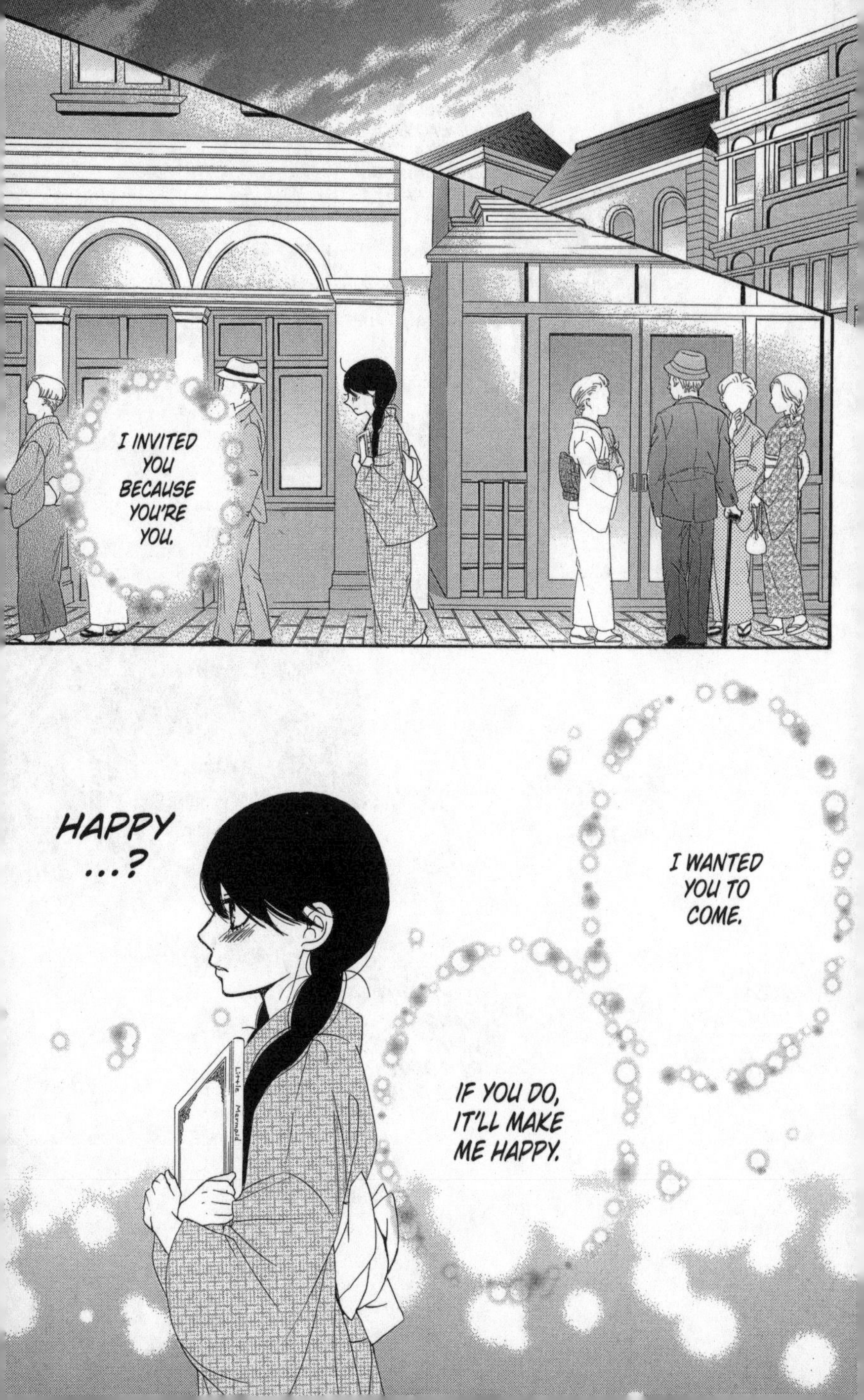
I INVITED YOU BECAUSE YOU'RE YOU.
I WANTED YOU TO COME.
IF YOU DO, IT'LL MAKE ME HAPPY.
HAPPY ...?
Little Mermaid

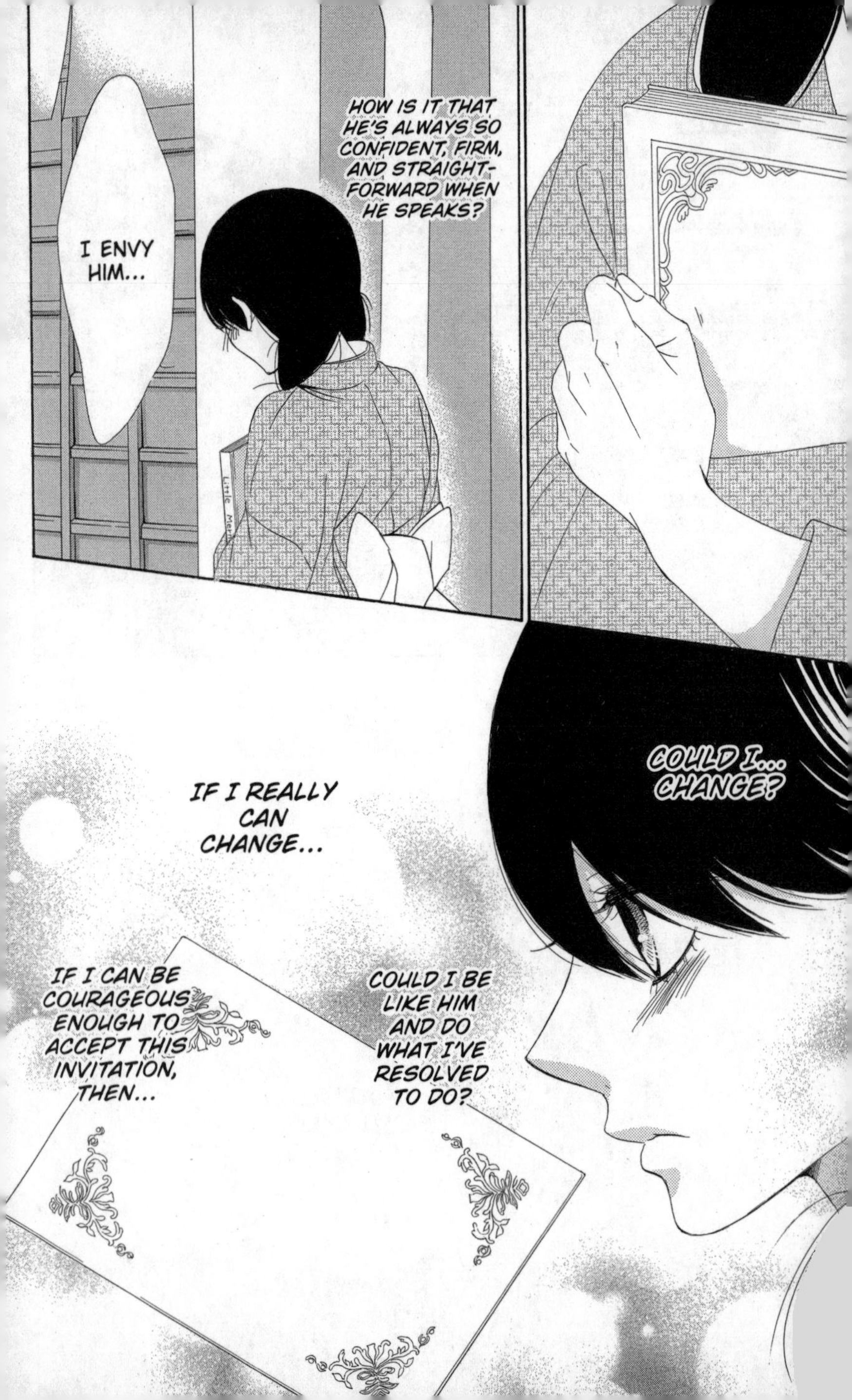
HOW IS IT THAT HE'S ALWAYS SO CONFIDENT, FIRM, AND STRAIGHT-FORWARD WHEN HE SPEAKS?
I ENVY HIM...
COULD I... CHANGE?
IF I REALLY CAN CHANGE...
COULD I BE LIKE HIM AND DO WHAT I'VE RESOLVED TO DO?
IF I CAN BE COURAGEOUS ENOUGH TO ACCEPT THIS INVITATION, THEN...

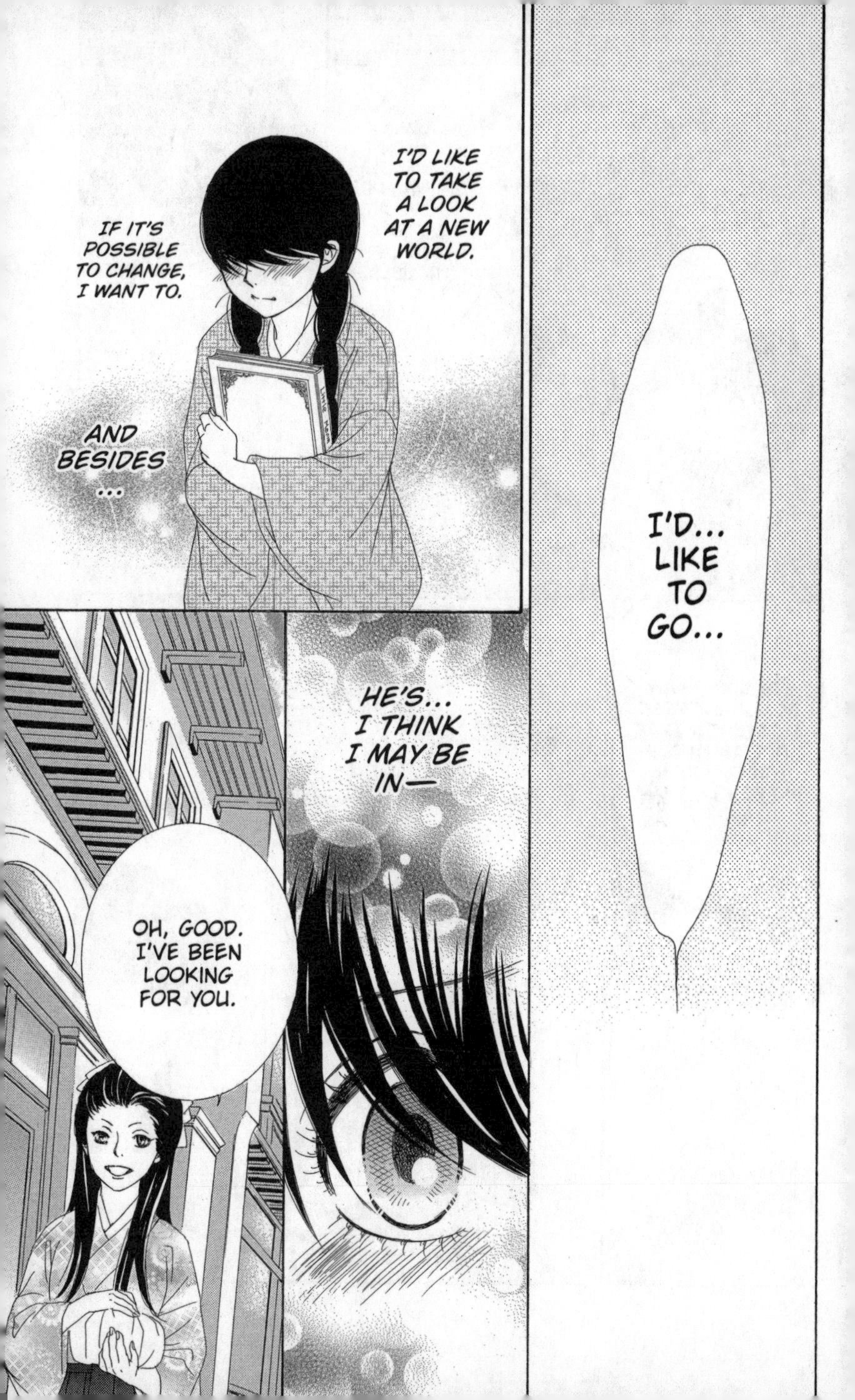
I'D... LIKE TO GO...
I'D LIKE TO TAKE A LOOK AT A NEW WORLD.
IF IT'S POSSIBLE TO CHANGE, I WANT TO.
AND BESIDES ...
HE'S... I THINK I MAY BE IN—
OH, GOOD. I'VE BEEN LOOKING FOR YOU.

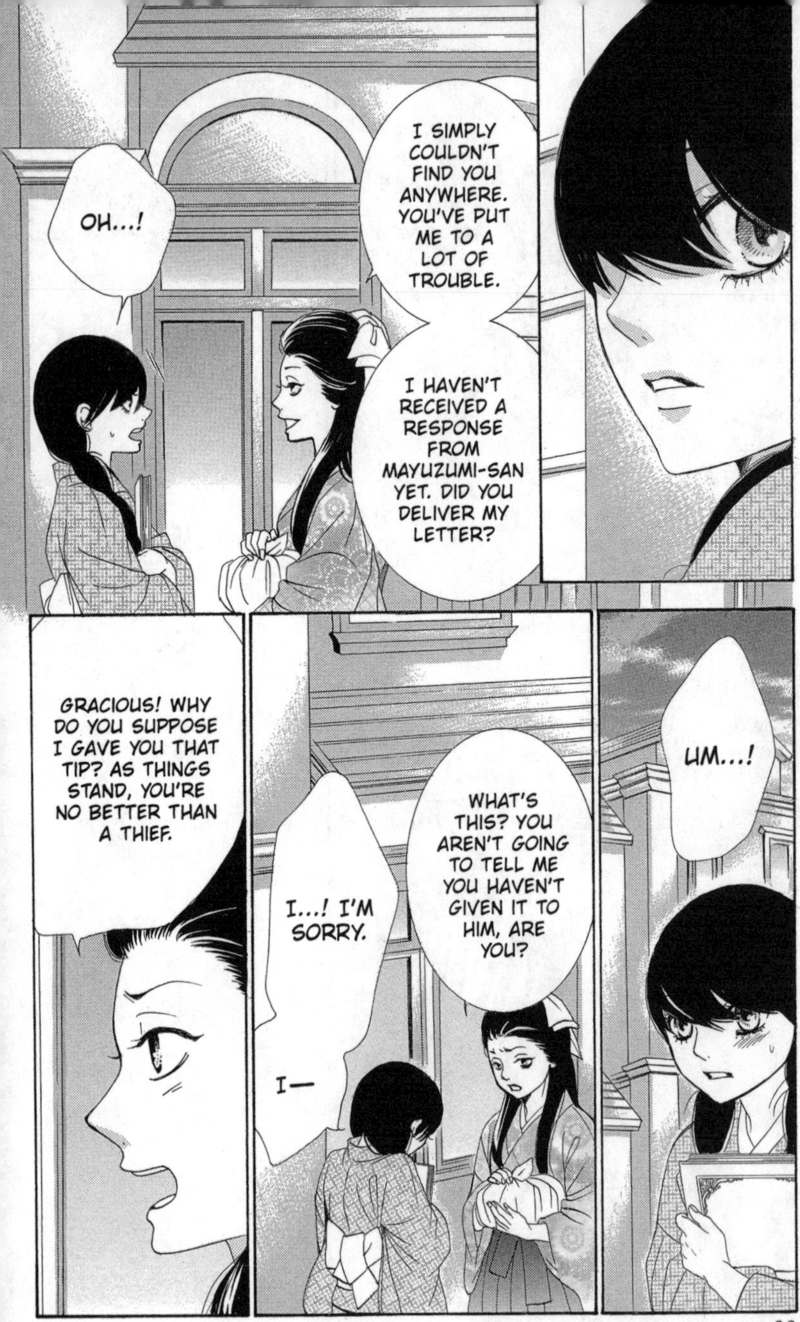
I SIMPLY COULDN'T FIND YOU ANYWHERE. YOU'VE PUT ME TO A LOT OF TROUBLE.
I HAVEN'T RECEIVED A RESPONSE FROM MAYUZUMI-SAN YET. DID YOU DELIVER MY LETTER?
OH...!
UM...!
WHAT'S THIS? YOU AREN'T GOING TO TELL ME YOU HAVEN'T GIVEN IT TO HIM, ARE YOU?
I...! I'M SORRY.
I—
GRACIOUS! WHY DO YOU SUPPOSE I GAVE YOU THAT TIP? AS THINGS STAND, YOU'RE NO BETTER THAN A THIEF.

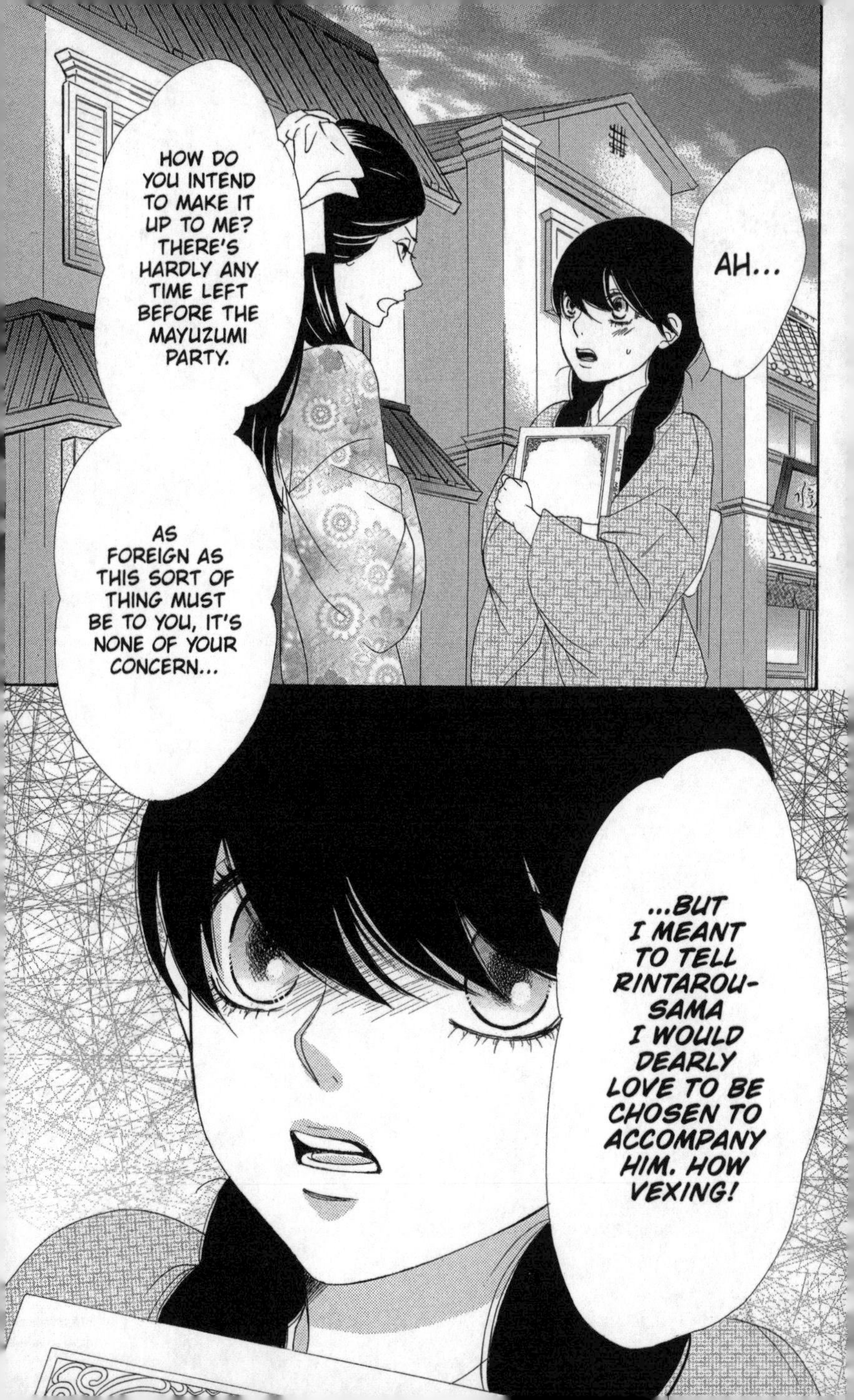
AH...
HOW DO YOU INTEND TO MAKE IT UP TO ME? THERE'S HARDLY ANY TIME LEFT BEFORE THE MAYUZUMI PARTY.
AS FOREIGN AS THIS SORT OF THING MUST BE TO YOU, IT'S NONE OF YOUR CONCERN...
...BUT I MEANT TO TELL RINTAROU-SAMA I WOULD DEARLY LOVE TO BE CHOSEN TO ACCOMPANY HIM. HOW VEXING!

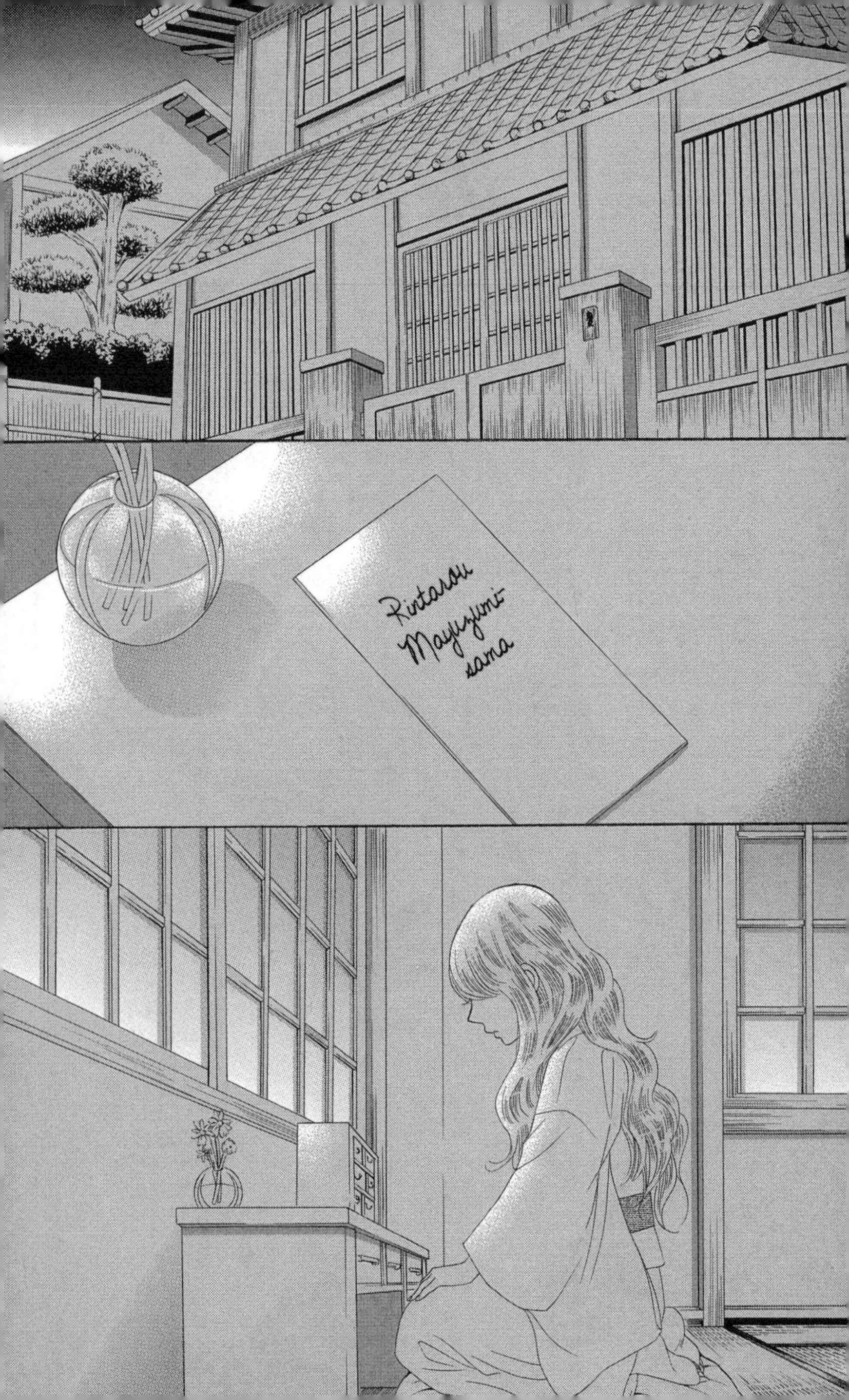
Rintarou Mayuzumi-sama

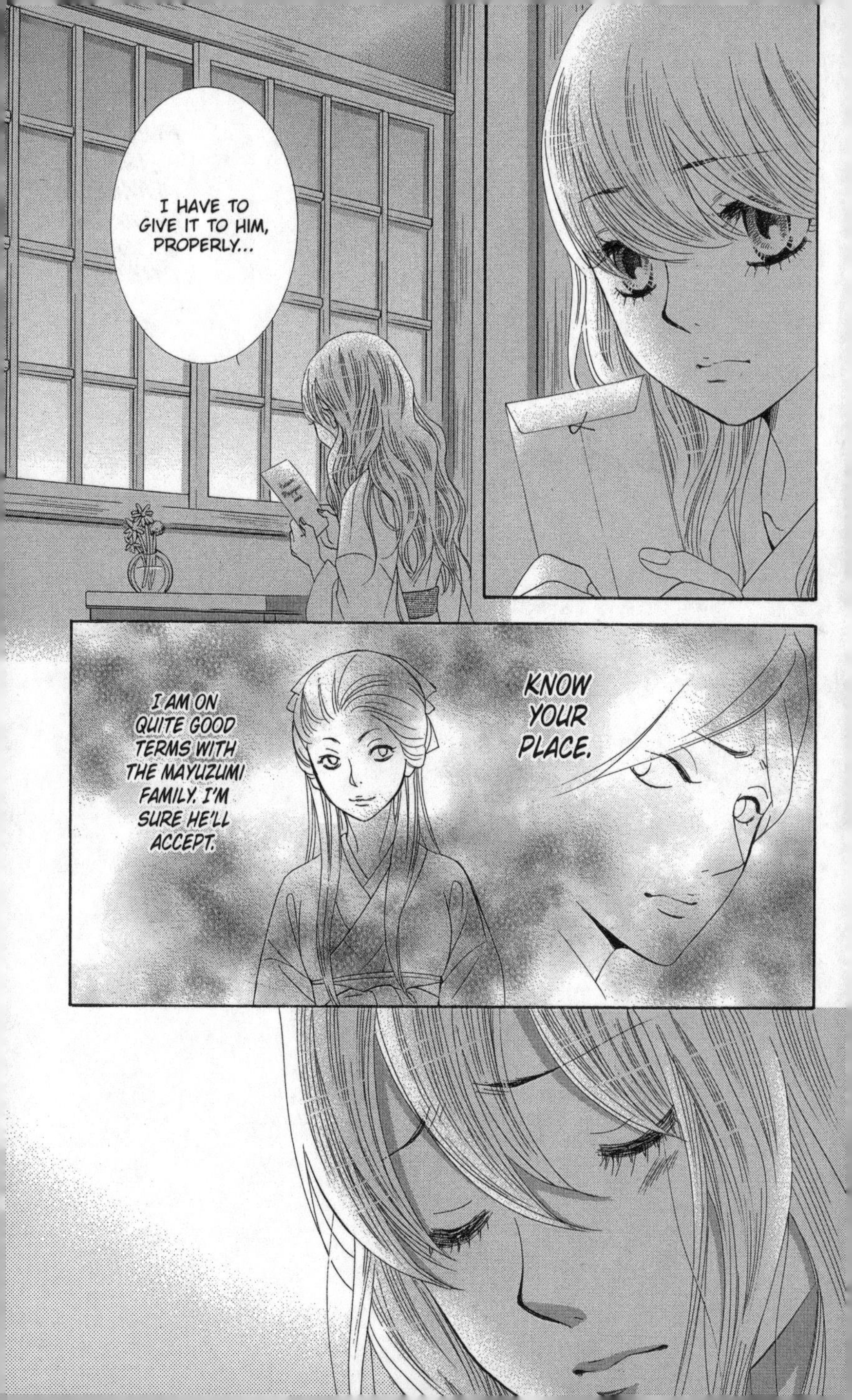
I HAVE TO GIVE IT TO HIM, PROPERLY...
KNOW YOUR PLACE.
I AM ON QUITE GOOD TERMS WITH THE MAYUZUMI FAMILY. I'M SURE HE'LL ACCEPT.

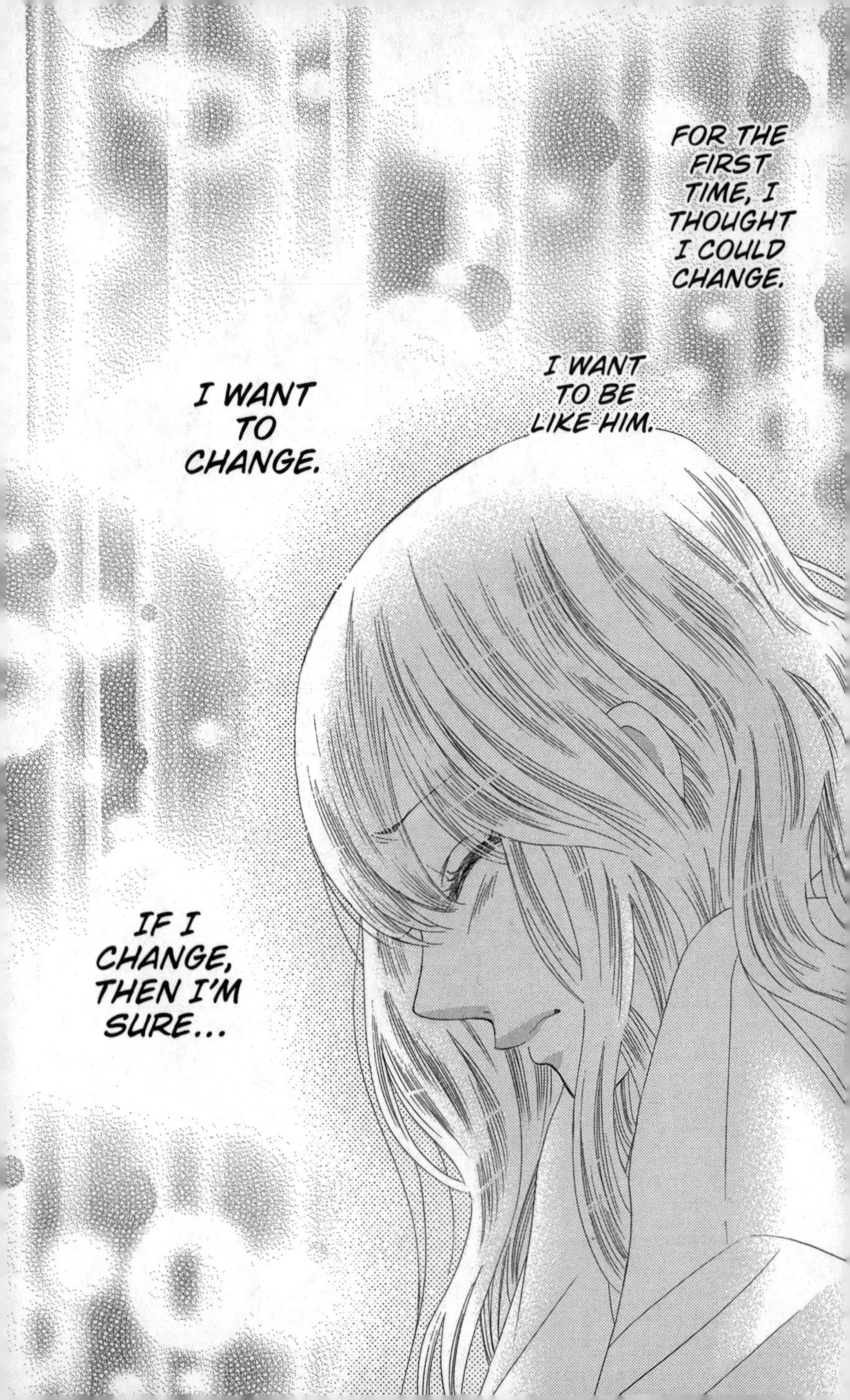
FOR THE FIRST TIME, I THOUGHT I COULD CHANGE.
I WANT TO BE LIKE HIM.
I WANT TO CHANGE.
IF I CHANGE, THEN I'M SURE...

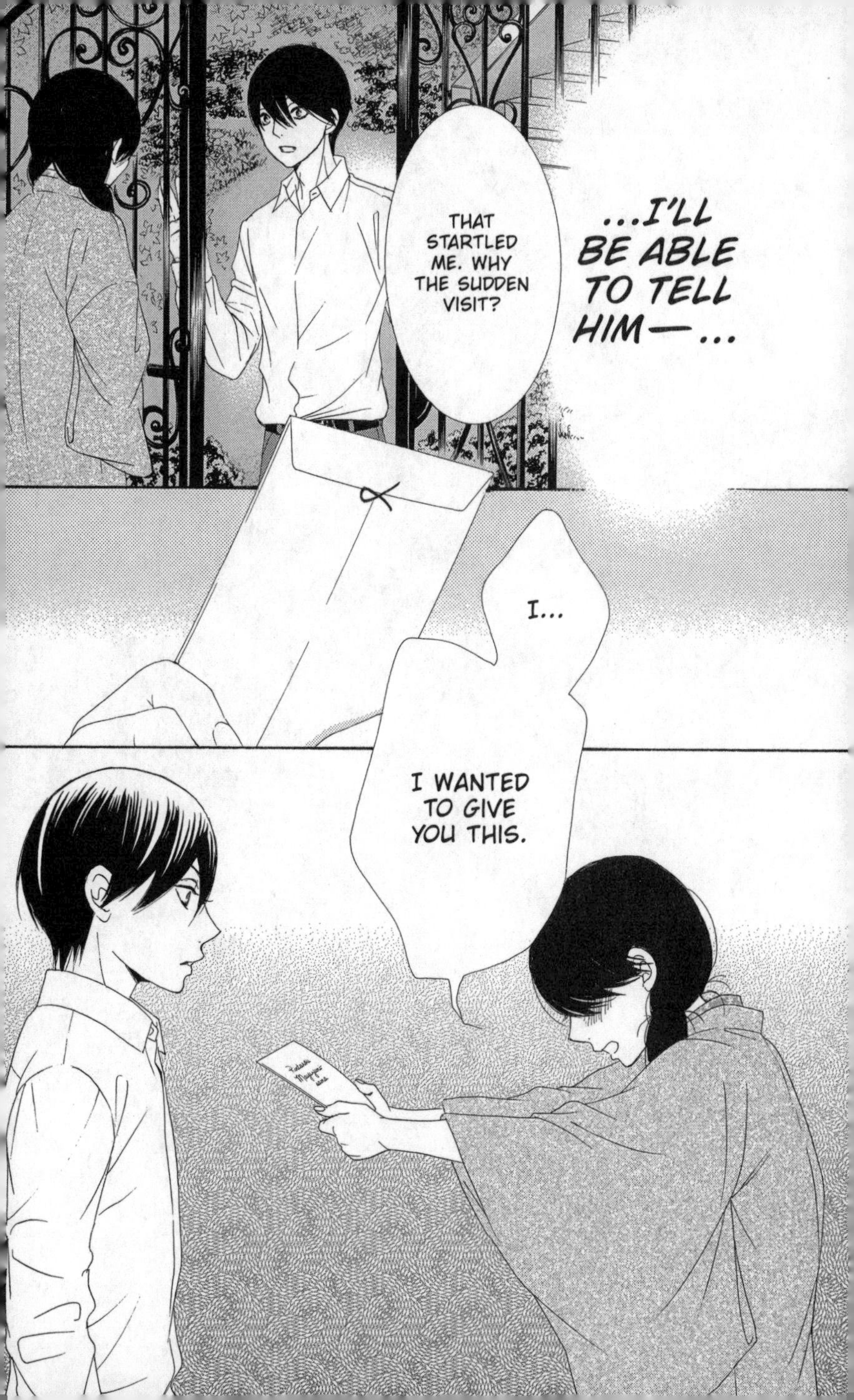
...I'LL BE ABLE TO TELL HIM—...
THAT STARTLED ME. WHY THE SUDDEN VISIT?
I...
I WANTED TO GIVE YOU THIS.

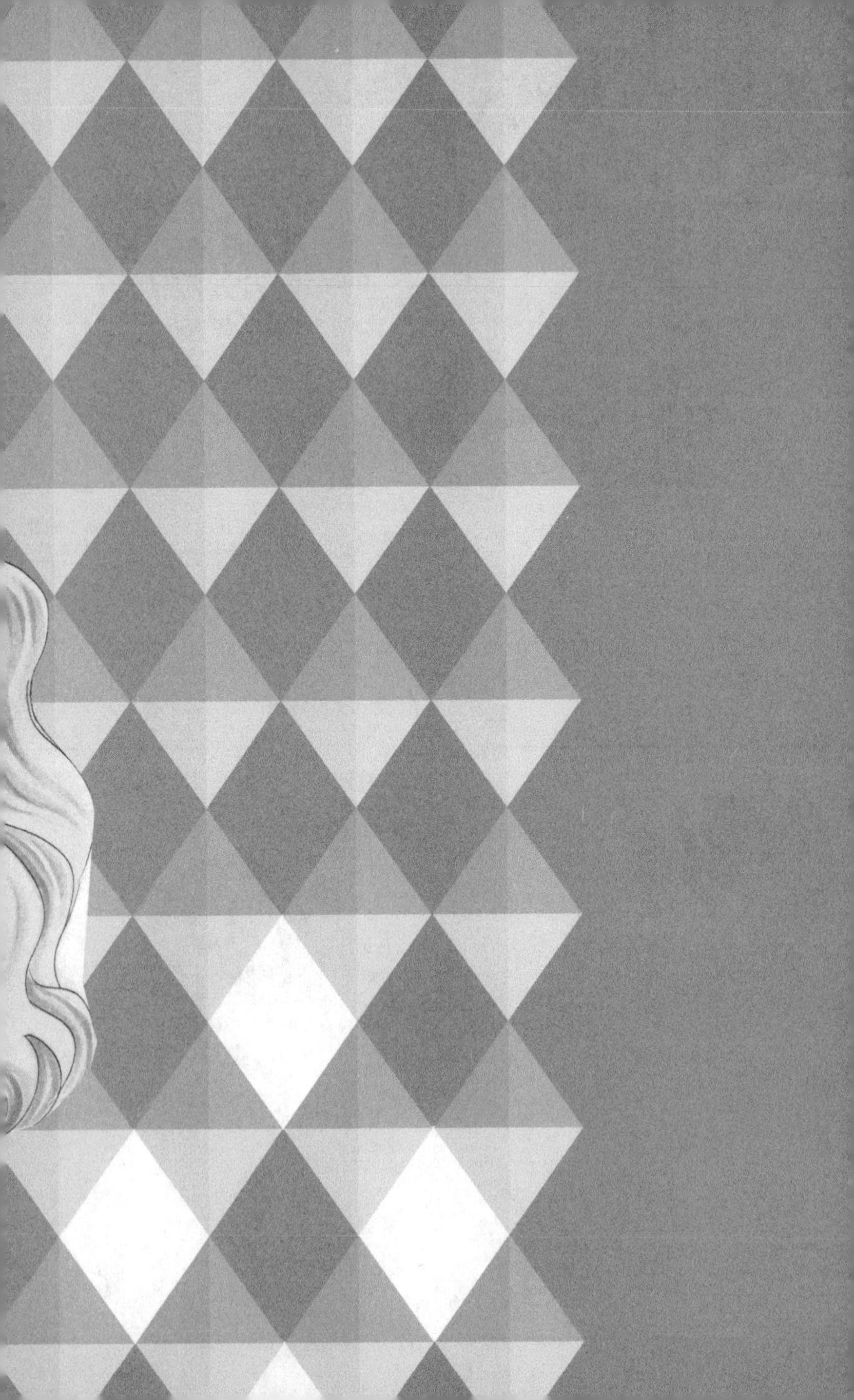

Episode 5

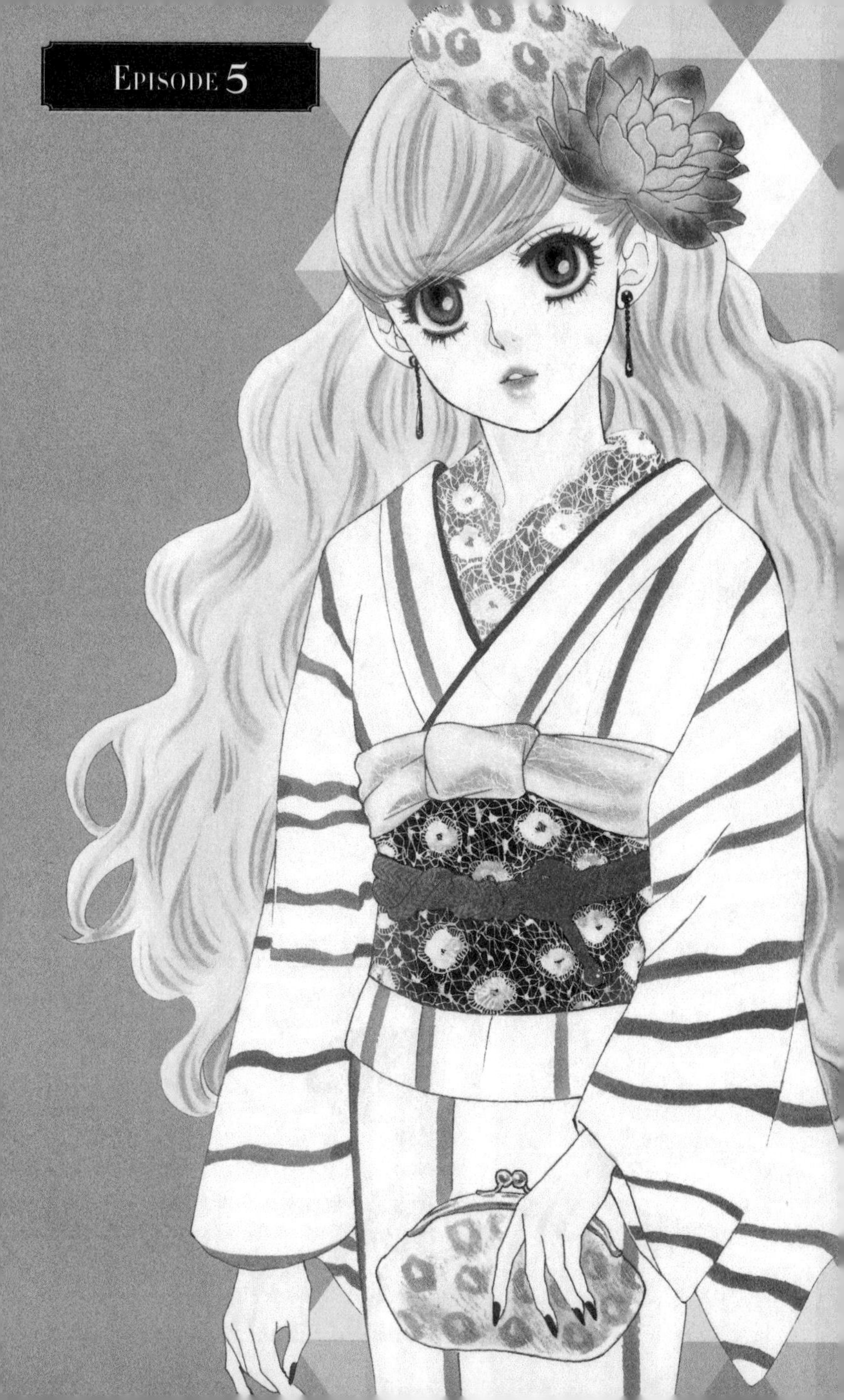

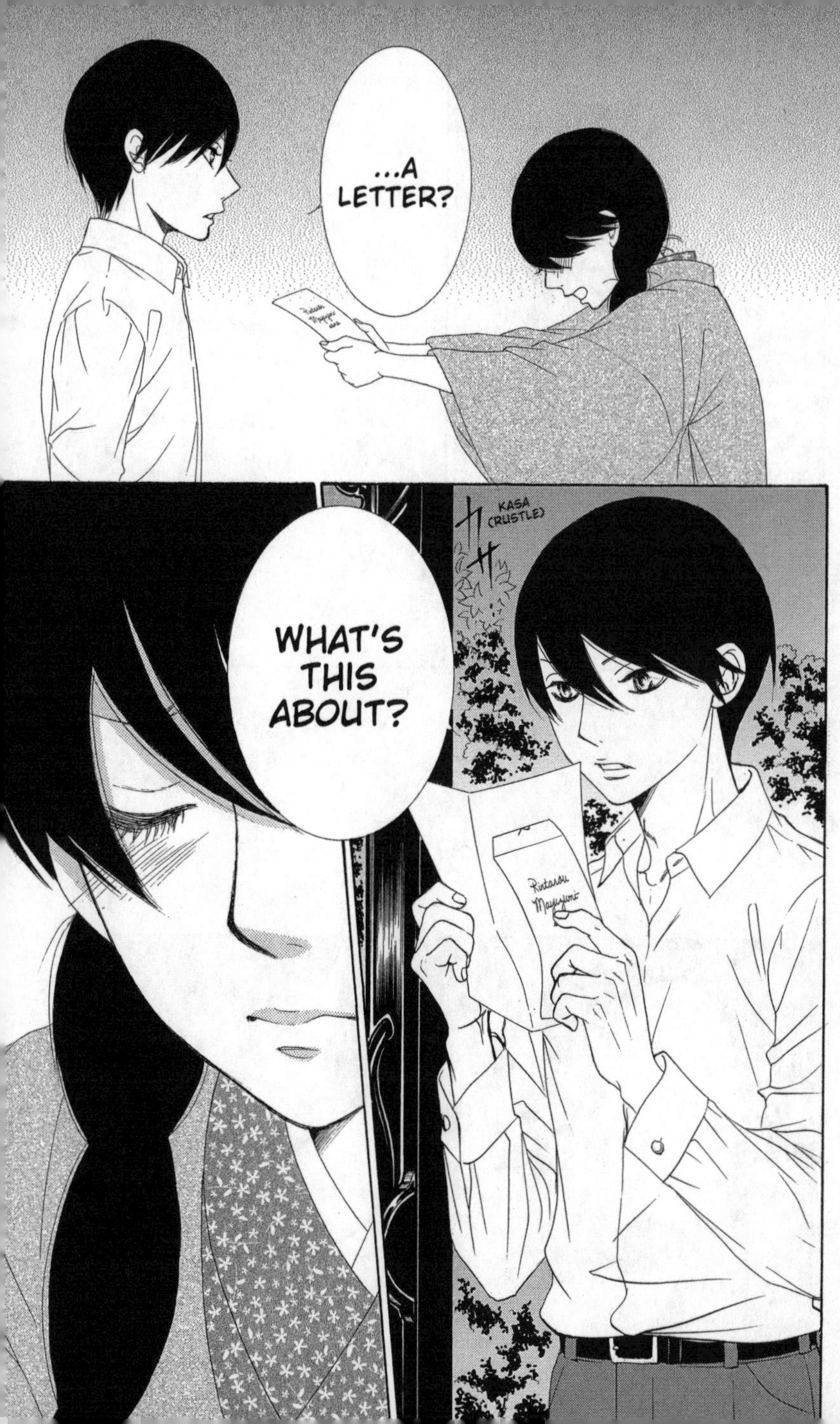
...A LETTER?
KASA (RUSTLE)
WHAT'S THIS ABOUT?

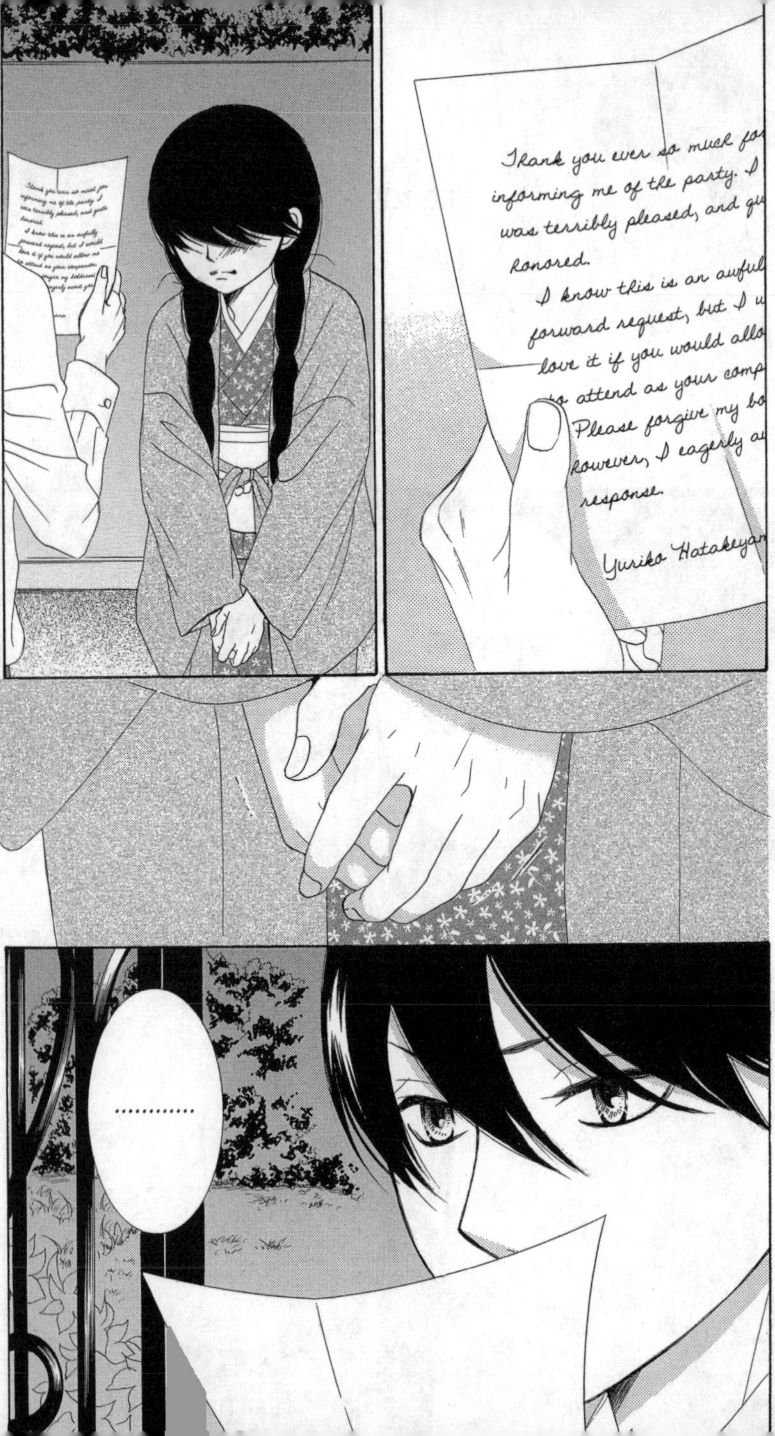
Thank you ever so much for
informing me of the party. I
was terribly pleased, and qu
honored.
I know this is an awful
forward request, but I w
love it if you would allo
to attend as your comp
Please forgive my bo
however, I eagerly a
response.
Yuriko Hatakeyam
....

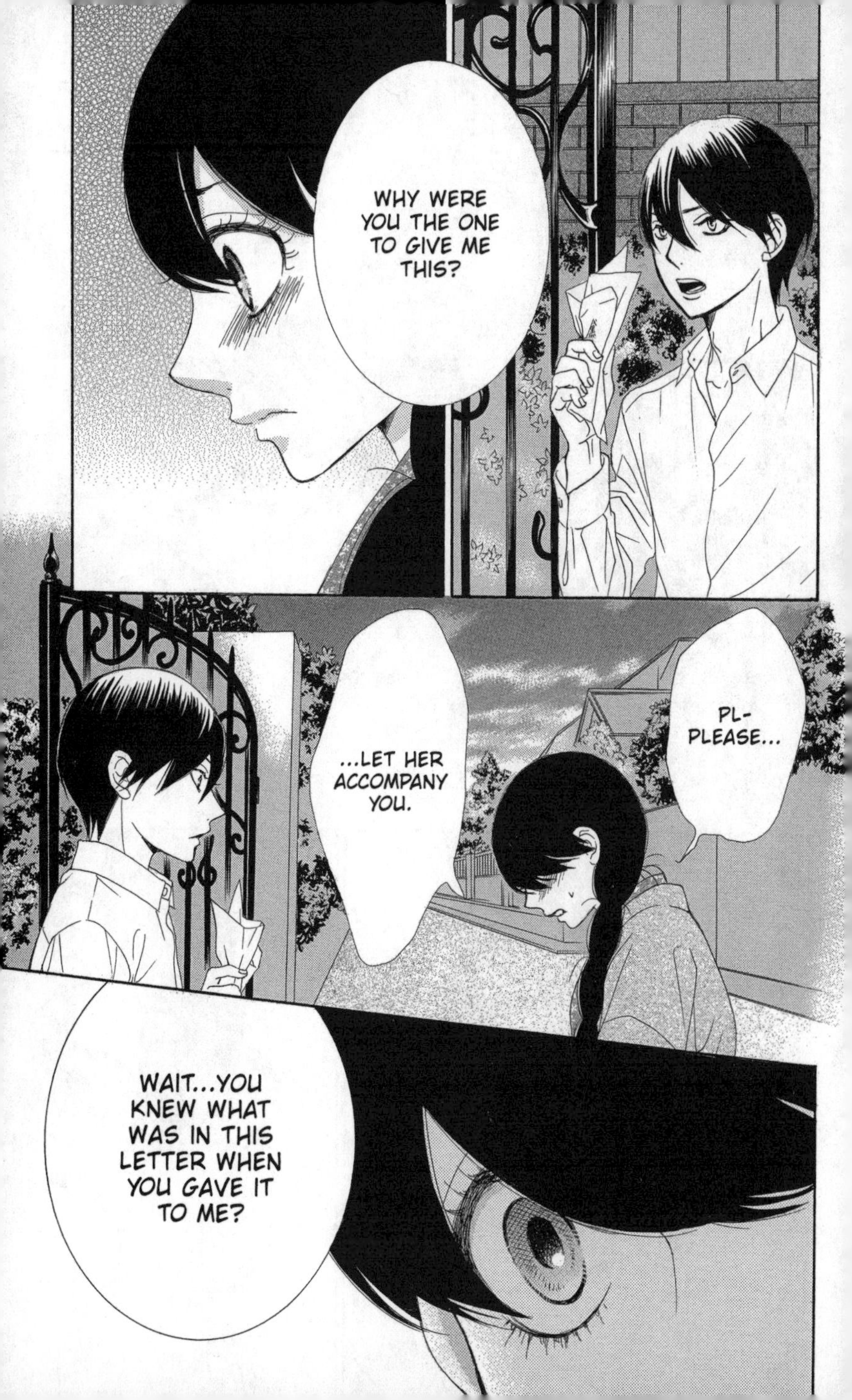
WHY WERE YOU THE ONE TO GIVE ME THIS?
PL- PLEASE...
...LET HER ACCOMPANY YOU.
WAIT...YOU KNEW WHAT WAS IN THIS LETTER WHEN YOU GAVE IT TO ME?

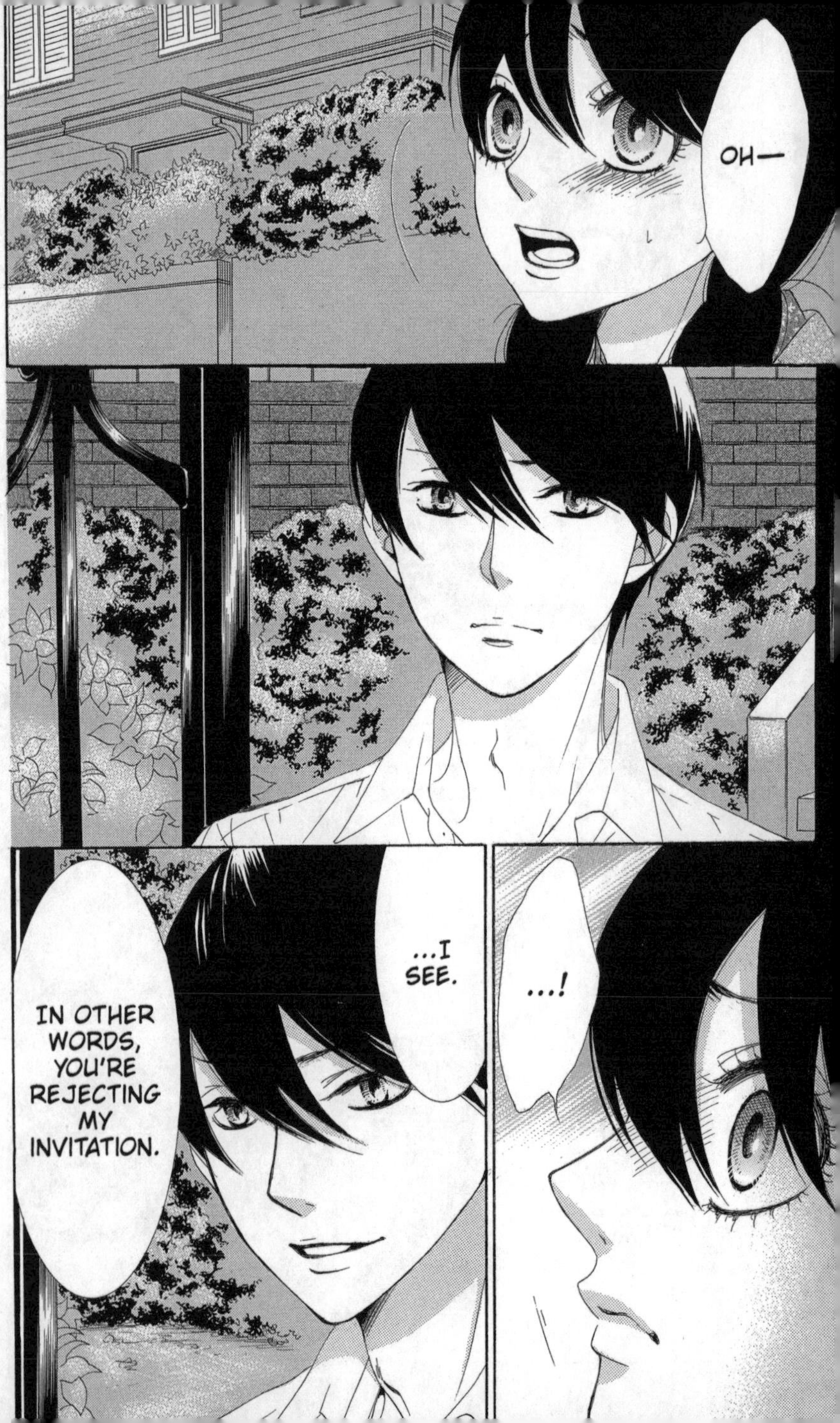
OH—
...!
...I SEE.
IN OTHER WORDS, YOU'RE REJECTING MY INVITATION.

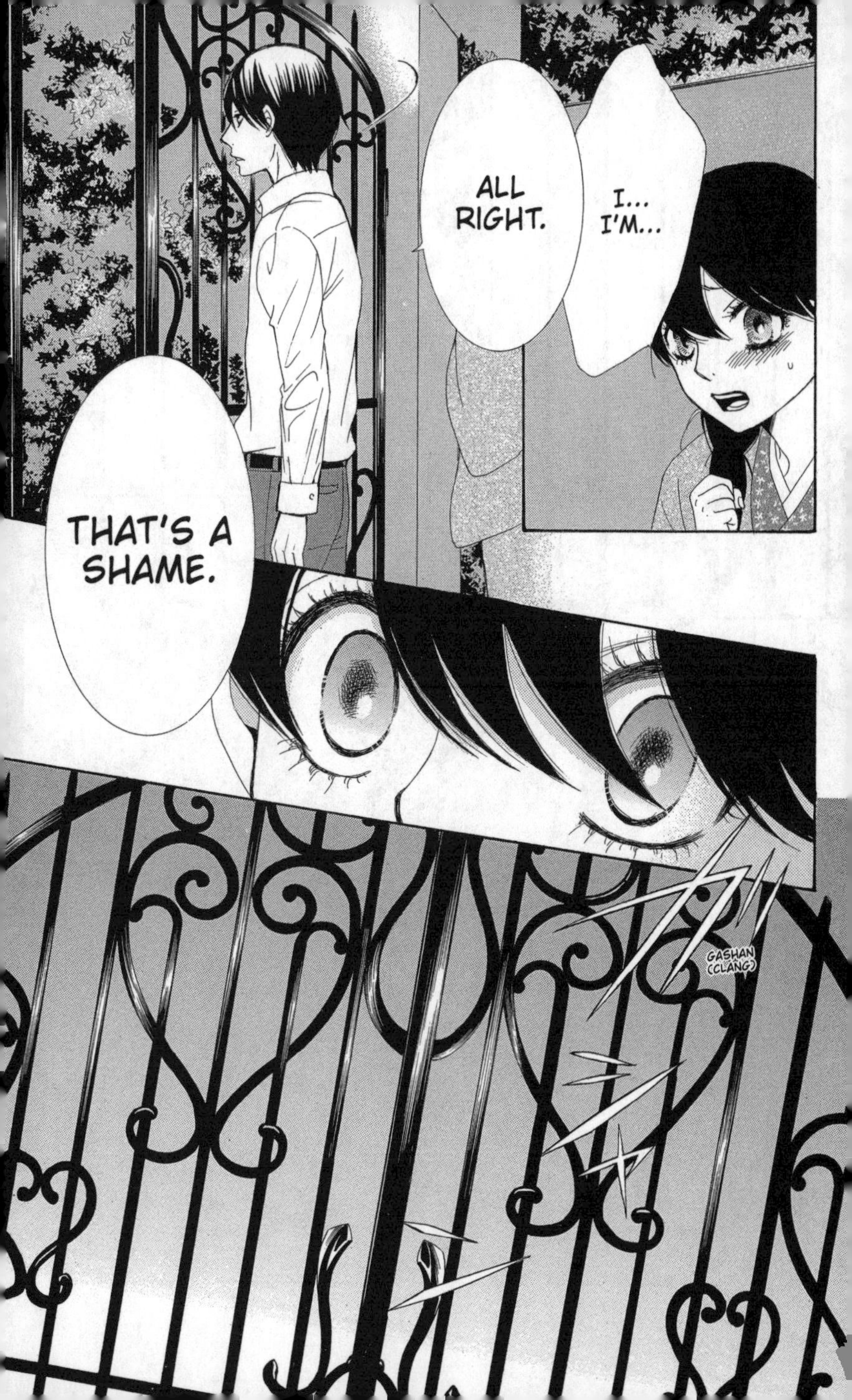
I... I'M...
ALL RIGHT.
THAT'S A SHAME.
GASHAN (CLANG)

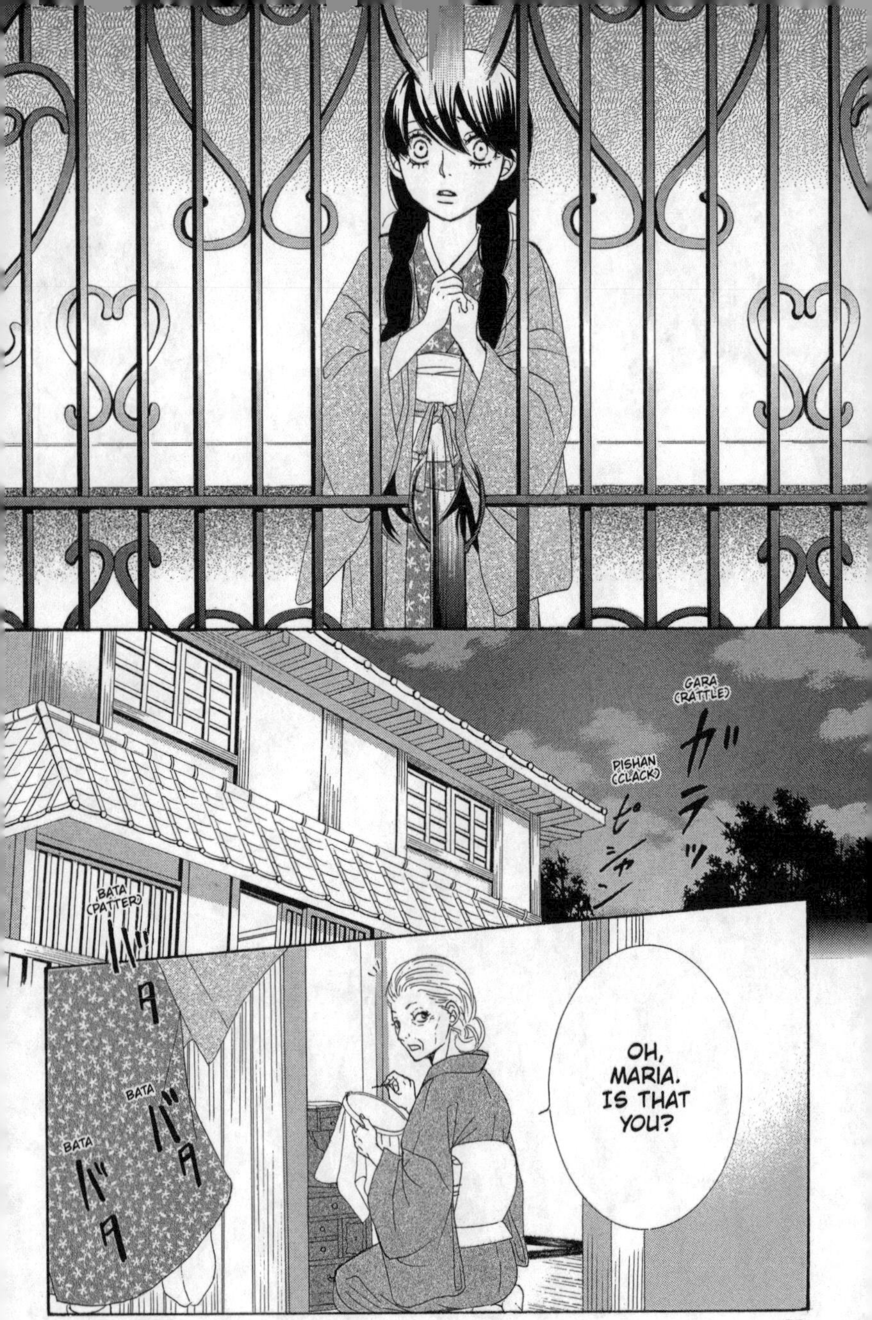
GARA (RATTLE)
PISHAN (CLACK)
BATA (PATTER)
OH, MARIA. IS THAT YOU?
BATA
BATA

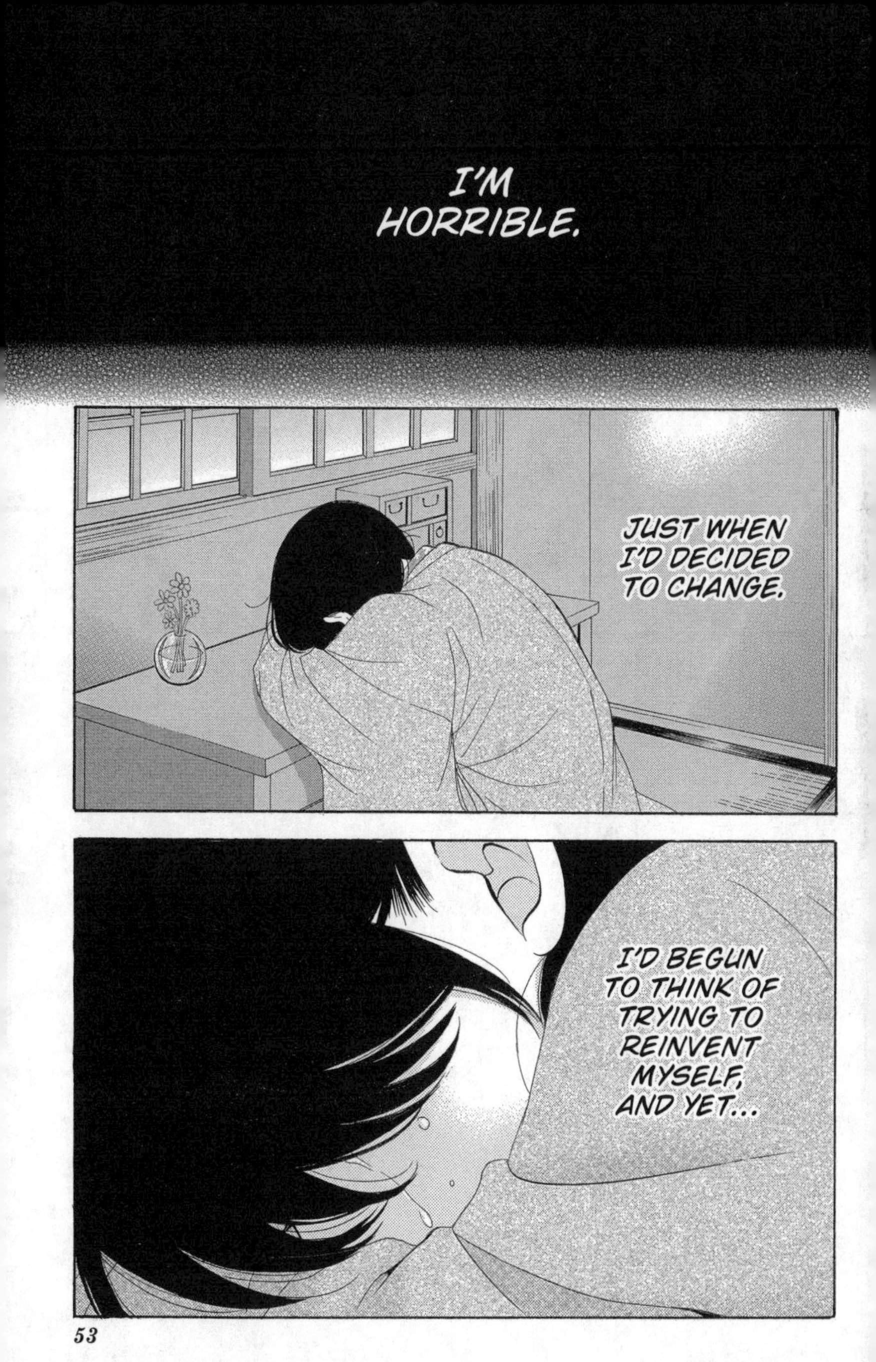
I'M HORRIBLE.
JUST WHEN I'D DECIDED TO CHANGE.
I'D BEGUN TO THINK OF TRYING TO REINVENT MYSELF, AND YET...

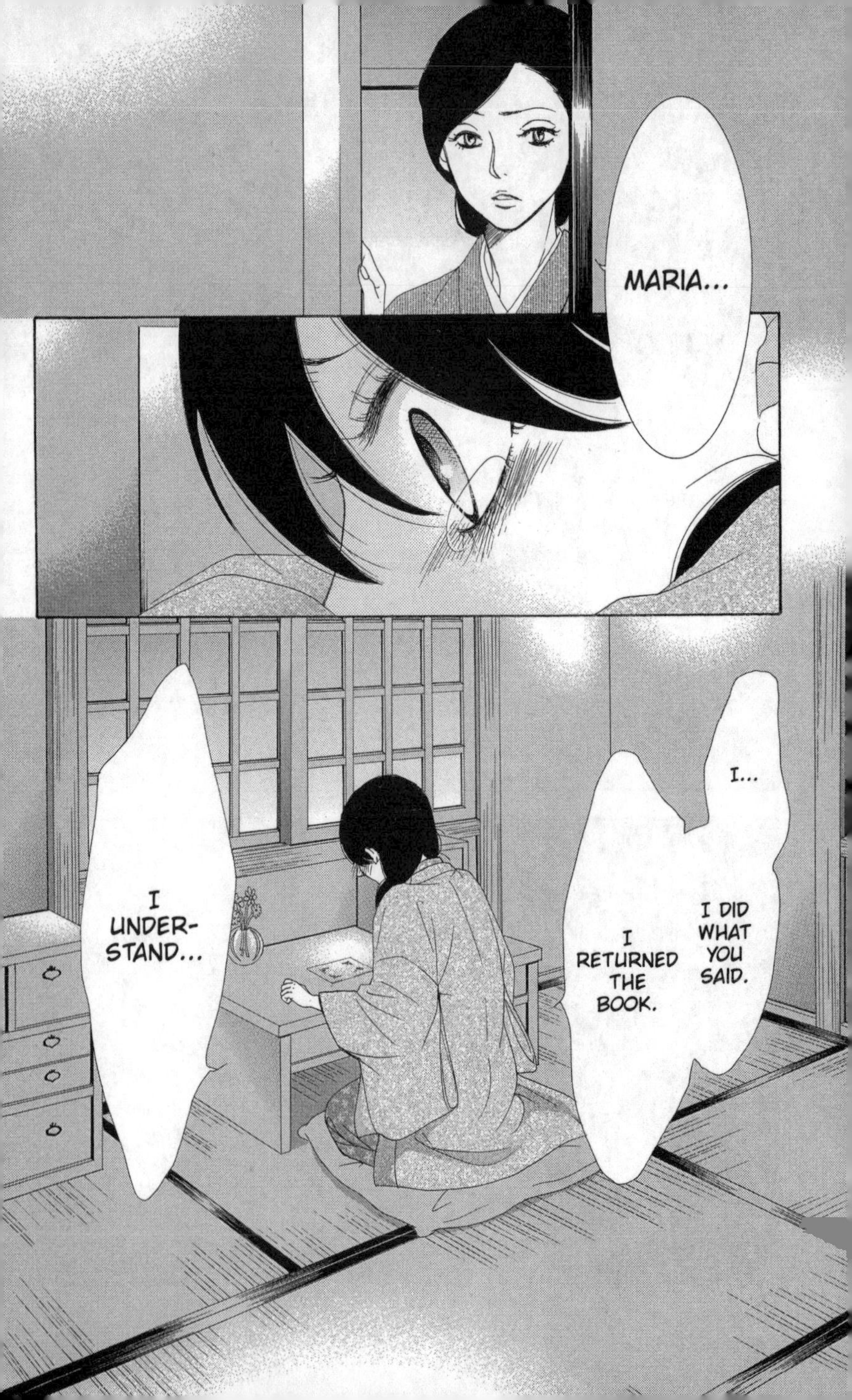
MARIA...
I...
I DID WHAT YOU SAID.
I RETURNED THE BOOK.
I UNDER-STAND...

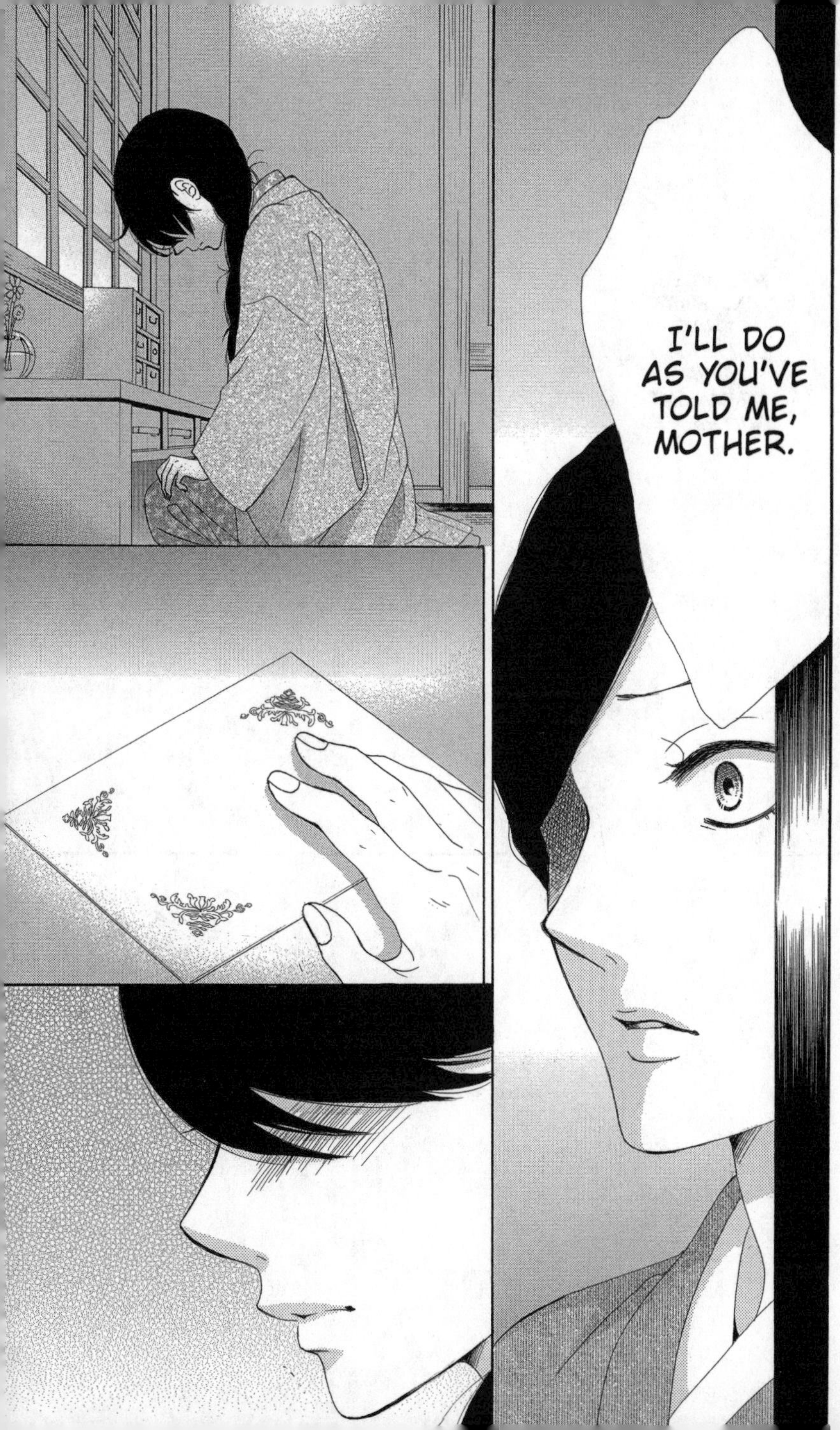
I'LL DO AS YOU'VE TOLD ME, MOTHER.

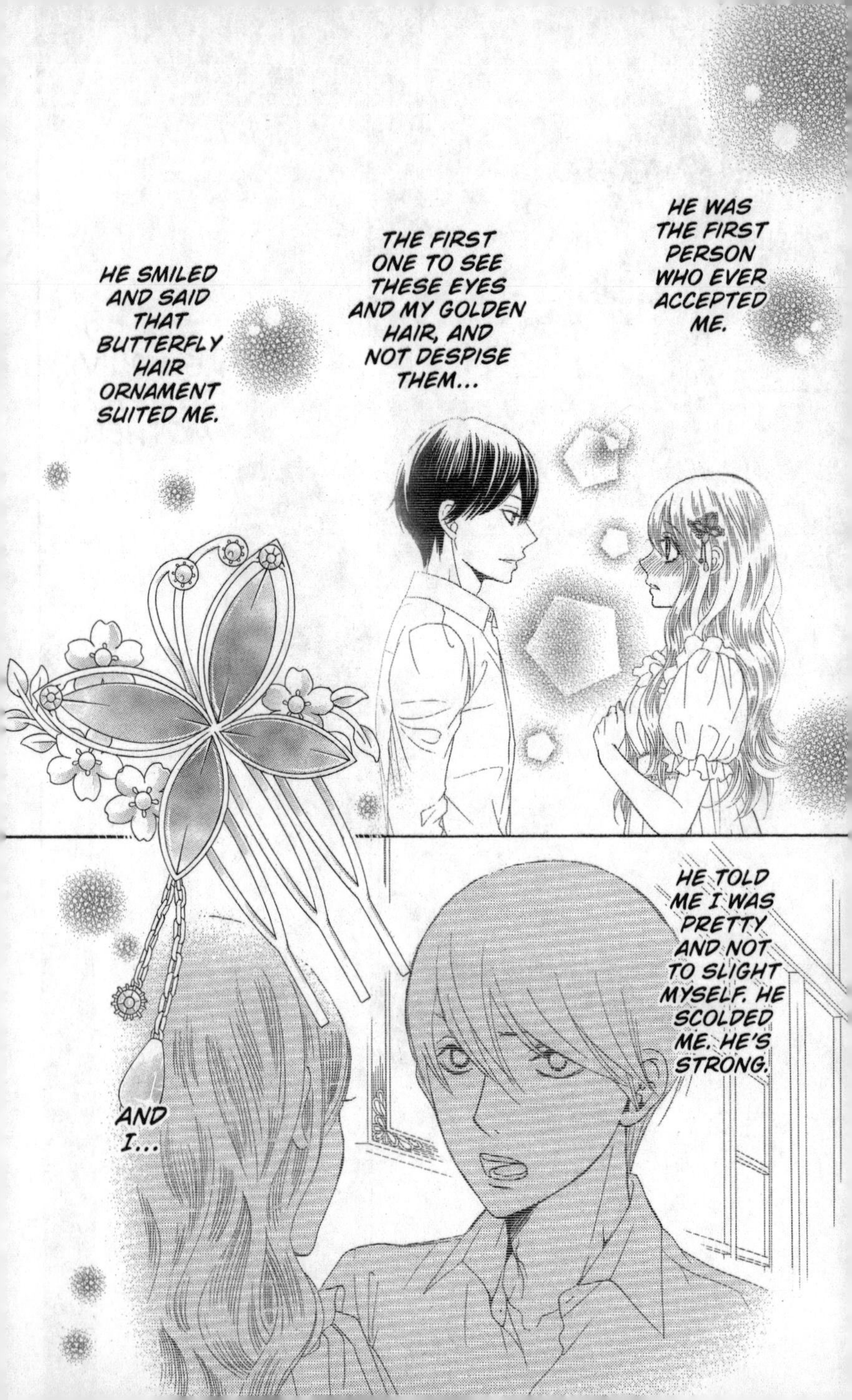
HE WAS THE FIRST PERSON WHO EVER ACCEPTED ME.
THE FIRST ONE TO SEE THESE EYES AND MY GOLDEN HAIR, AND NOT DESPISE THEM...
HE SMILED AND SAID THAT BUTTERFLY HAIR ORNAMENT SUITED ME.
HE TOLD ME I WAS PRETTY AND NOT TO SLIGHT MYSELF. HE SCOLDED ME. HE'S STRONG.
AND I...

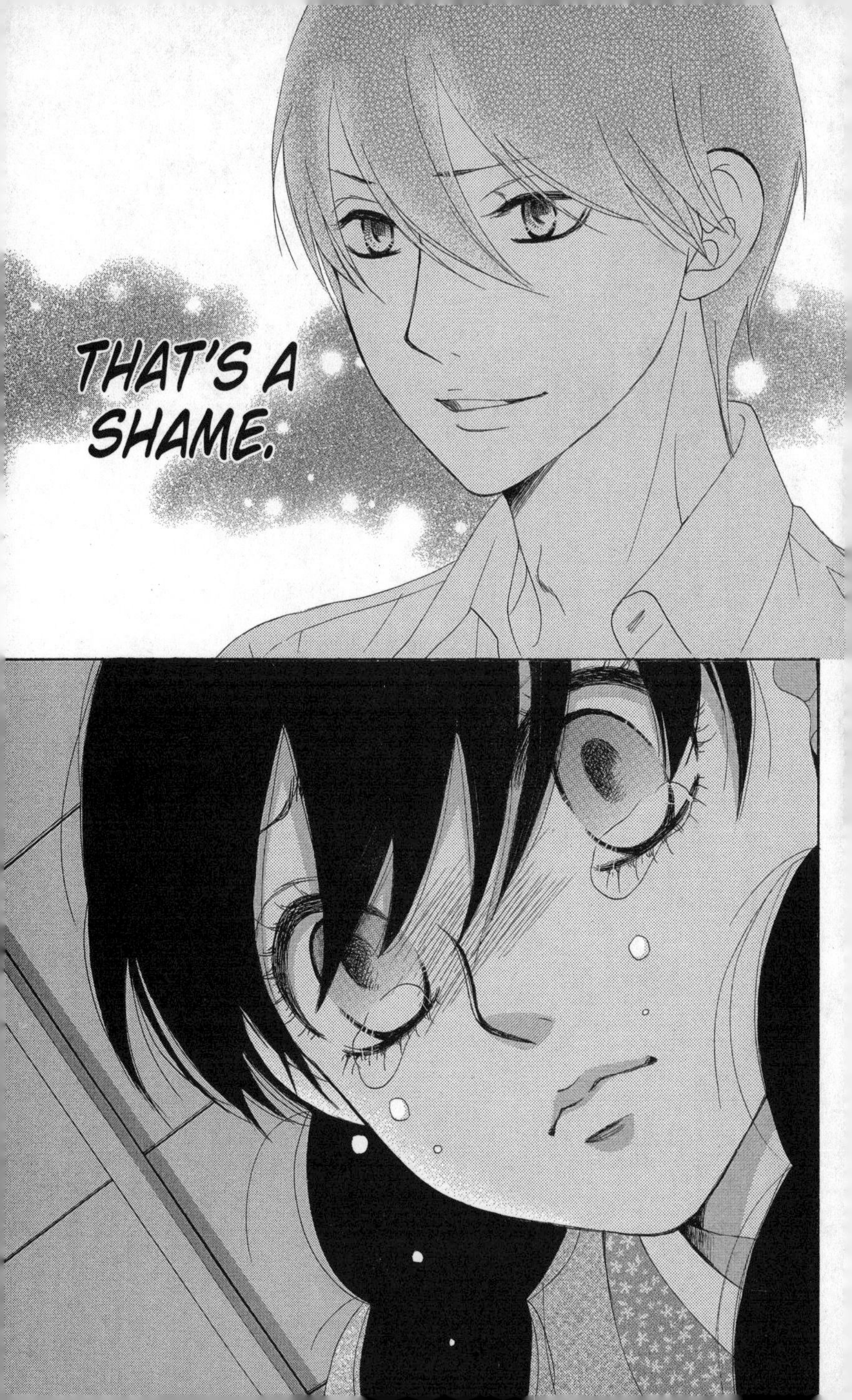
THAT'S A SHAME.

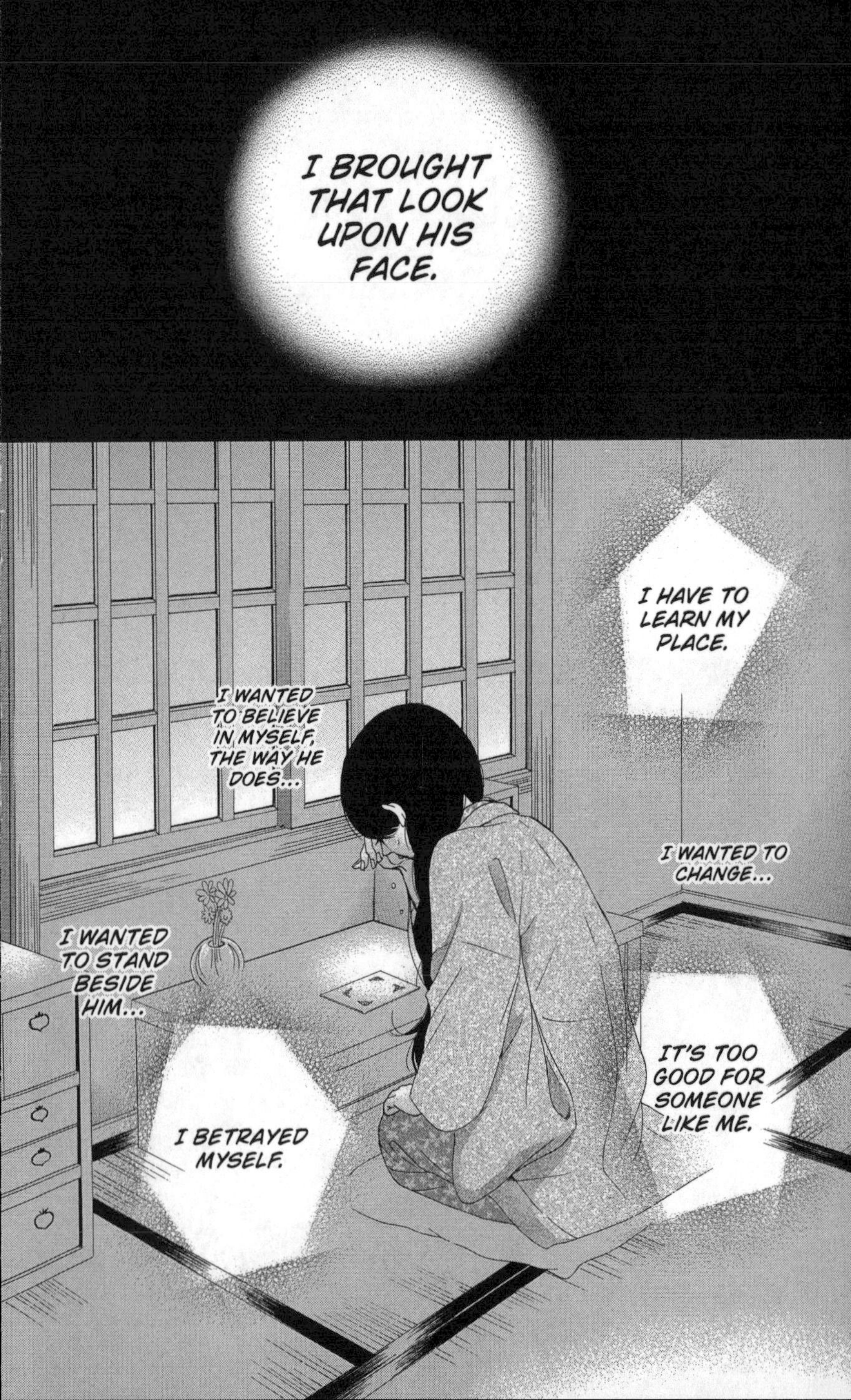
I BROUGHT THAT LOOK UPON HIS FACE.
I HAVE TO LEARN MY PLACE.
I WANTED TO BELIEVE IN MYSELF, THE WAY HE DOES...
I WANTED TO CHANGE...
I WANTED TO STAND BESIDE HIM...
IT'S TOO GOOD FOR SOMEONE LIKE ME.
I BETRAYED MYSELF.

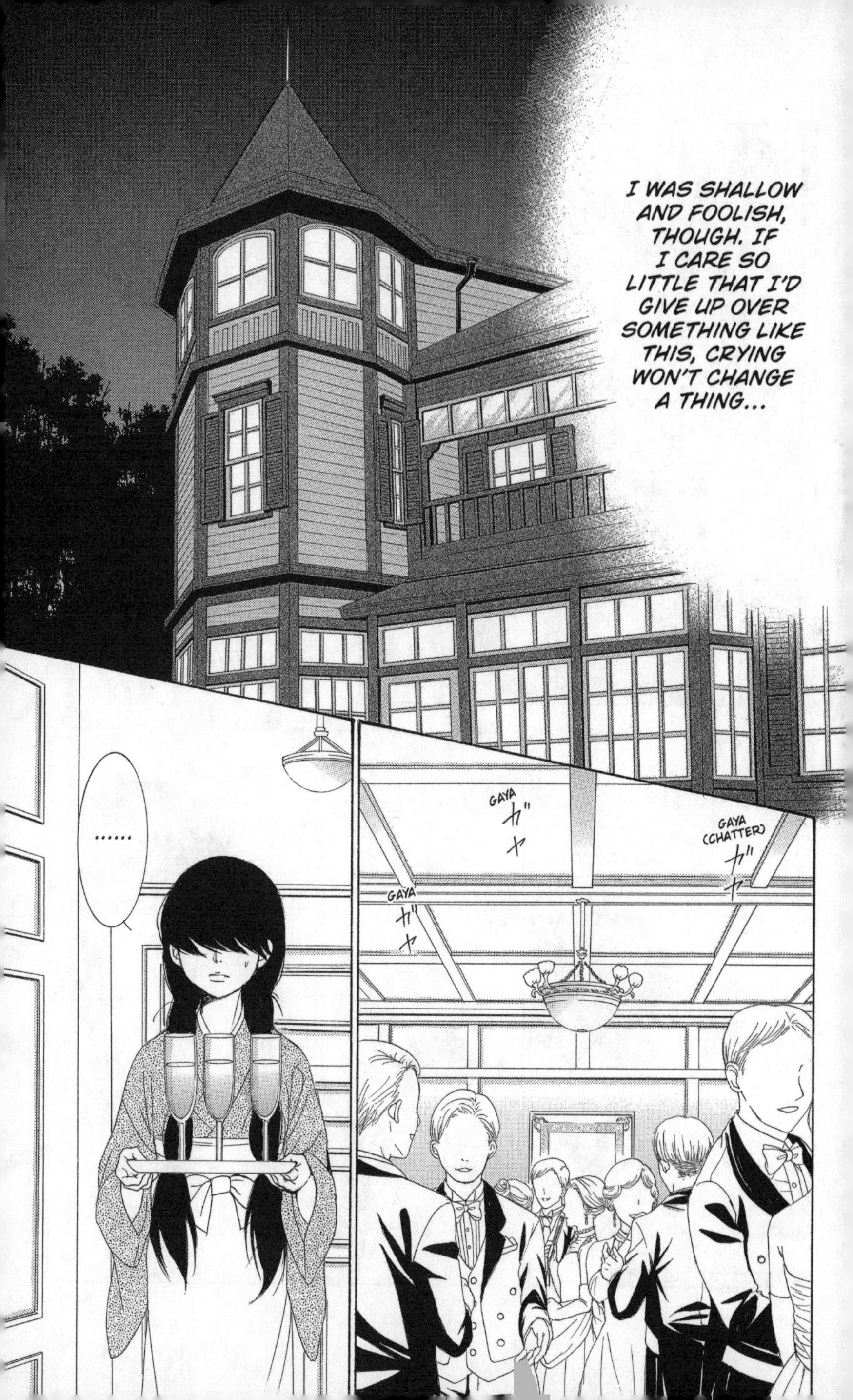
I WAS SHALLOW AND FOOLISH, THOUGH. IF I CARE SO LITTLE THAT I'D GIVE UP OVER SOMETHING LIKE THIS, CRYING WON'T CHANGE A THING...
GAYA (CHATTER)
ガヤ
GAYA
ガヤ
GAYA
ガヤ
......

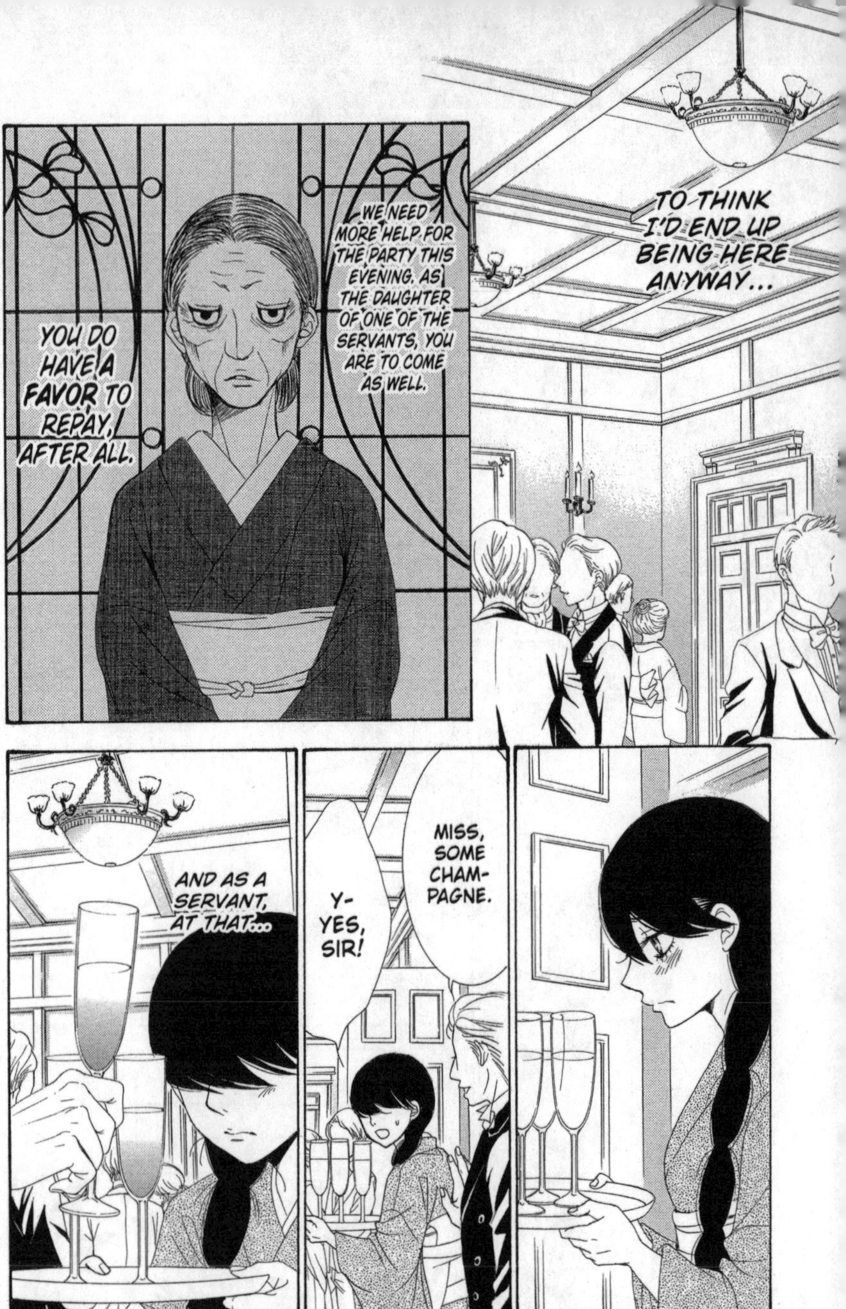
TO THINK I'D END UP BEING HERE ANYWAY...
WE NEED MORE HELP FOR THE PARTY THIS EVENING. AS THE DAUGHTER OF ONE OF THE SERVANTS, YOU ARE TO COME AS WELL.
YOU DO HAVE A FAVOR TO REPAY, AFTER ALL.
MISS, SOME CHAMPAGNE.
Y-YES, SIR!
AND AS A SERVANT, AT THAT...

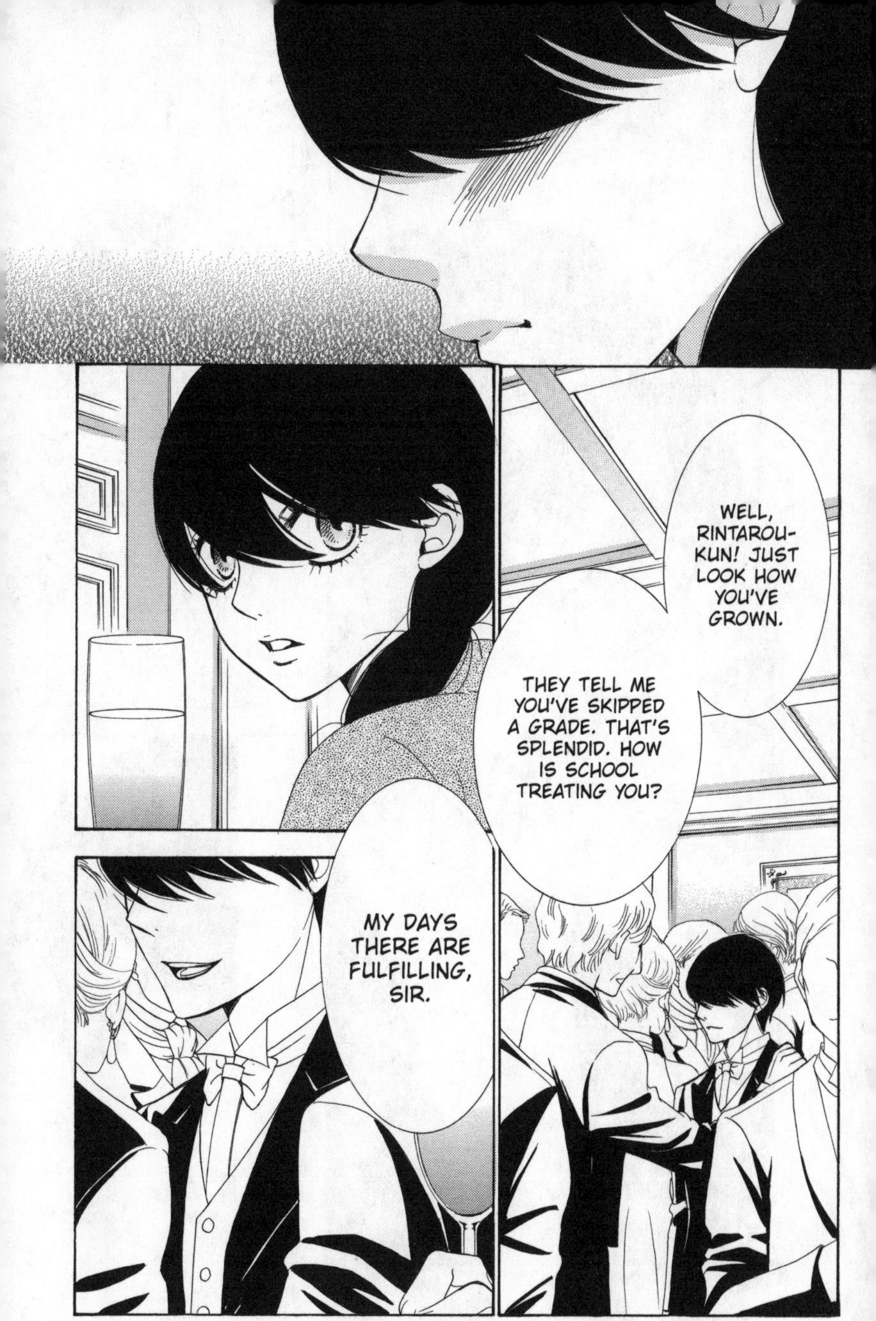
WELL, RINTAROU-KUN! JUST LOOK HOW YOU'VE GROWN.
THEY TELL ME YOU'VE SKIPPED A GRADE. THAT'S SPLENDID. HOW IS SCHOOL TREATING YOU?
MY DAYS THERE ARE FULFILLING, SIR.

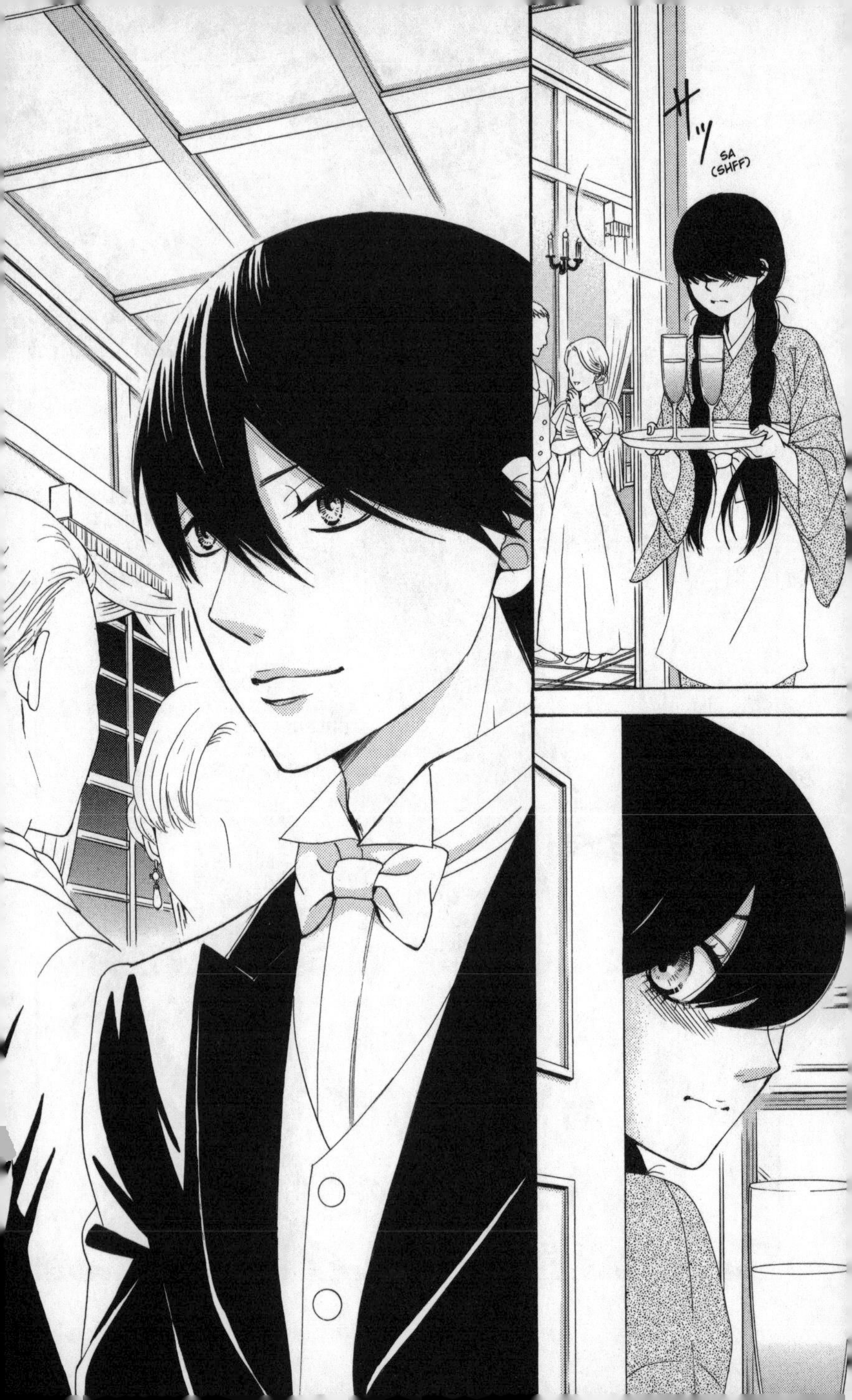
サッ
SA
(SHFF)

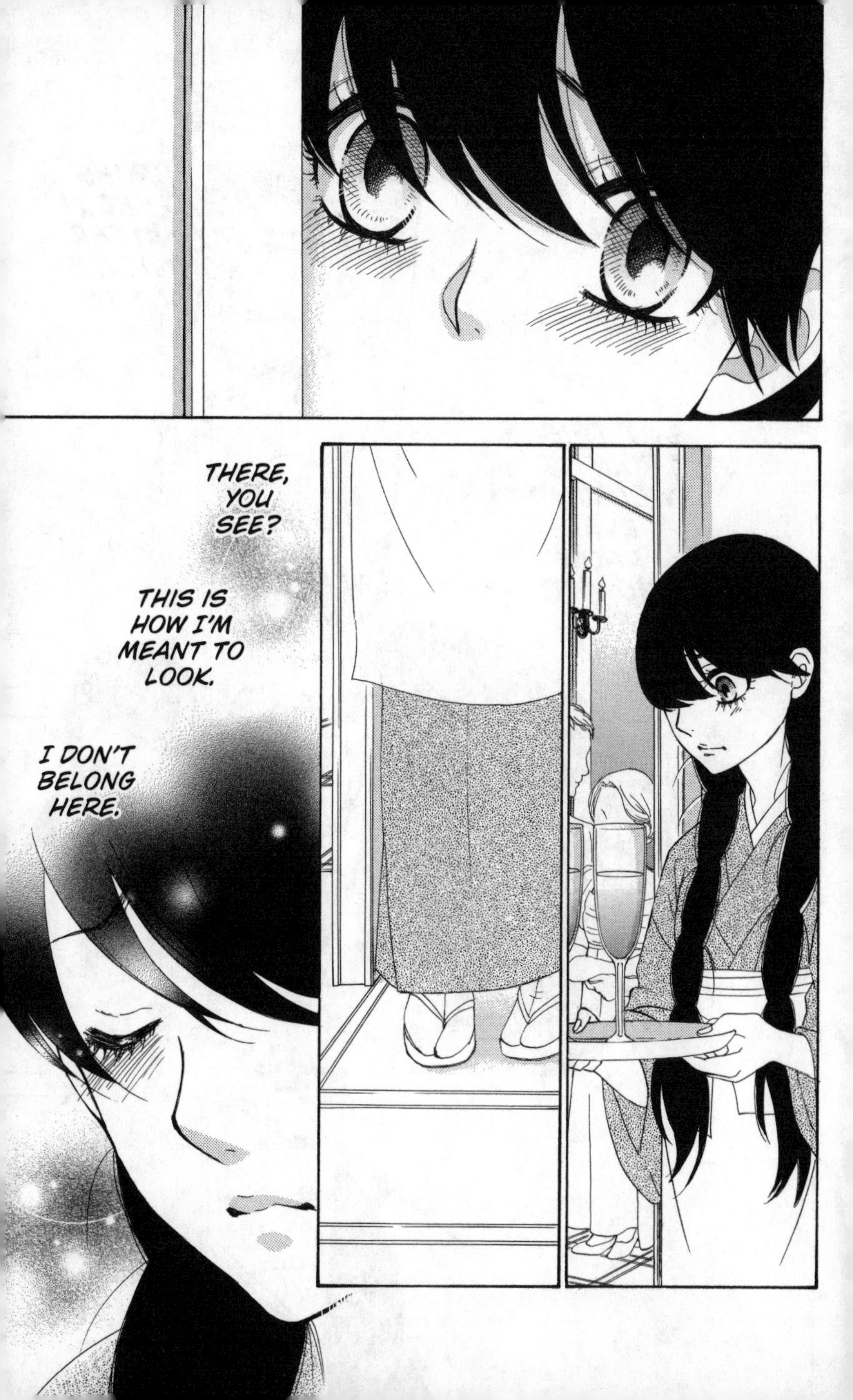
THERE, YOU SEE?
THIS IS HOW I'M MEANT TO LOOK.
I DON'T BELONG HERE.

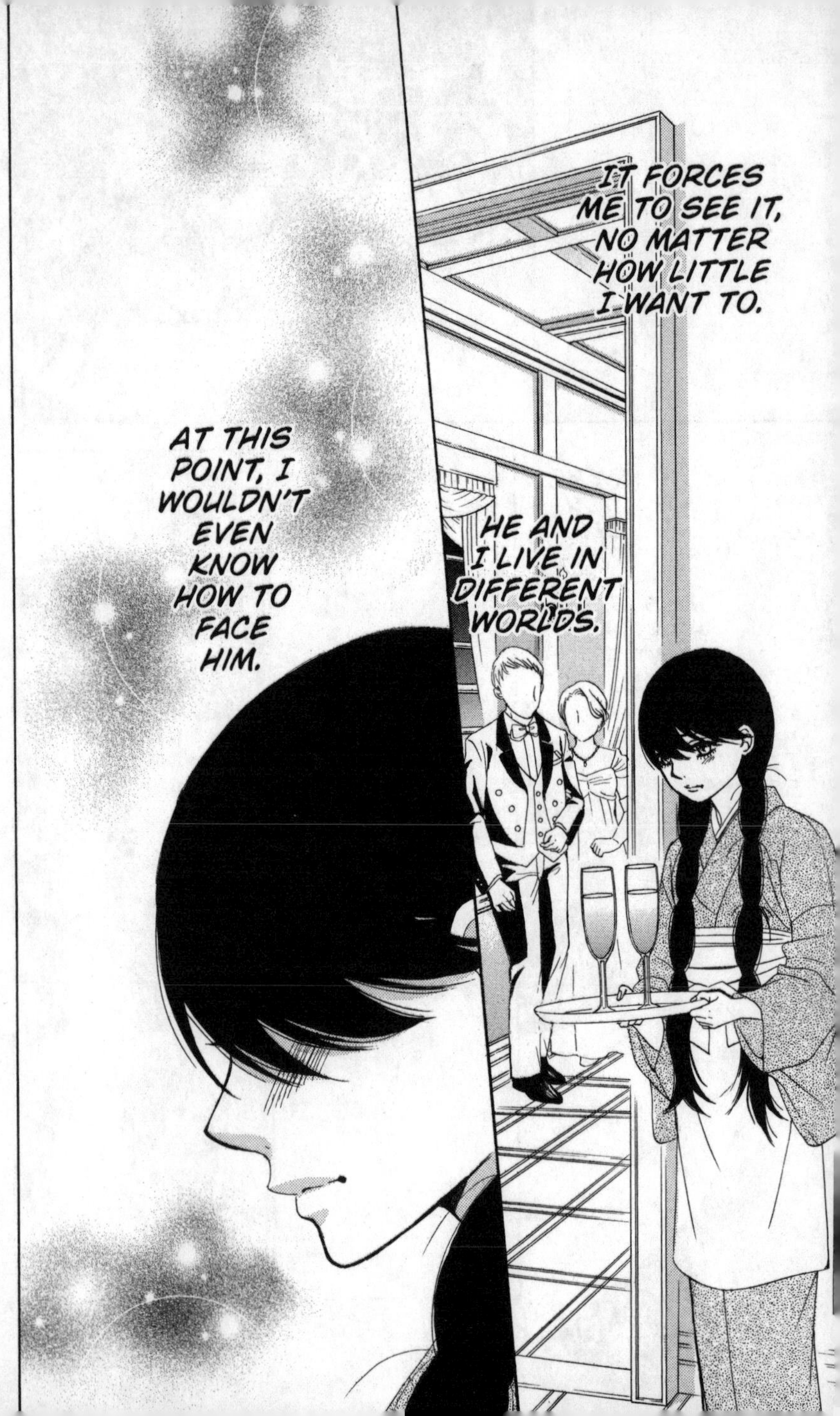
IT FORCES ME TO SEE IT, NO MATTER HOW LITTLE I WANT TO.
HE AND I LIVE IN DIFFERENT WORLDS.
AT THIS POINT, I WOULDN'T EVEN KNOW HOW TO FACE HIM.

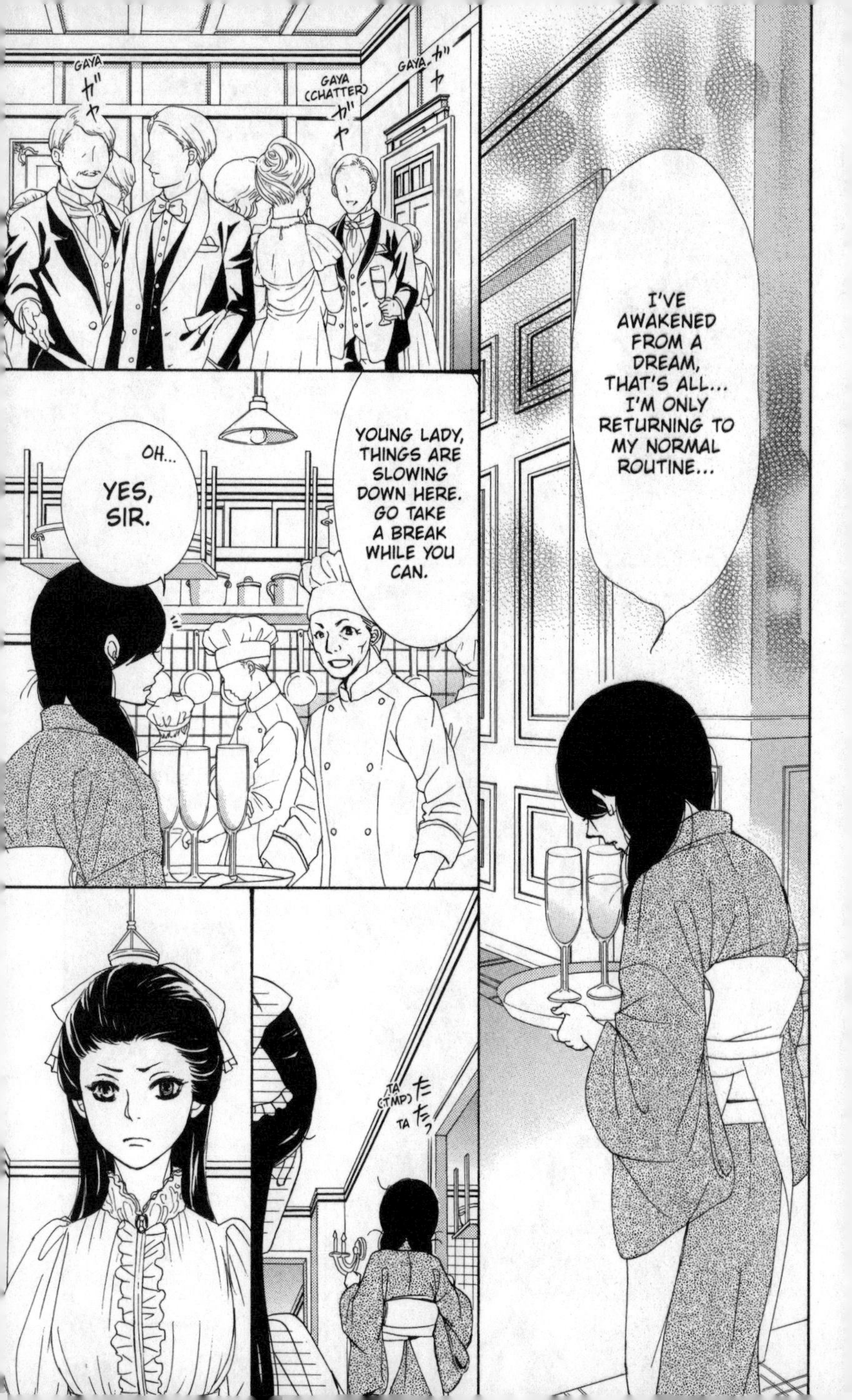

I'VE AWAKENED FROM A DREAM, THAT'S ALL... I'M ONLY RETURNING TO MY NORMAL ROUTINE...
GAYA ガヤ
GAYA (CHATTER) ガヤ
GAYA ガヤ
YOUNG LADY, THINGS ARE SLOWING DOWN HERE. GO TAKE A BREAK WHILE YOU CAN.
OH... YES, SIR.
TA (TMP) TA たたっ

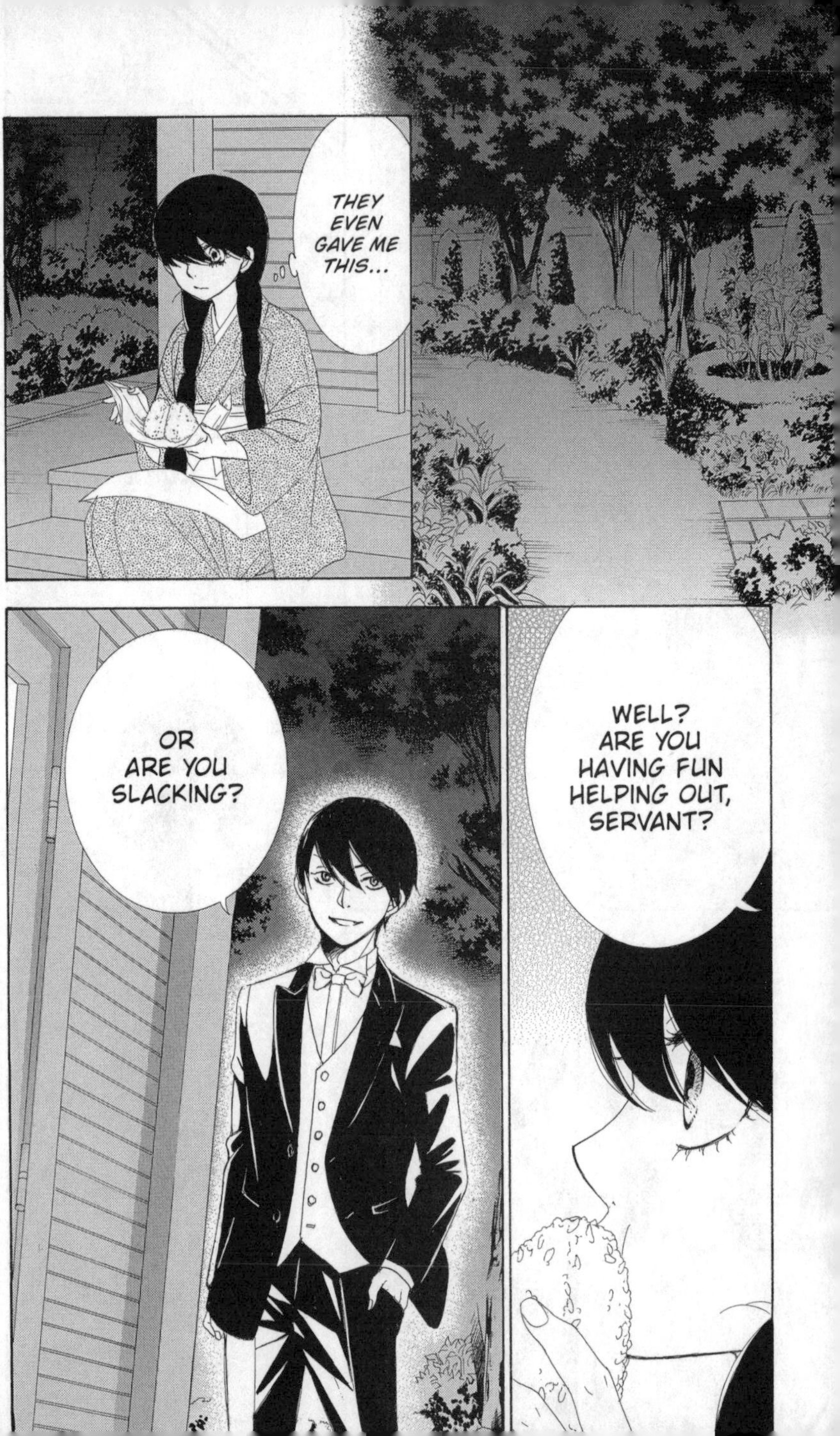
THEY EVEN GAVE ME THIS...
WELL? ARE YOU HAVING FUN HELPING OUT, SERVANT?
OR ARE YOU SLACKING?

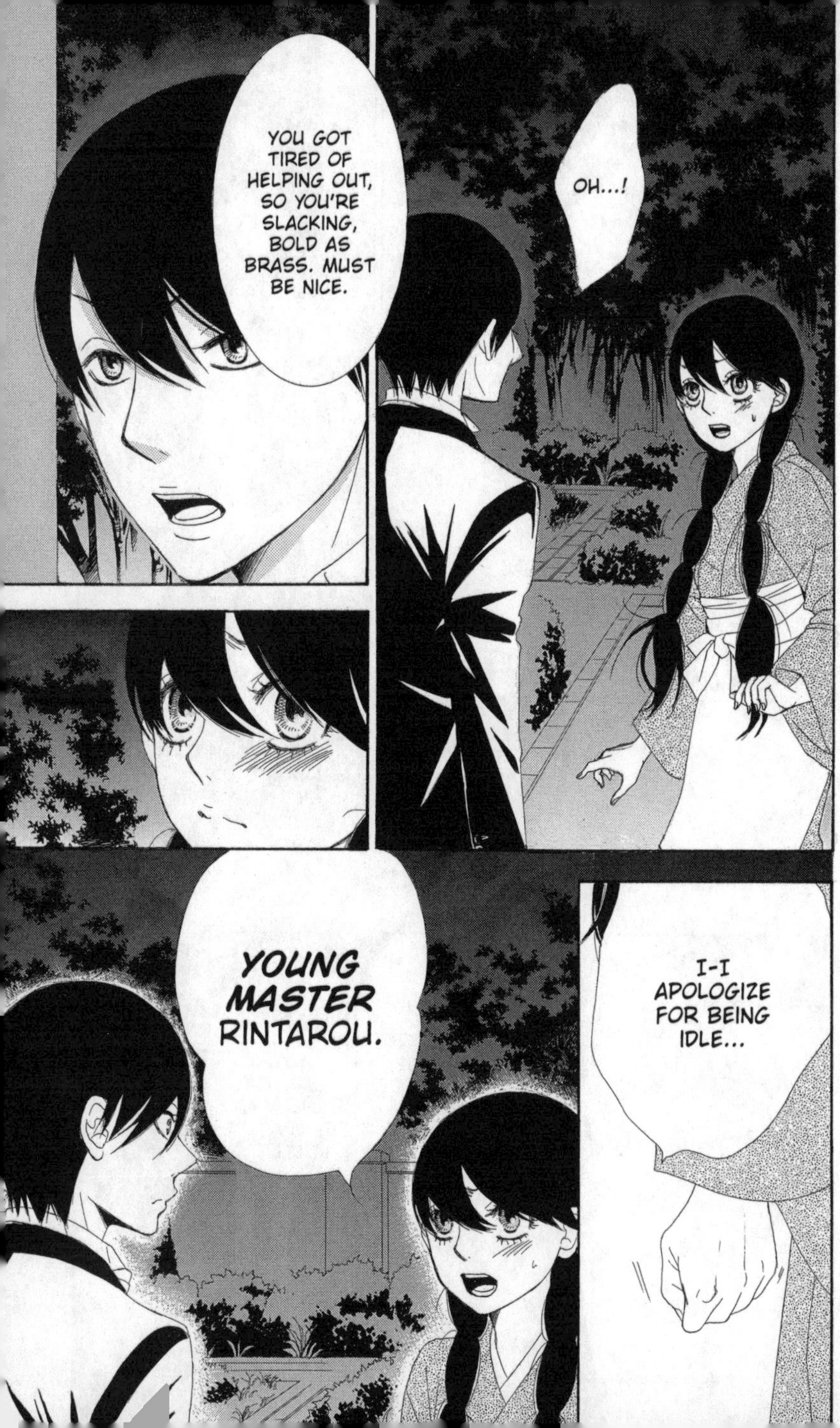
OH...!
YOU GOT TIRED OF HELPING OUT, SO YOU'RE SLACKING, BOLD AS BRASS. MUST BE NICE.
I-I APOLOGIZE FOR BEING IDLE...
YOUNG MASTER RINTAROU.

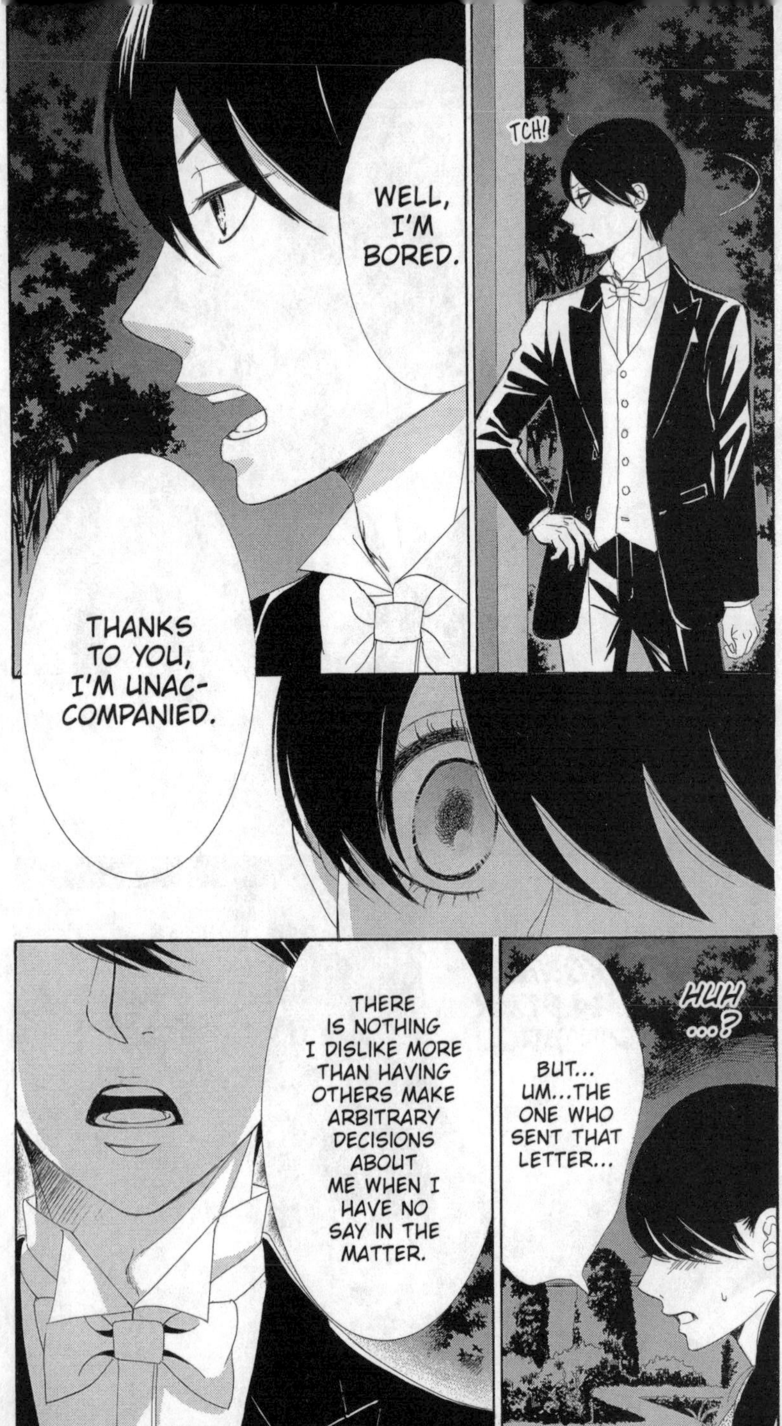
TCH!
WELL, I'M BORED.
THANKS TO YOU, I'M UNAC-COMPANIED.
HUH...?
BUT... UM...THE ONE WHO SENT THAT LETTER...
THERE IS NOTHING I DISLIKE MORE THAN HAVING OTHERS MAKE ARBITRARY DECISIONS ABOUT ME WHEN I HAVE NO SAY IN THE MATTER.

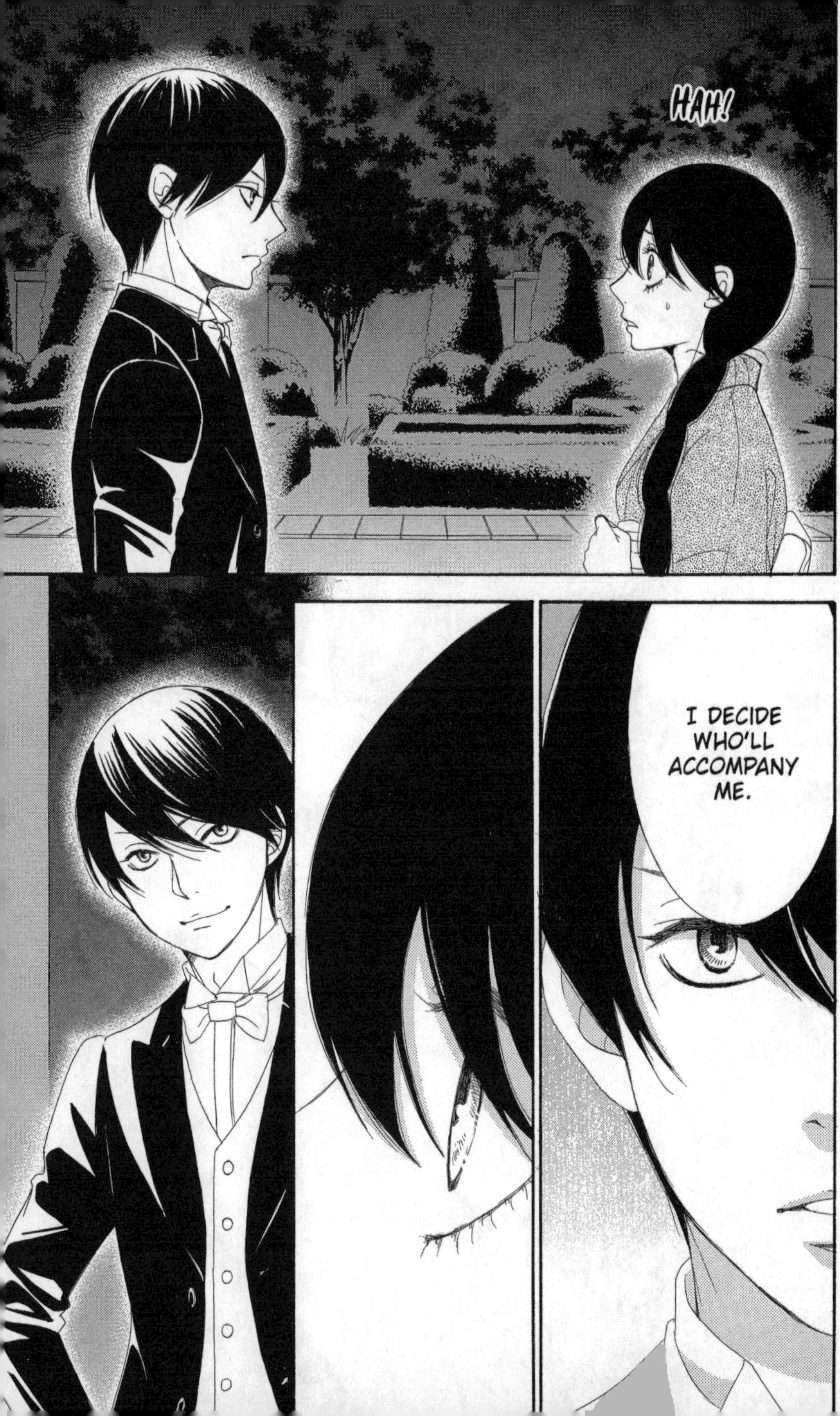
HAH!
I DECIDE WHO'LL ACCOMPANY ME.

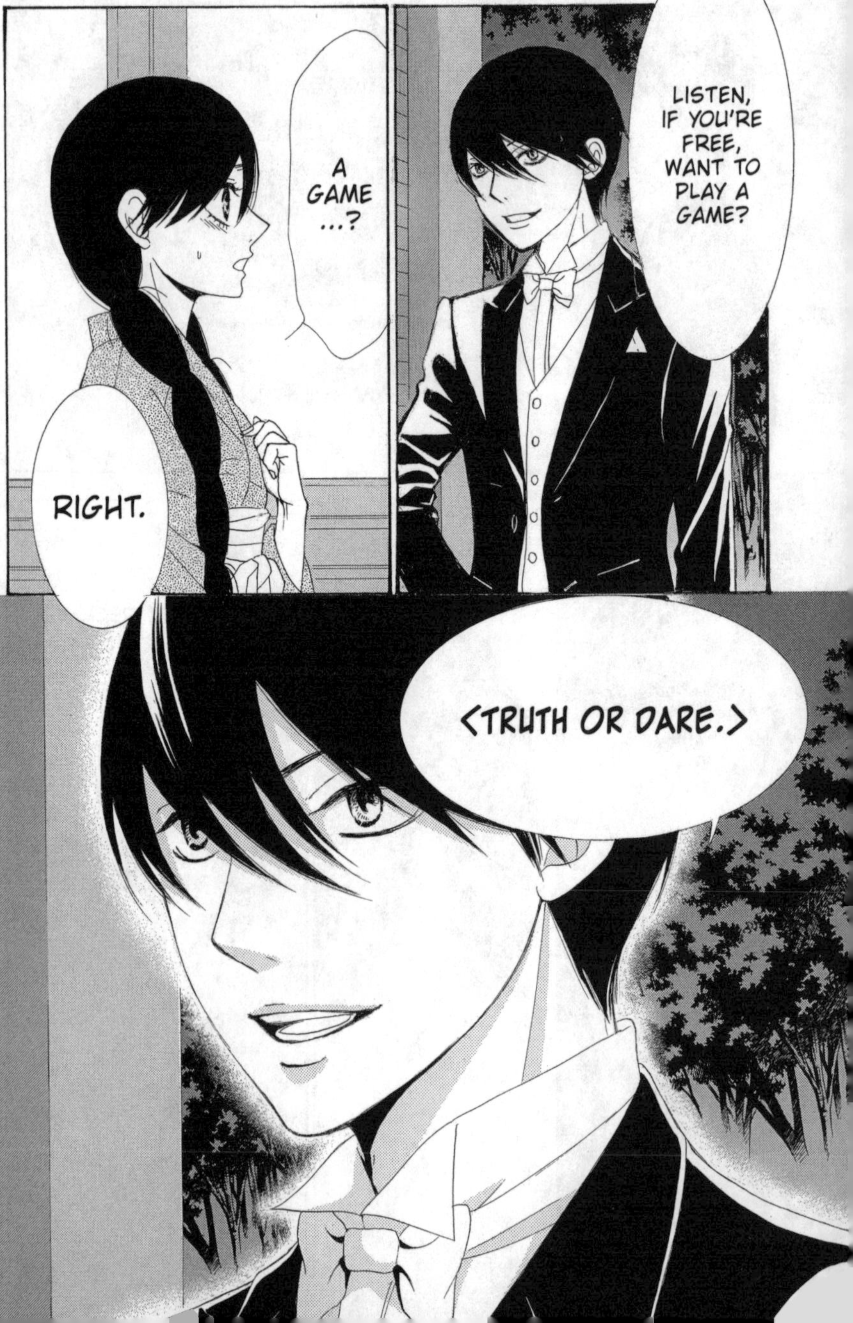
LISTEN, IF YOU'RE FREE, WANT TO PLAY A GAME?
A GAME ...?
RIGHT.
<TRUTH OR DARE.>

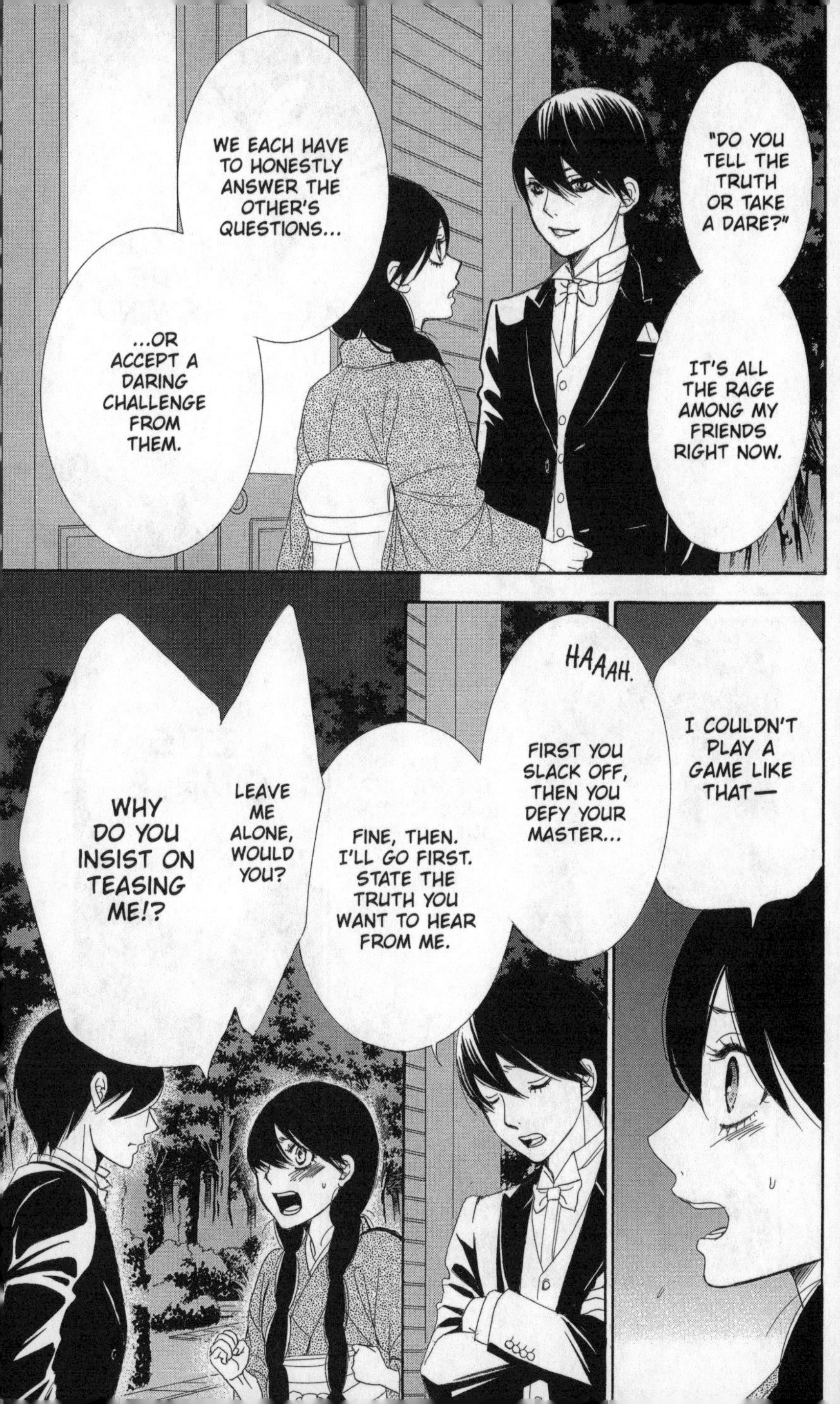
"DO YOU TELL THE TRUTH OR TAKE A DARE?"
IT'S ALL THE RAGE AMONG MY FRIENDS RIGHT NOW.
WE EACH HAVE TO HONESTLY ANSWER THE OTHER'S QUESTIONS...
...OR ACCEPT A DARING CHALLENGE FROM THEM.
I COULDN'T PLAY A GAME LIKE THAT—
HAAAH.
FIRST YOU SLACK OFF, THEN YOU DEFY YOUR MASTER...
FINE, THEN. I'LL GO FIRST. STATE THE TRUTH YOU WANT TO HEAR FROM ME.
LEAVE ME ALONE, WOULD YOU?
WHY DO YOU INSIST ON TEASING ME!?

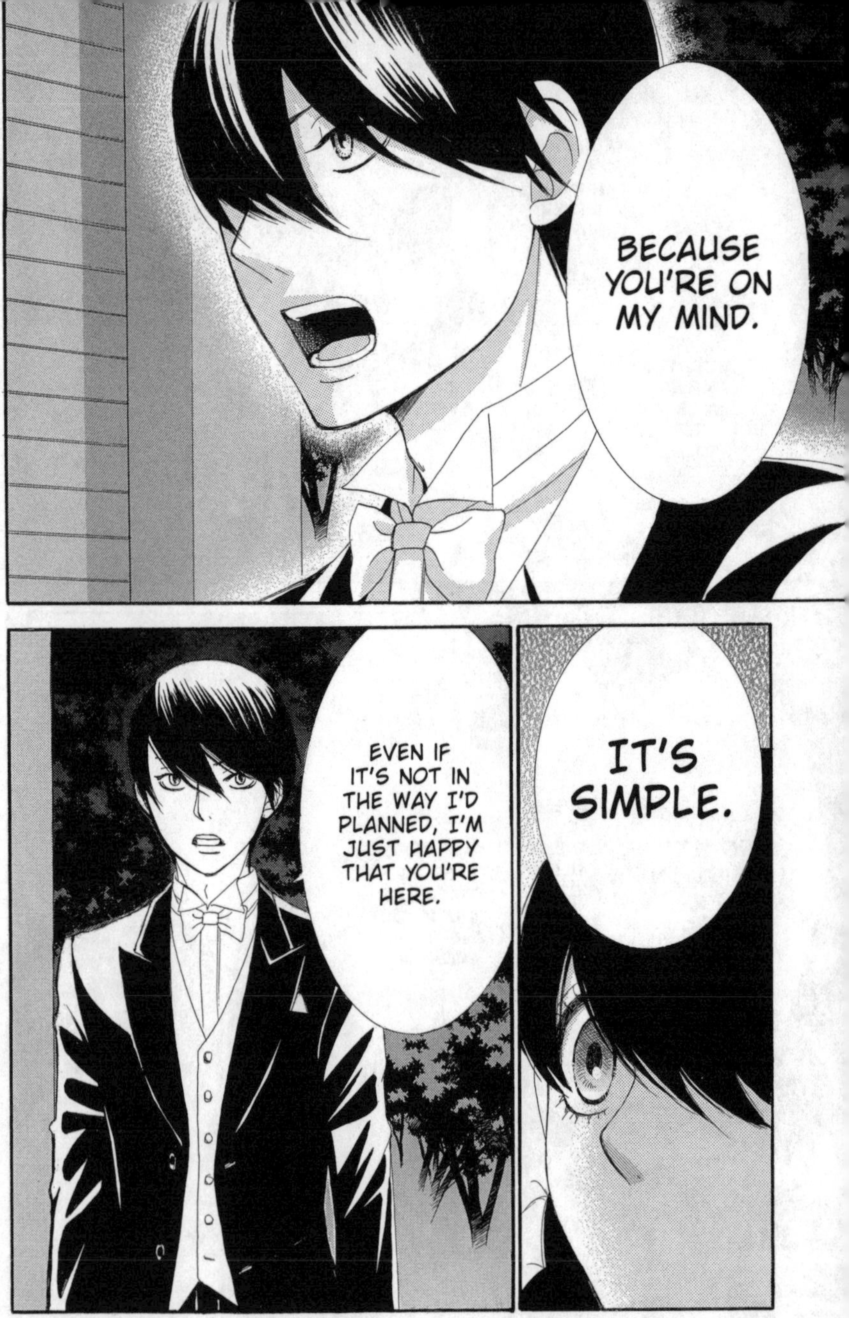
BECAUSE YOU'RE ON MY MIND.
IT'S SIMPLE.
EVEN IF IT'S NOT IN THE WAY I'D PLANNED, I'M JUST HAPPY THAT YOU'RE HERE.

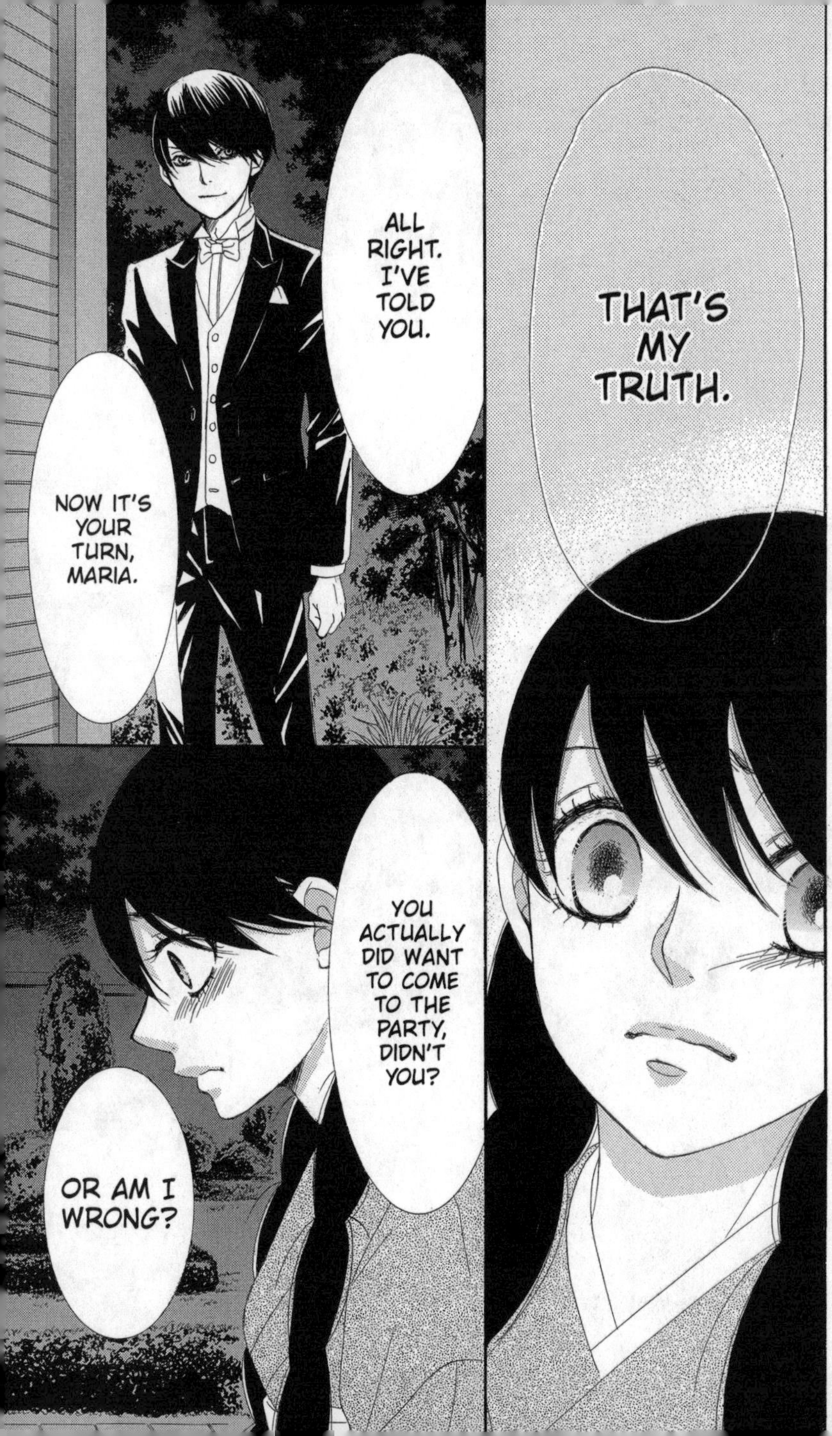
THAT'S MY TRUTH.
ALL RIGHT. I'VE TOLD YOU.
NOW IT'S YOUR TURN, MARIA.
YOU ACTUALLY DID WANT TO COME TO THE PARTY, DIDN'T YOU?
OR AM I WRONG?

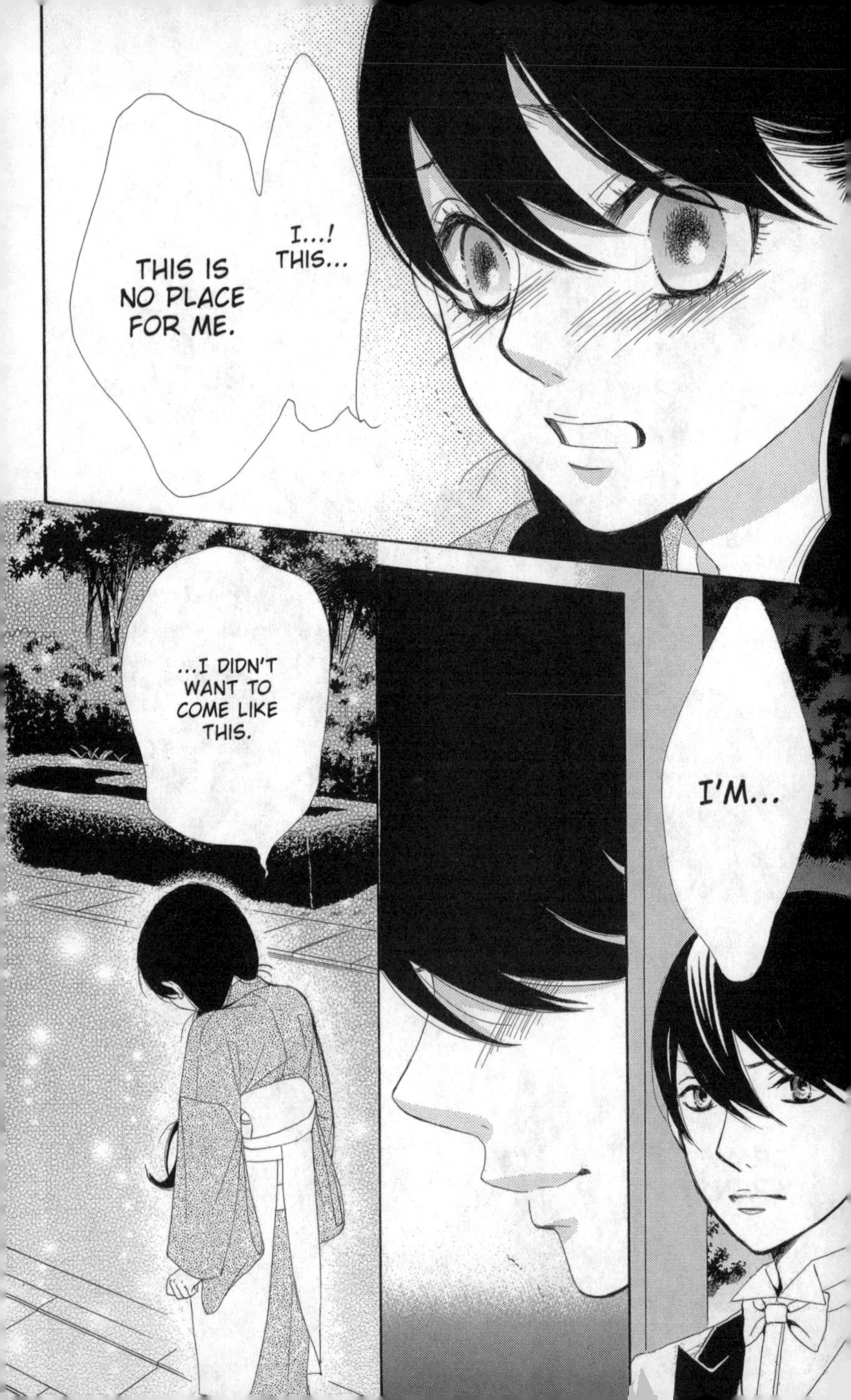
I...! THIS...
THIS IS NO PLACE FOR ME.
I'M...
...I DIDN'T WANT TO COME LIKE THIS.

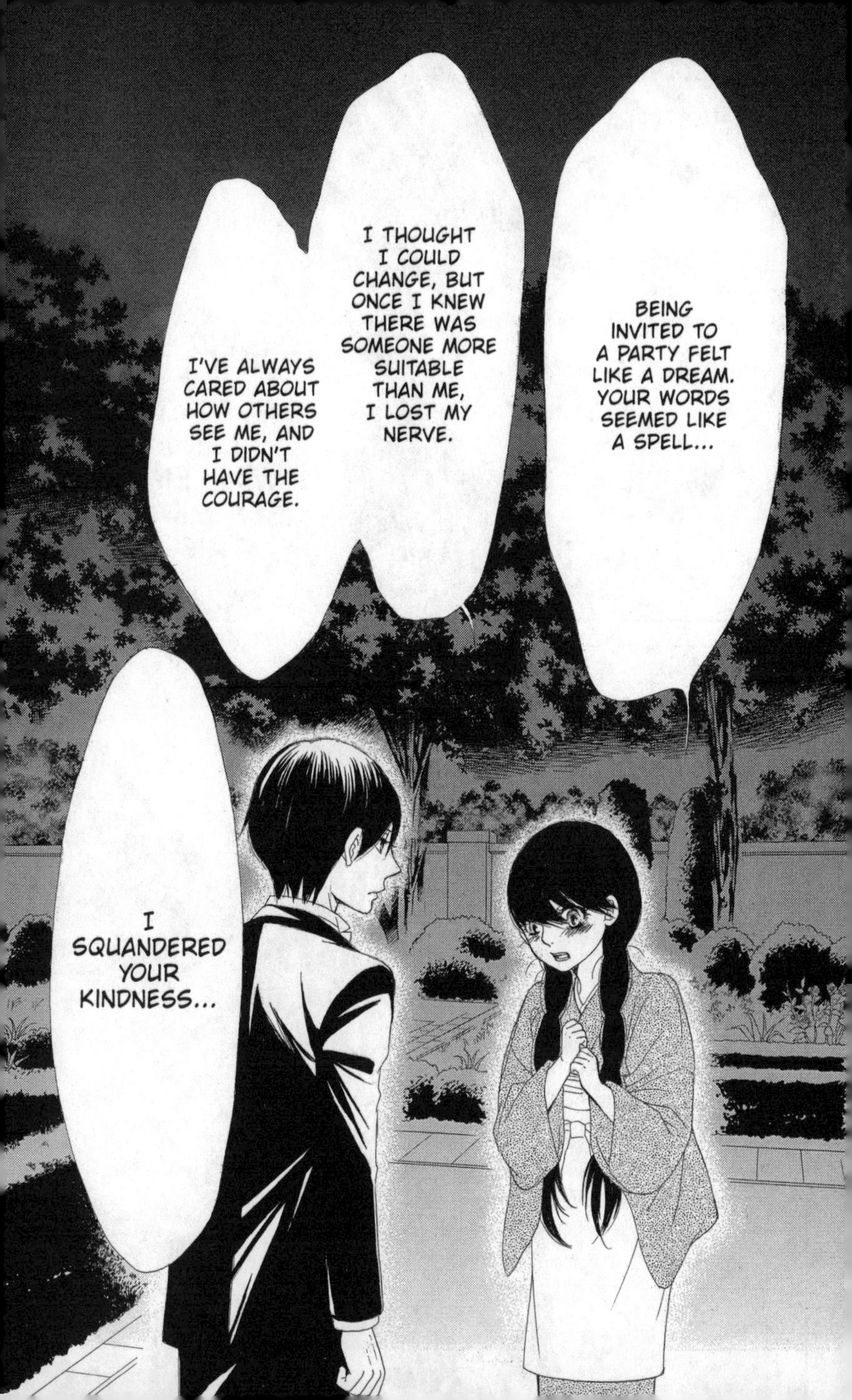
BEING INVITED TO A PARTY FELT LIKE A DREAM. YOUR WORDS SEEMED LIKE A SPELL...
I THOUGHT I COULD CHANGE, BUT ONCE I KNEW THERE WAS SOMEONE MORE SUITABLE THAN ME, I LOST MY NERVE.
I'VE ALWAYS CARED ABOUT HOW OTHERS SEE ME, AND I DIDN'T HAVE THE COURAGE.
I SQUANDERED YOUR KINDNESS...

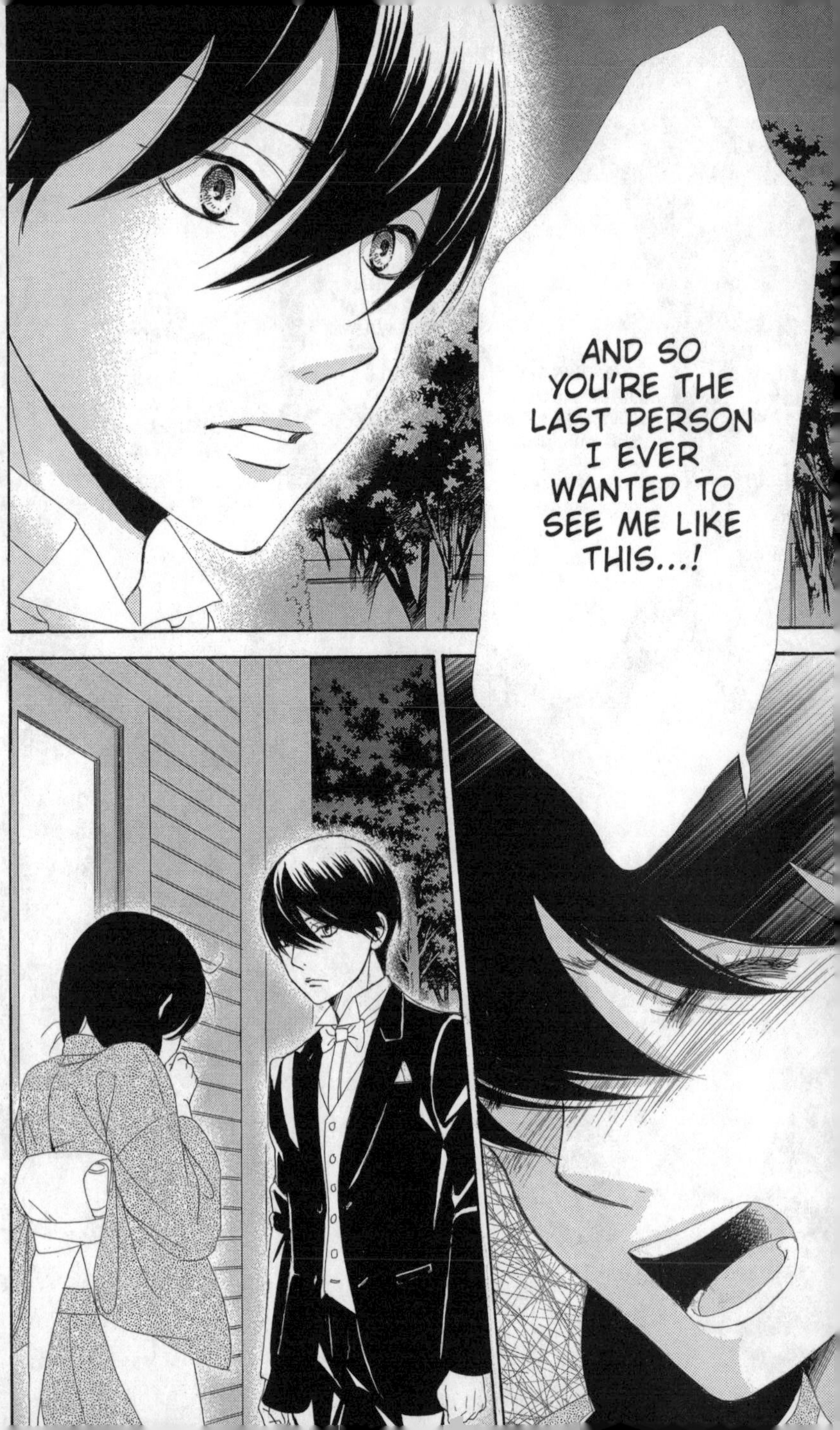
AND SO YOU'RE THE LAST PERSON I EVER WANTED TO SEE ME LIKE THIS...!

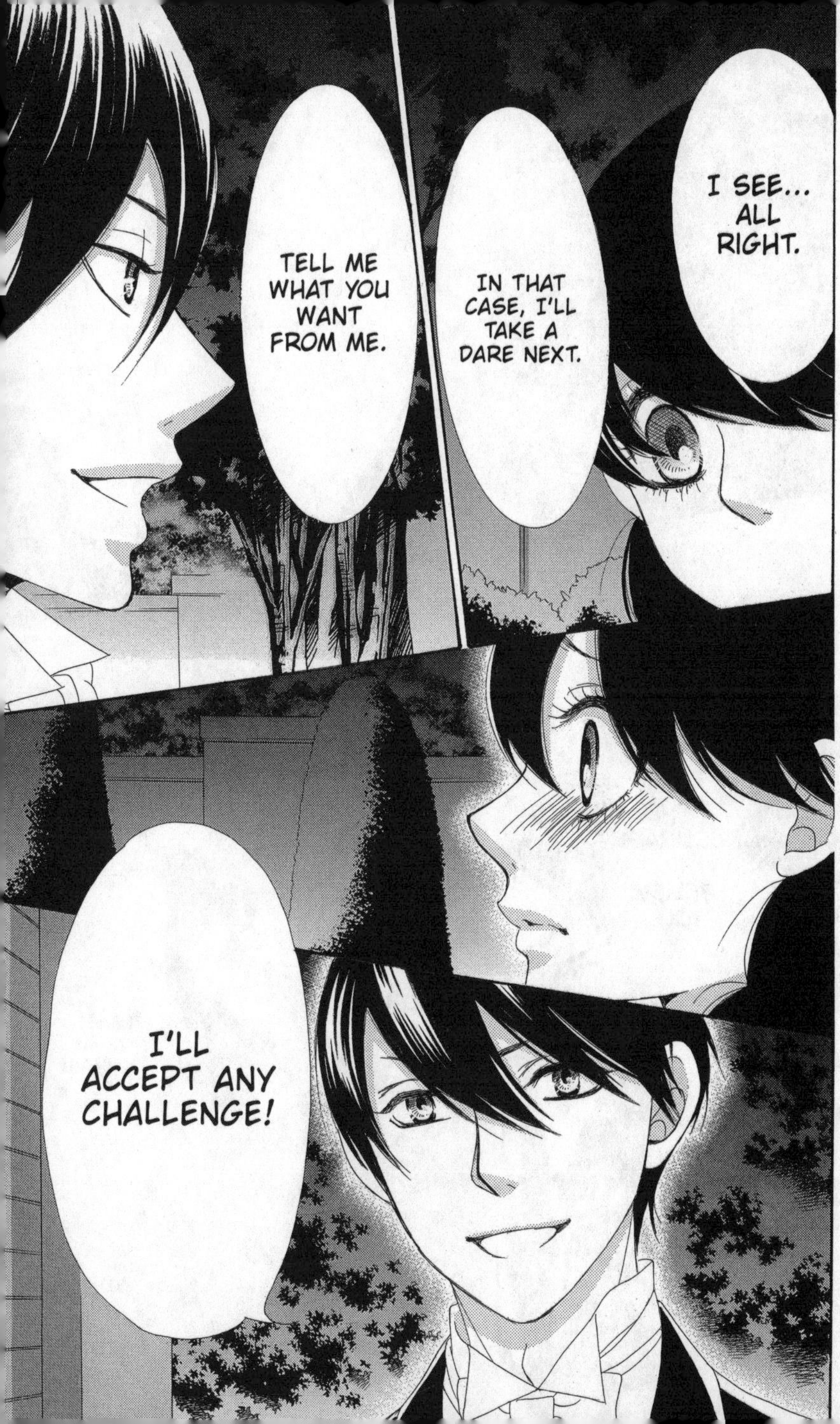
I SEE... ALL RIGHT.
IN THAT CASE, I'LL TAKE A DARE NEXT.
TELL ME WHAT YOU WANT FROM ME.
I'LL ACCEPT ANY CHALLENGE!

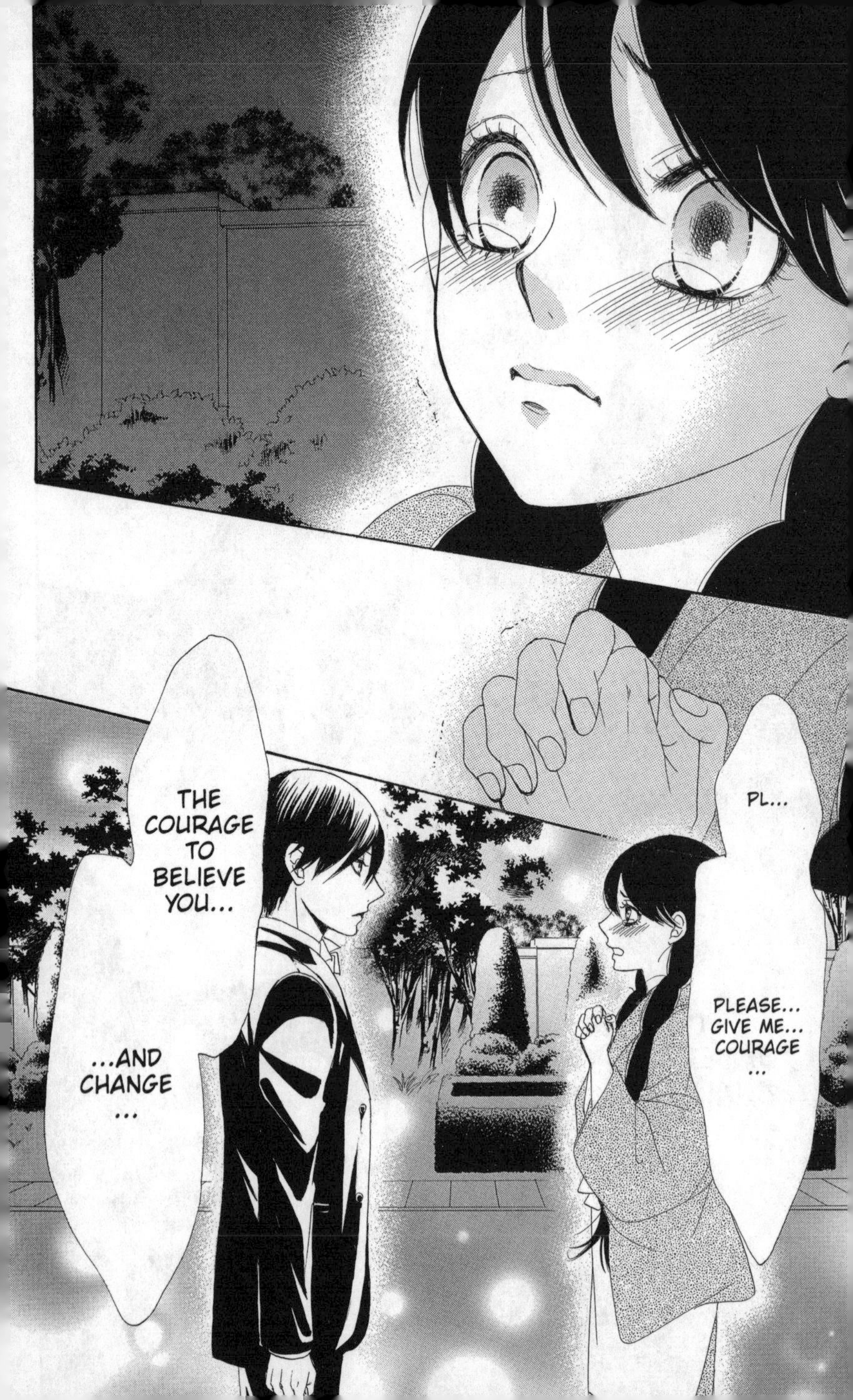
PL...
PLEASE... GIVE ME... COURAGE ...
THE COURAGE TO BELIEVE YOU...
...AND CHANGE ...

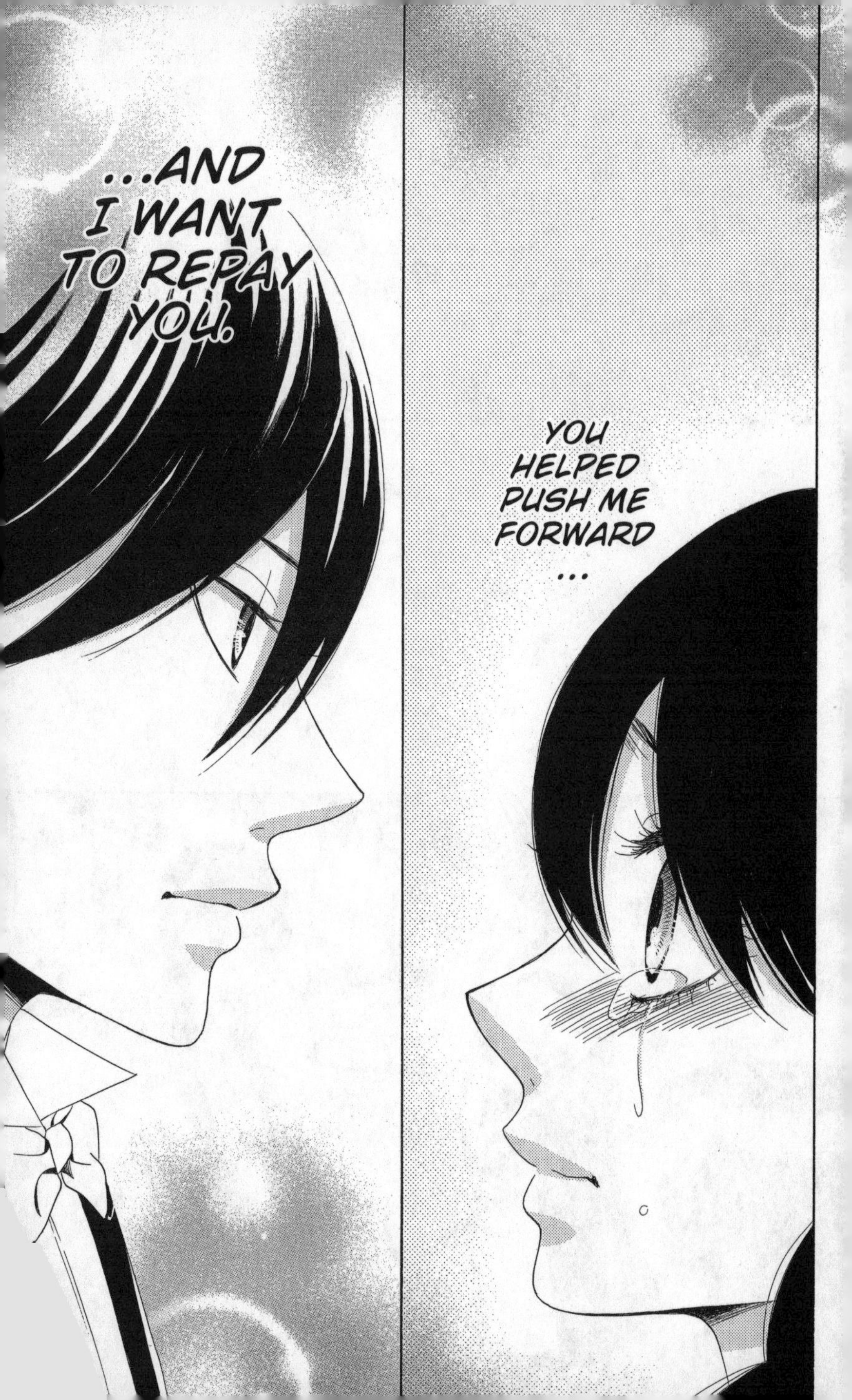
YOU HELPED PUSH ME FORWARD ...
...AND I WANT TO REPAY YOU.

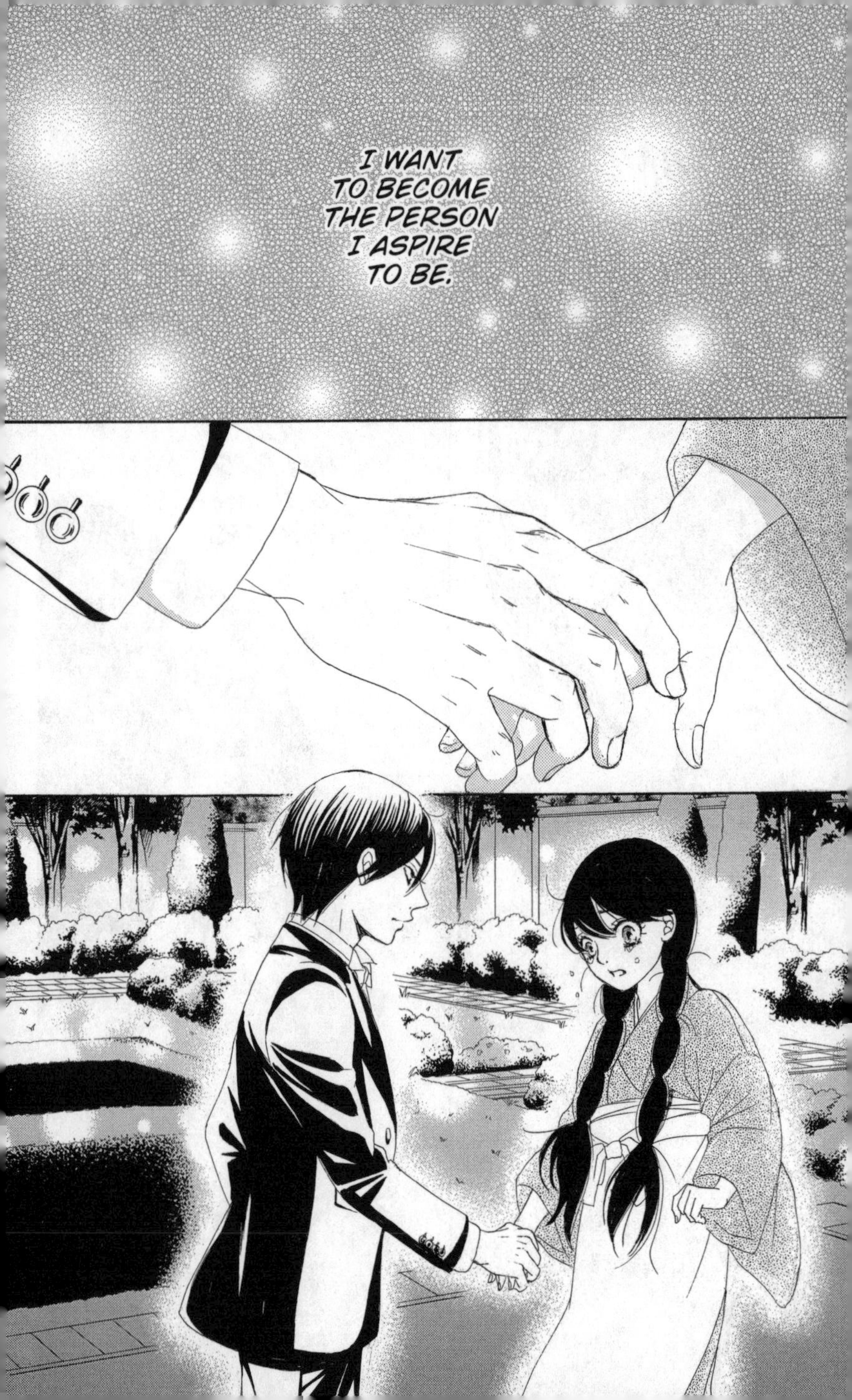
I WANT TO BECOME THE PERSON I ASPIRE TO BE.

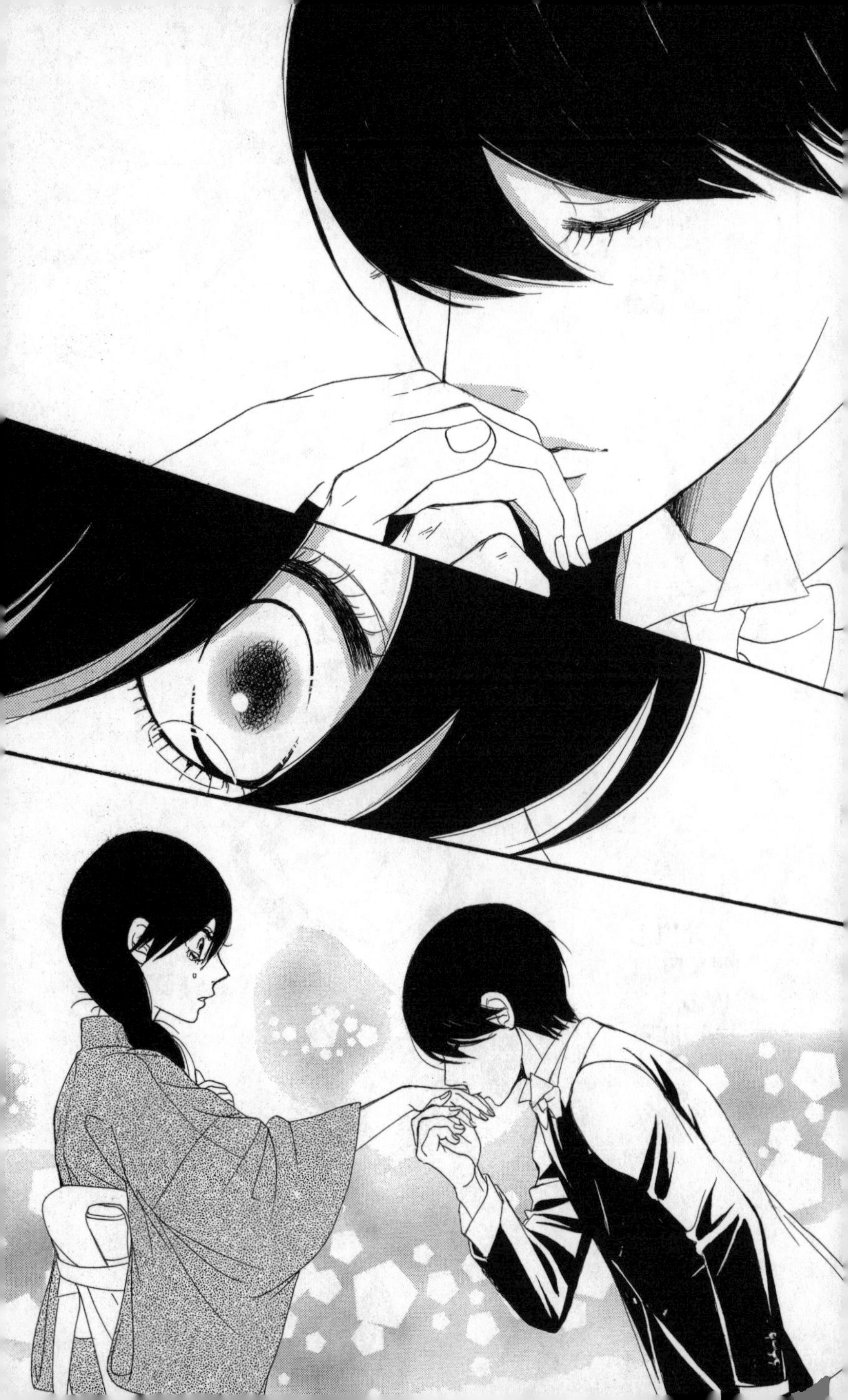

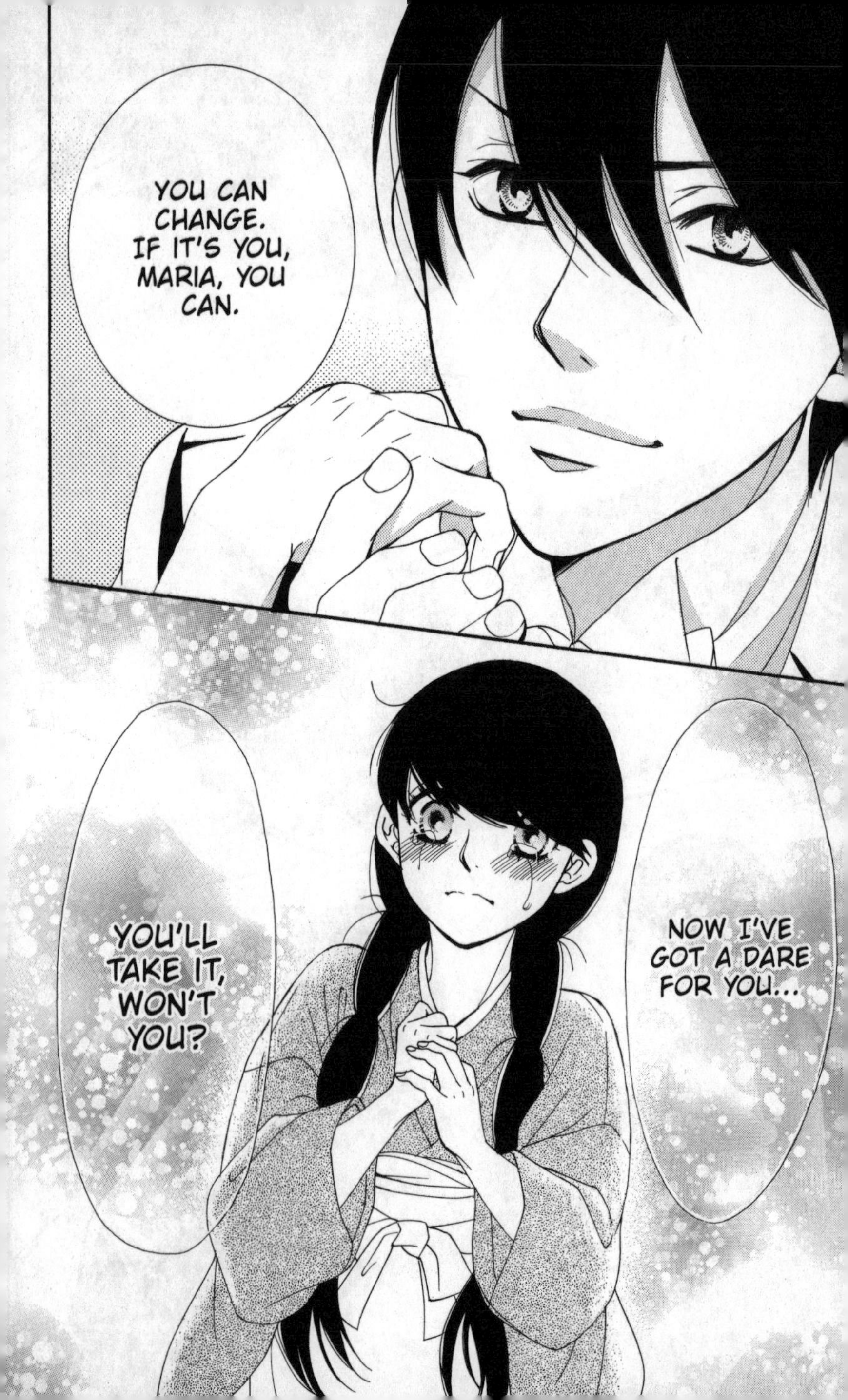
YOU CAN CHANGE. IF IT'S YOU, MARIA, YOU CAN.
NOW I'VE GOT A DARE FOR YOU...
YOU'LL TAKE IT, WON'T YOU?

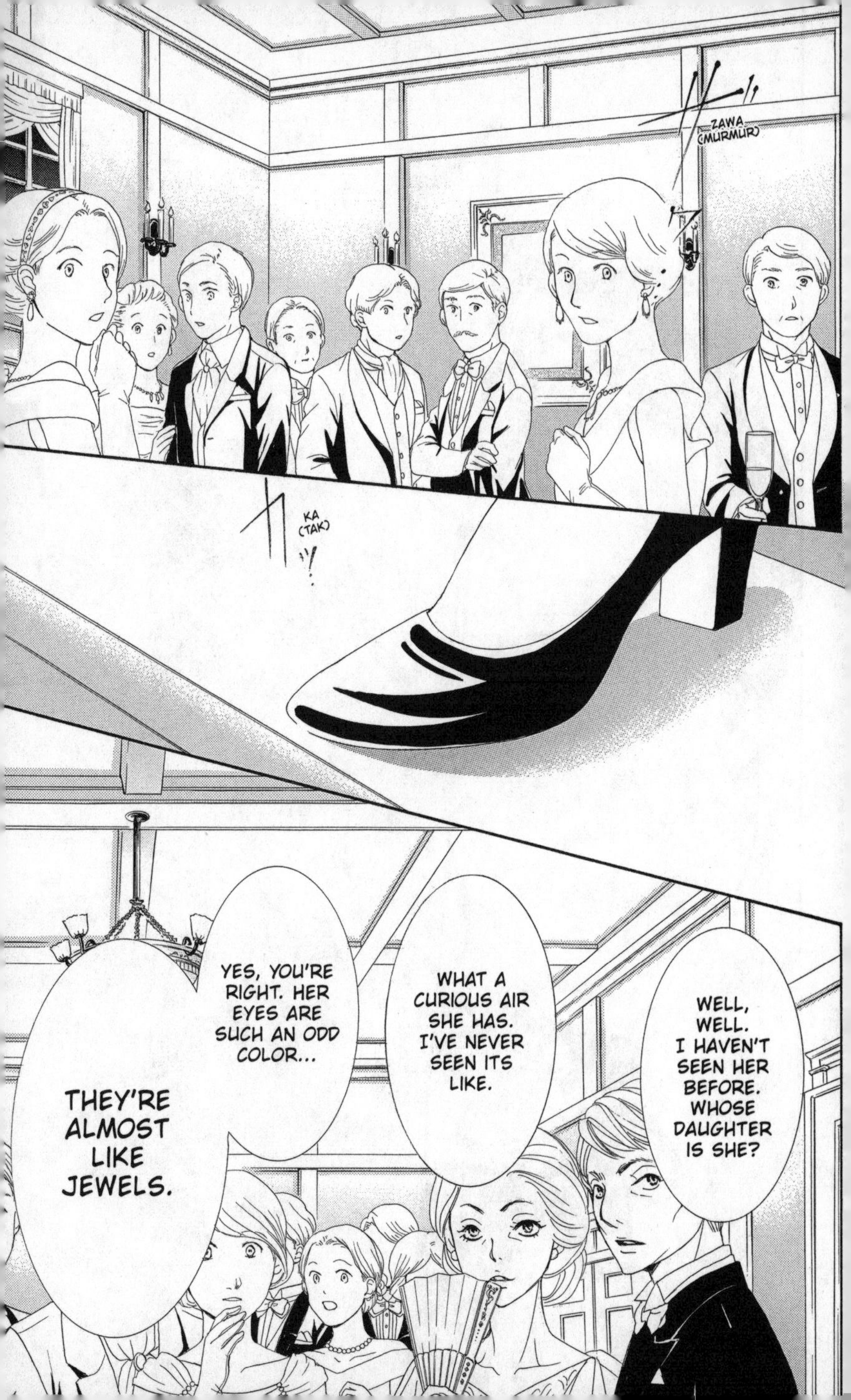
ZAWA (MURMUR)
KA (TAK)
WELL, WELL. I HAVEN'T SEEN HER BEFORE. WHOSE DAUGHTER IS SHE?
WHAT A CURIOUS AIR SHE HAS. I'VE NEVER SEEN ITS LIKE.
YES, YOU'RE RIGHT. HER EYES ARE SUCH AN ODD COLOR...
THEY'RE ALMOST LIKE JEWELS.

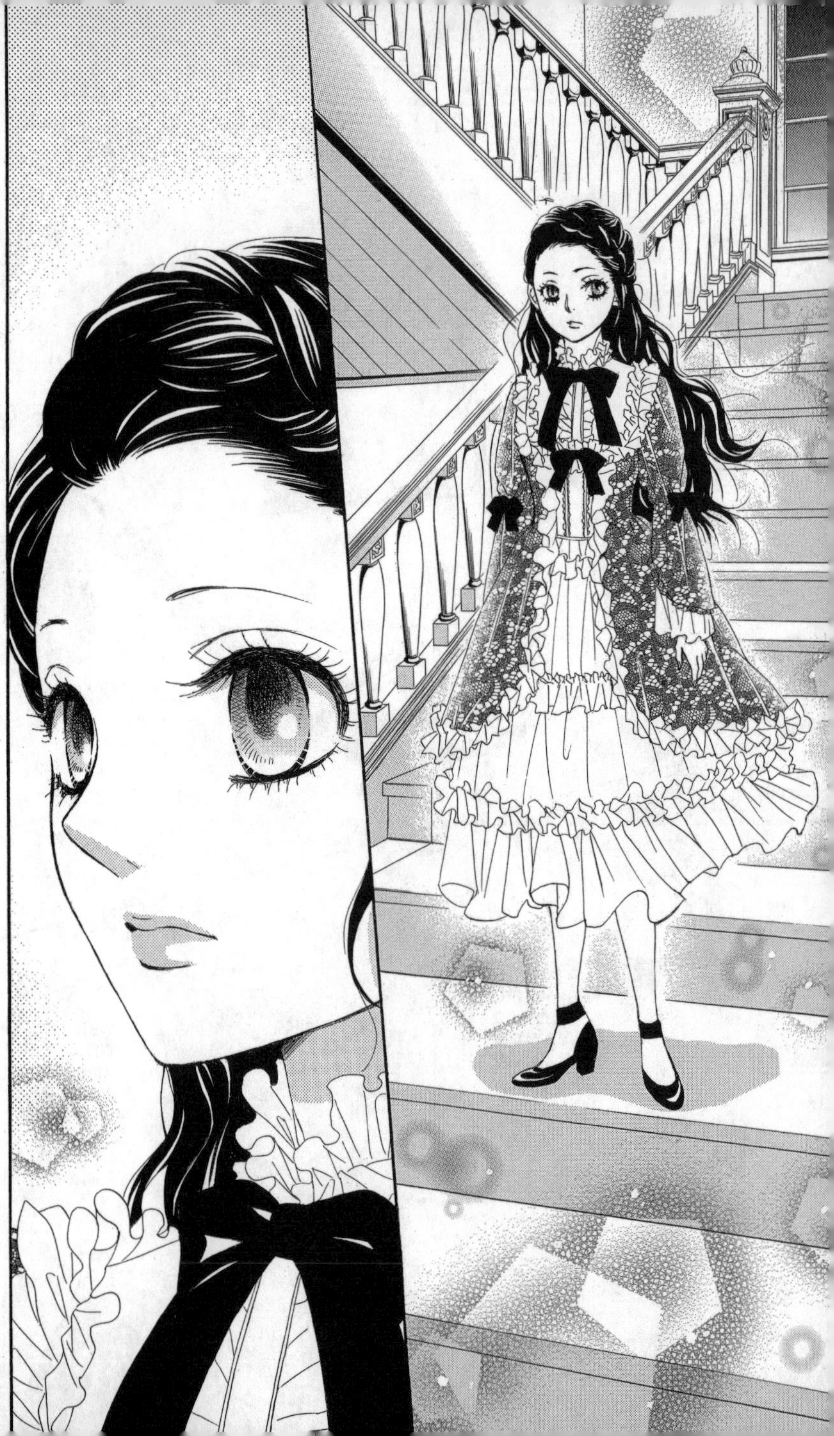

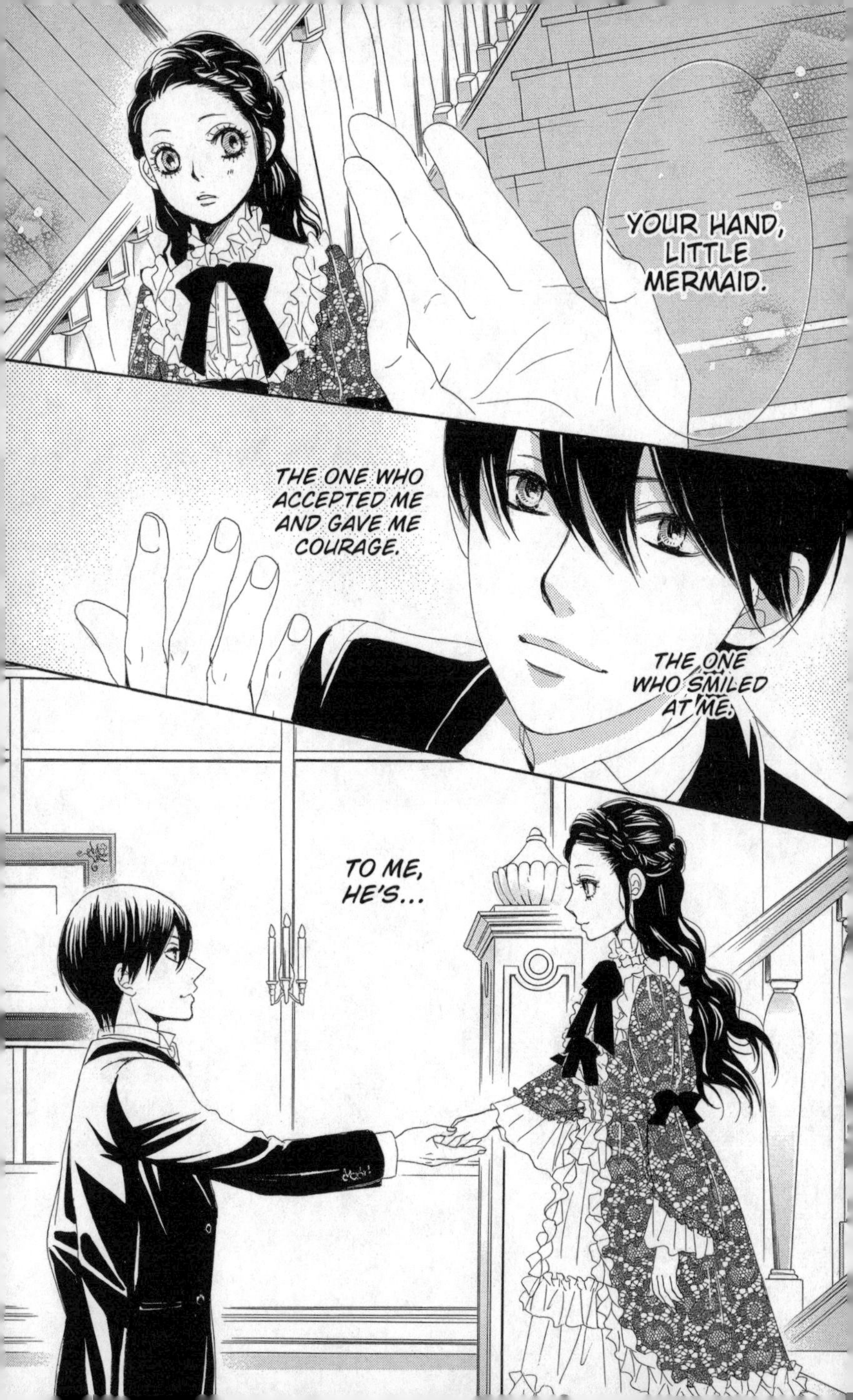
YOUR HAND, LITTLE MERMAID.
THE ONE WHO SMILED AT ME.
THE ONE WHO ACCEPTED ME AND GAVE ME COURAGE.
TO ME, HE'S...

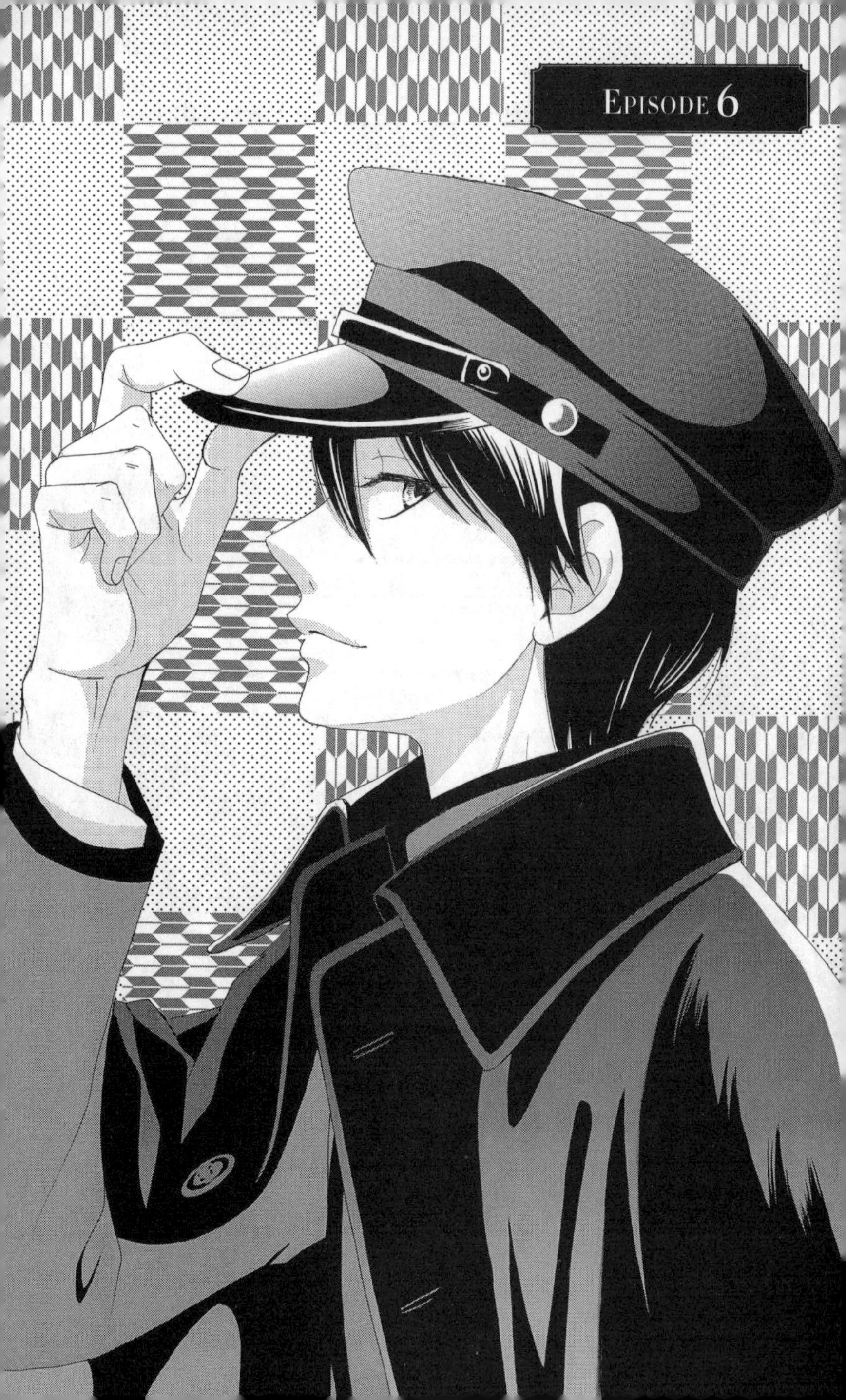
Episode 6

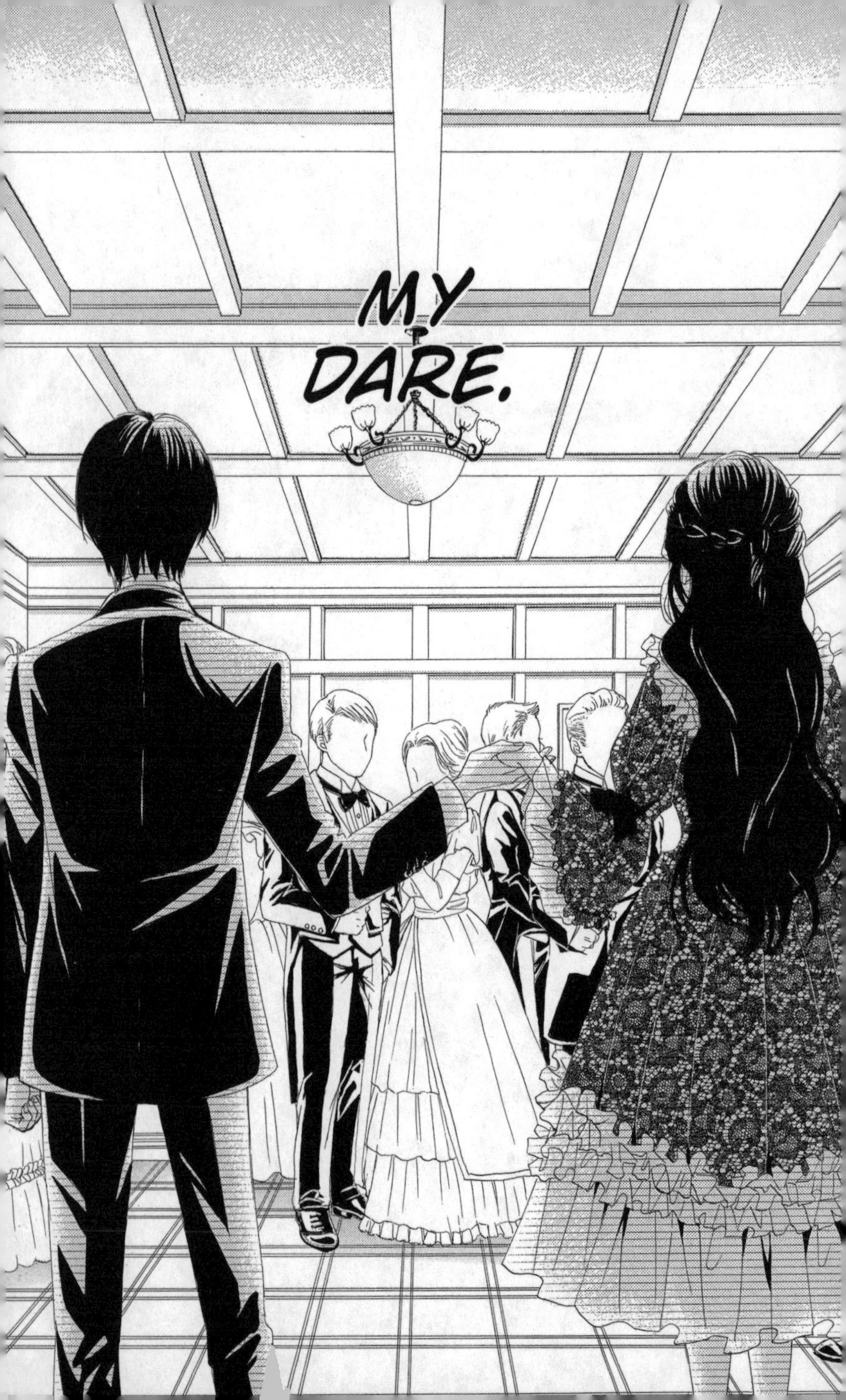
MY DARE.

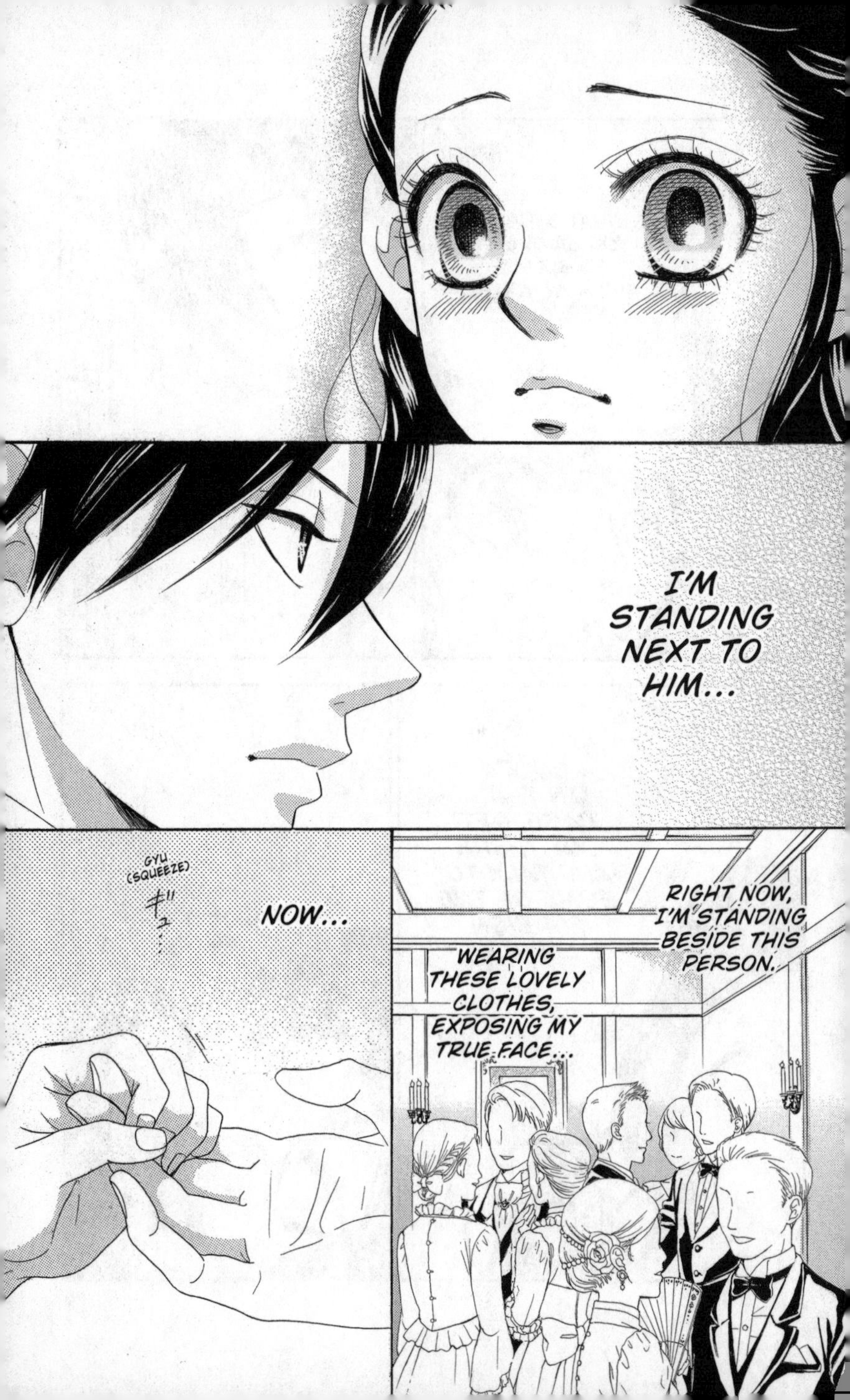
I'M STANDING NEXT TO HIM...
RIGHT NOW, I'M STANDING BESIDE THIS PERSON.
WEARING THESE LOVELY CLOTHES, EXPOSING MY TRUE FACE...
NOW...
ギュ…
GYU (SQUEEZE)

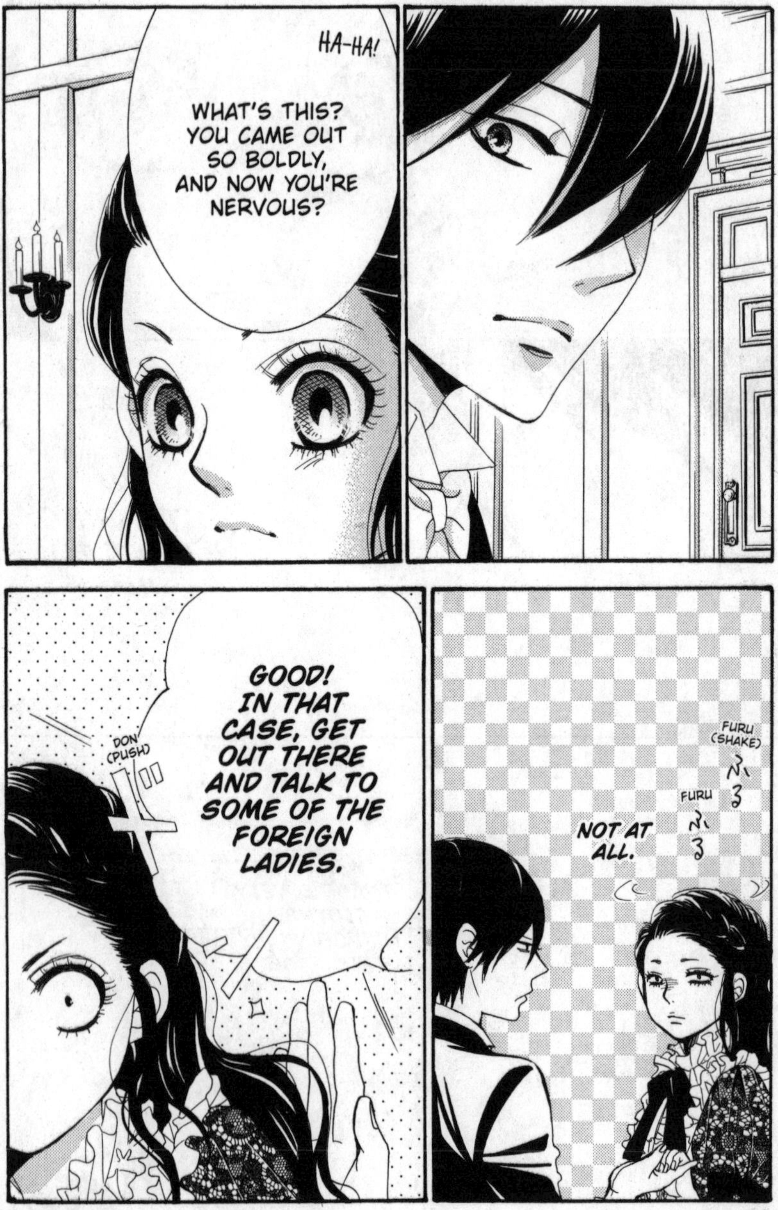
HA-HA!
WHAT'S THIS? YOU CAME OUT SO BOLDLY, AND NOW YOU'RE NERVOUS?
FURU (SHAKE)
ふる
FURU
ふる
NOT AT ALL.
GOOD! IN THAT CASE, GET OUT THERE AND TALK TO SOME OF THE FOREIGN LADIES.
DON (PUSH)

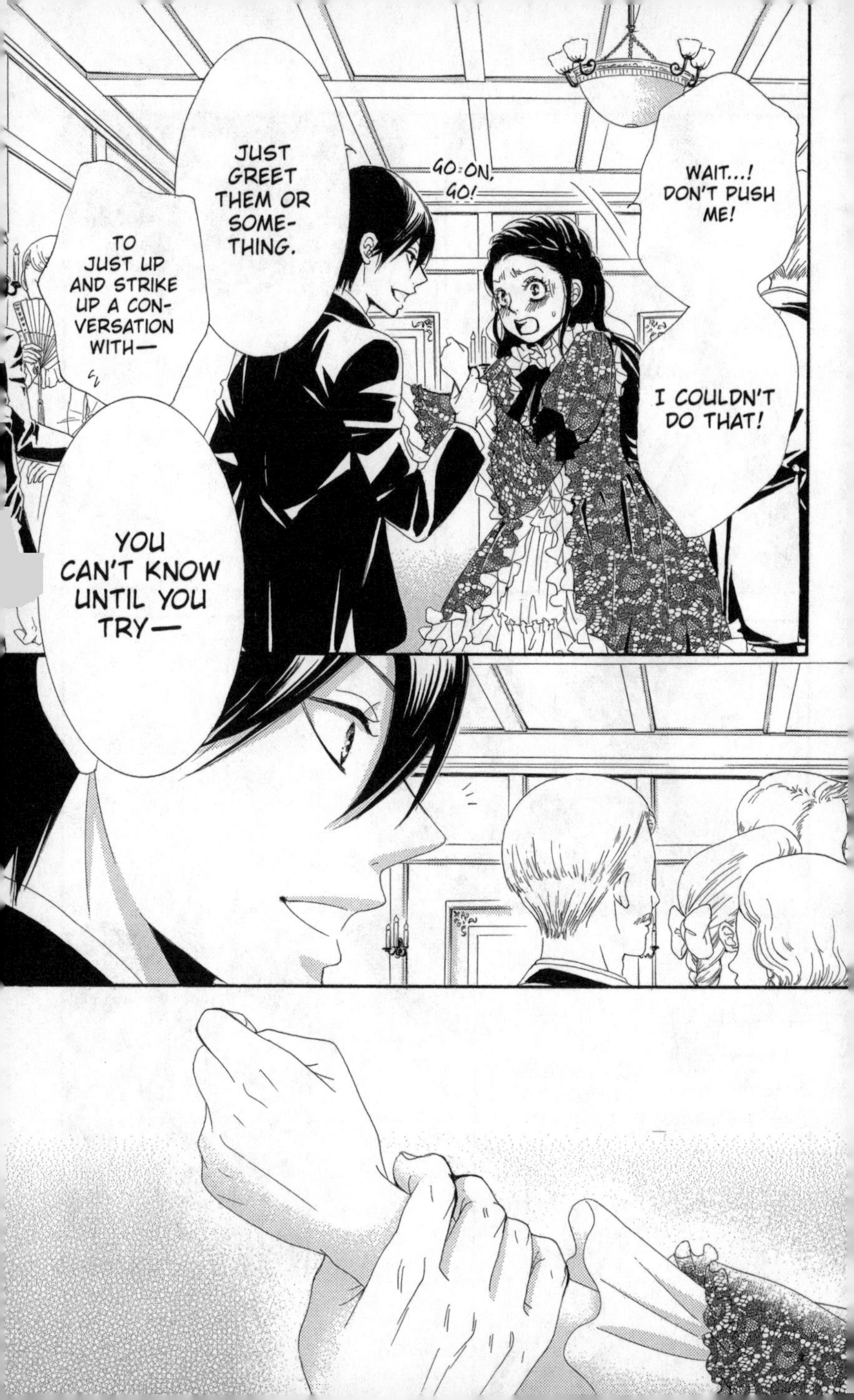
WAIT...! DON'T PUSH ME!
GO ON, GO!
JUST GREET THEM OR SOME-THING.
I COULDN'T DO THAT!
TO JUST UP AND STRIKE UP A CON-VERSATION WITH—
YOU CAN'T KNOW UNTIL YOU TRY—

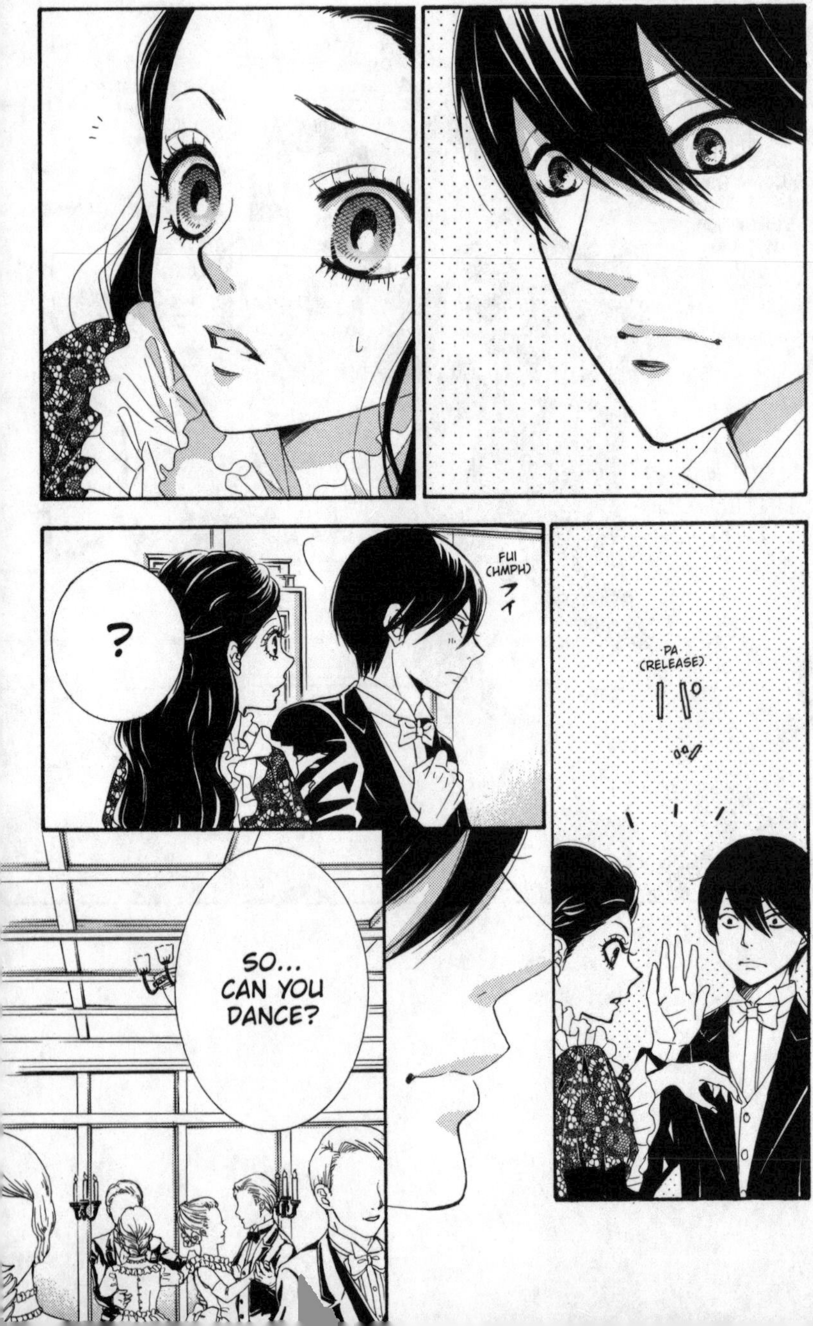
PA (RELEASE)
FUI (HMPH)
フイ
?
SO... CAN YOU DANCE?

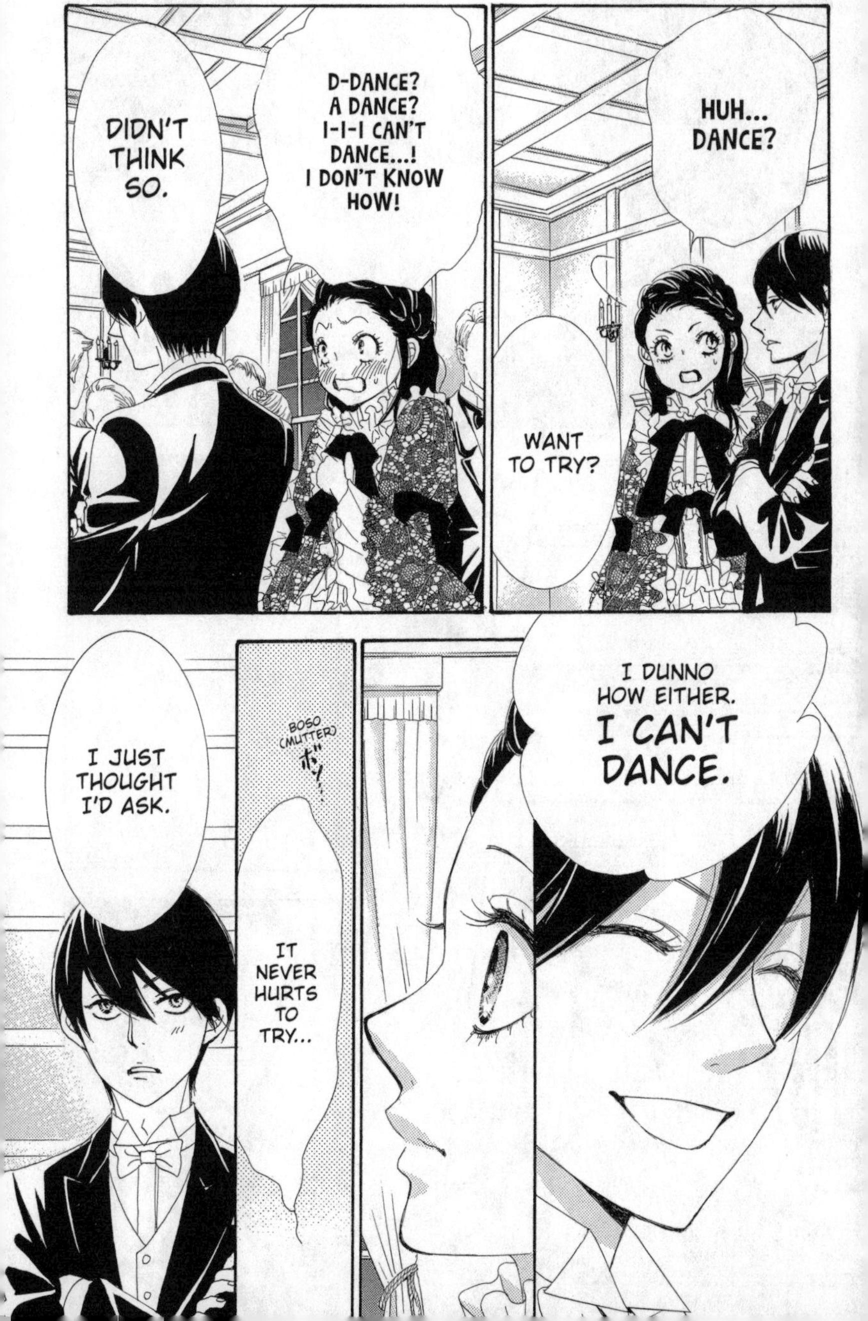
HUH... DANCE?
WANT TO TRY?
D-DANCE? A DANCE? I-I-I CAN'T DANCE...! I DON'T KNOW HOW!
DIDN'T THINK SO.
I DUNNO HOW EITHER. I CAN'T DANCE.
BOSO (MUTTER)
IT NEVER HURTS TO TRY...
I JUST THOUGHT I'D ASK.

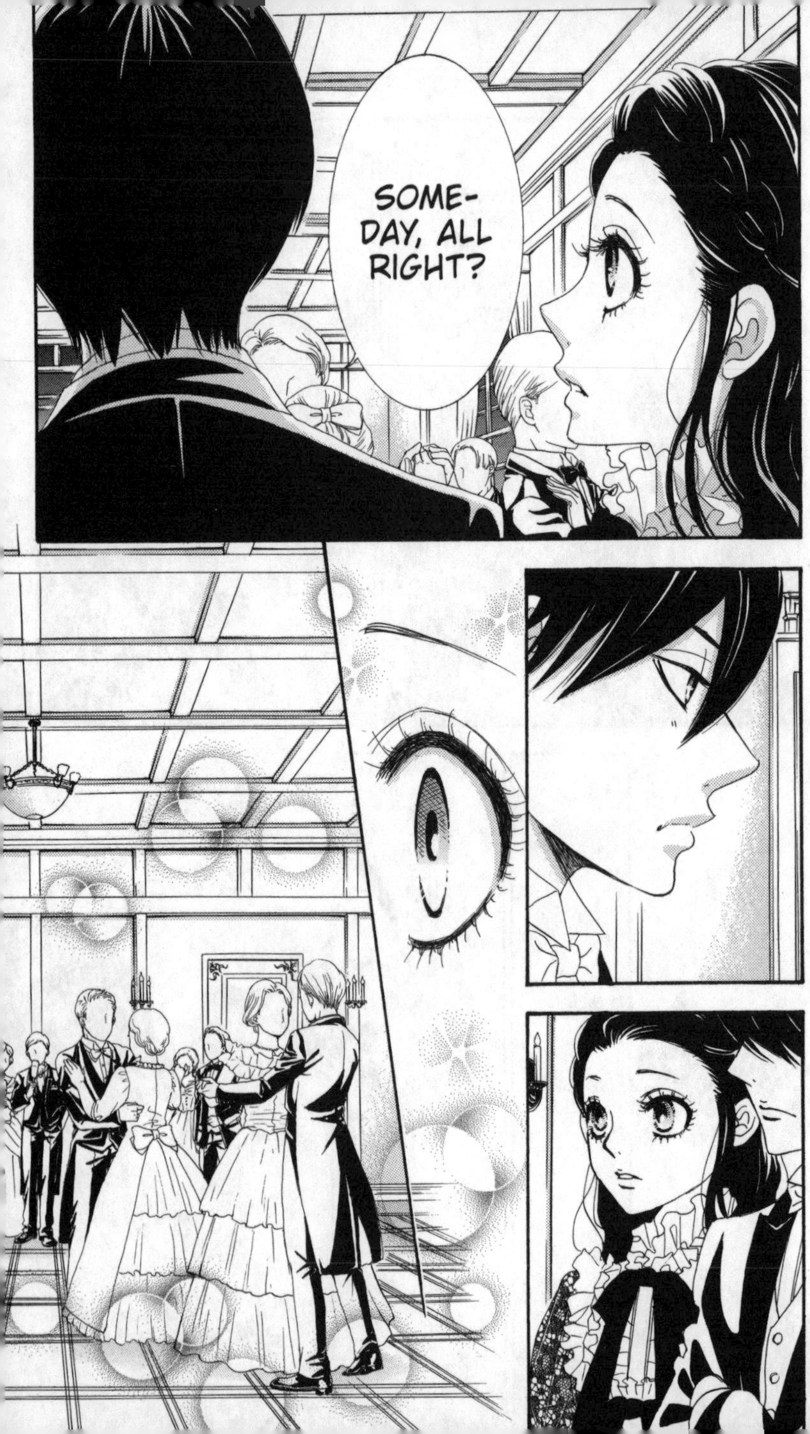
SOME-
DAY, ALL
RIGHT?

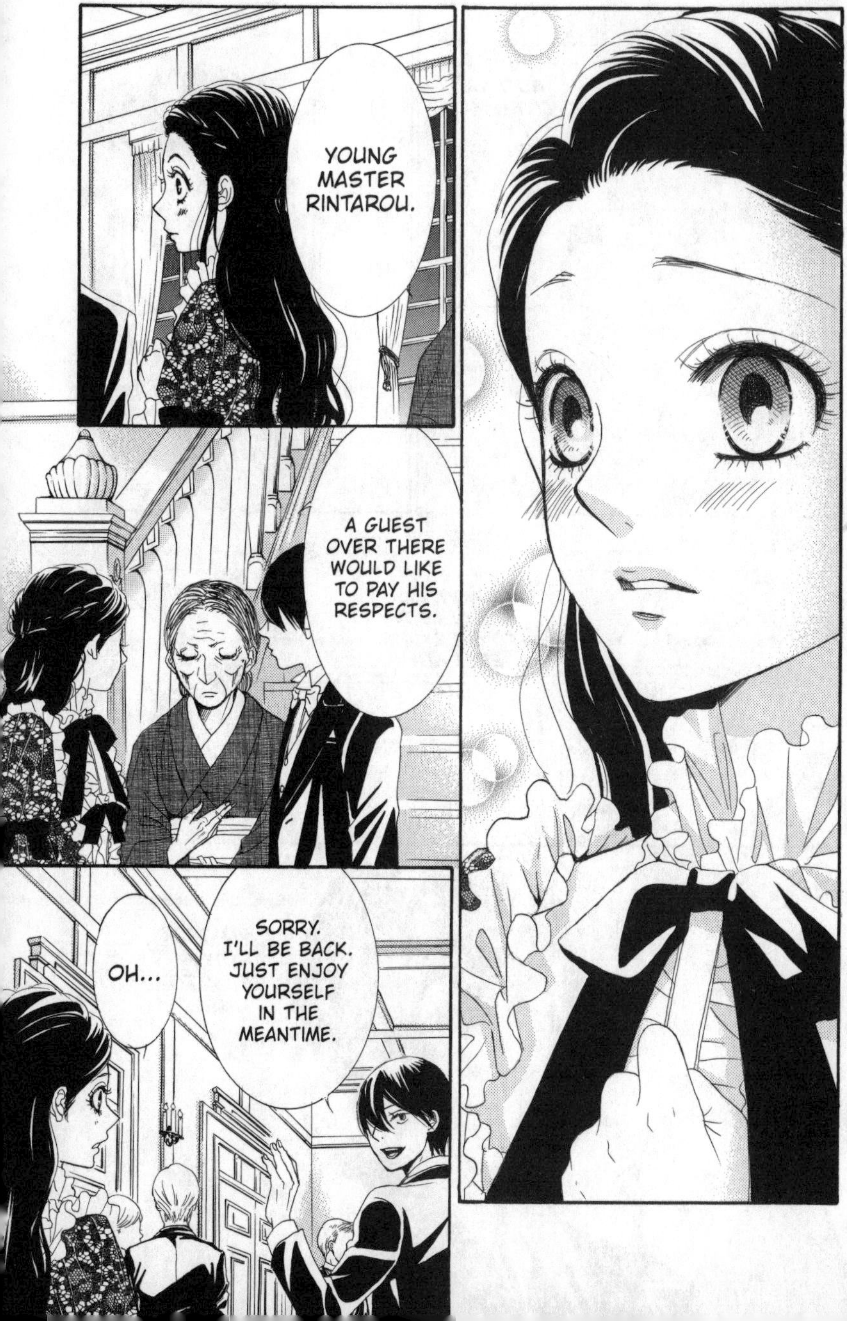
YOUNG MASTER RINTAROU.
A GUEST OVER THERE WOULD LIKE TO PAY HIS RESPECTS.
SORRY. I'LL BE BACK. JUST ENJOY YOURSELF IN THE MEANTIME.
OH...

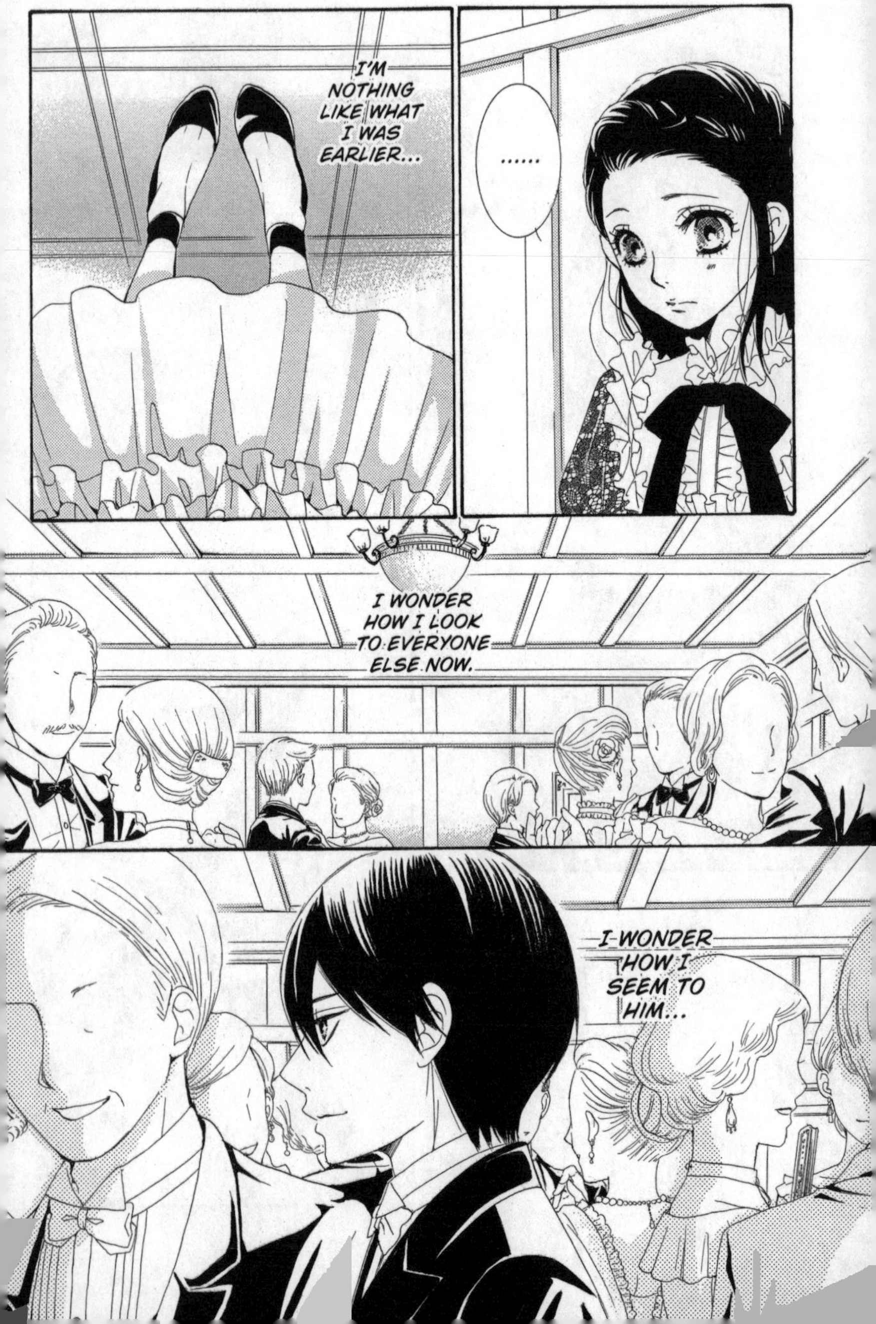
......
I'M NOTHING LIKE WHAT I WAS EARLIER...
I WONDER HOW I LOOK TO EVERYONE ELSE NOW.
I WONDER HOW I SEEM TO HIM...

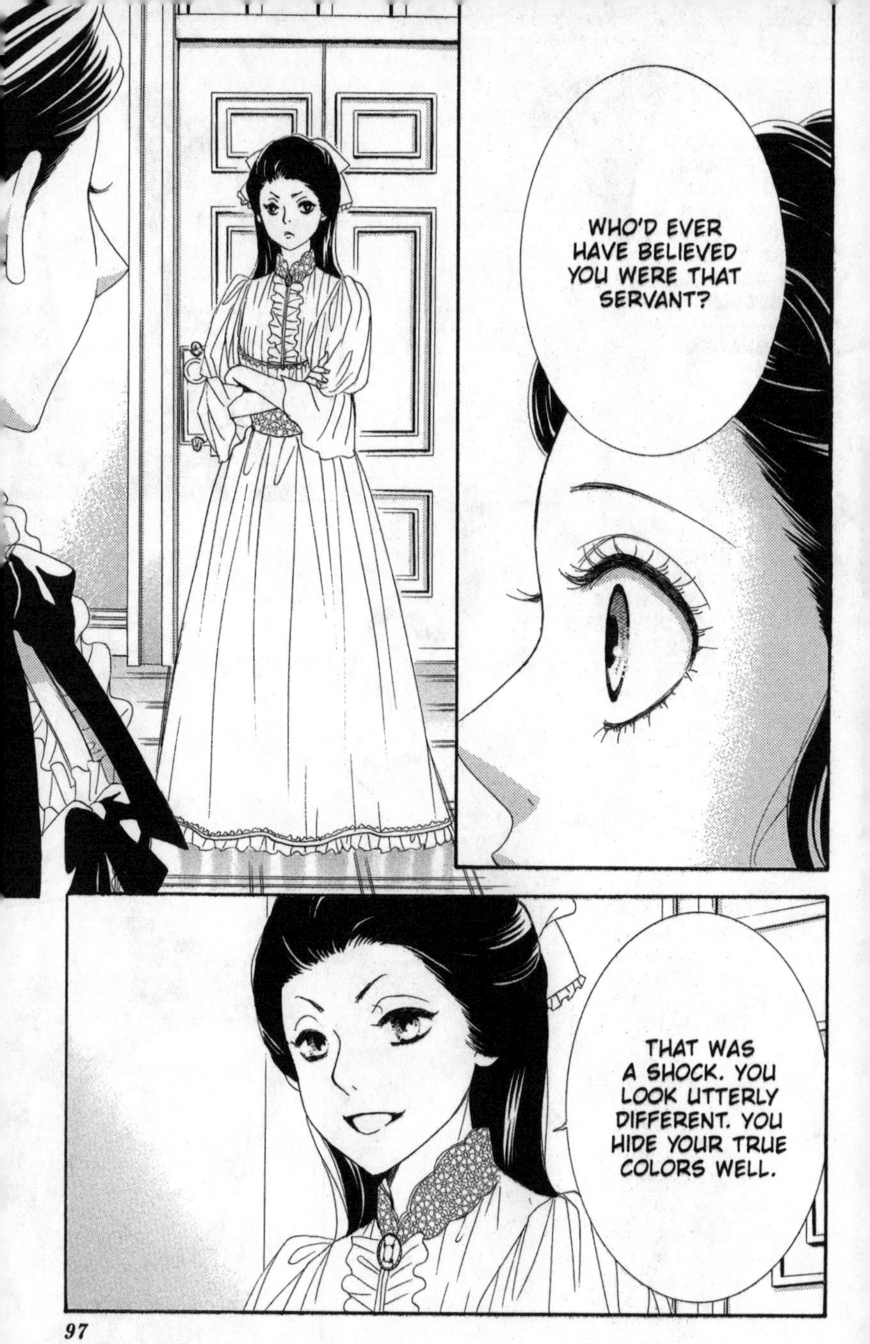
WHO'D EVER HAVE BELIEVED YOU WERE THAT SERVANT?
THAT WAS A SHOCK. YOU LOOK UTTERLY DIFFERENT. YOU HIDE YOUR TRUE COLORS WELL.

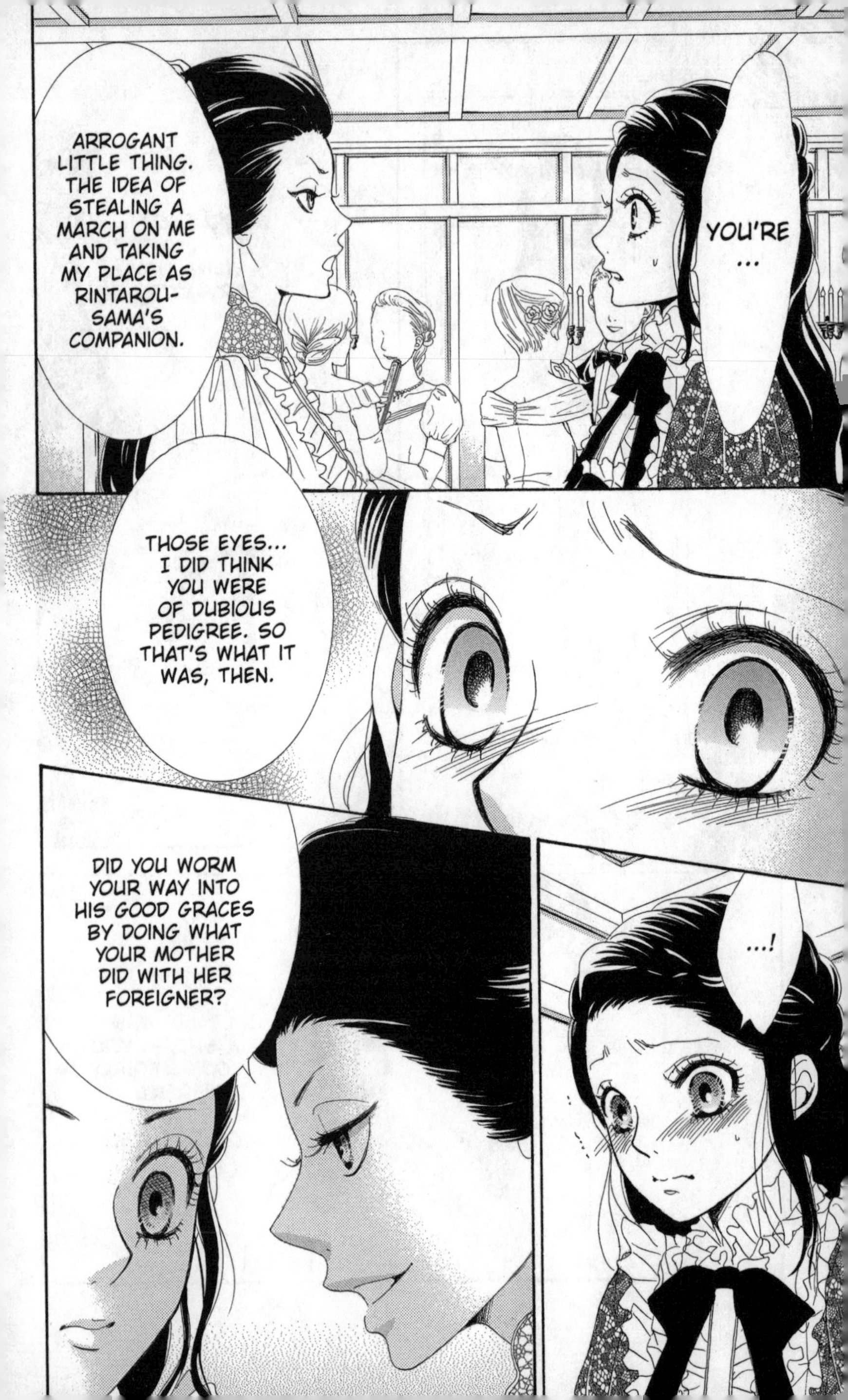
YOU'RE ...
ARROGANT LITTLE THING. THE IDEA OF STEALING A MARCH ON ME AND TAKING MY PLACE AS RINTAROU-SAMA'S COMPANION.
THOSE EYES... I DID THINK YOU WERE OF DUBIOUS PEDIGREE. SO THAT'S WHAT IT WAS, THEN.
...!
DID YOU WORM YOUR WAY INTO HIS GOOD GRACES BY DOING WHAT YOUR MOTHER DID WITH HER FOREIGNER?

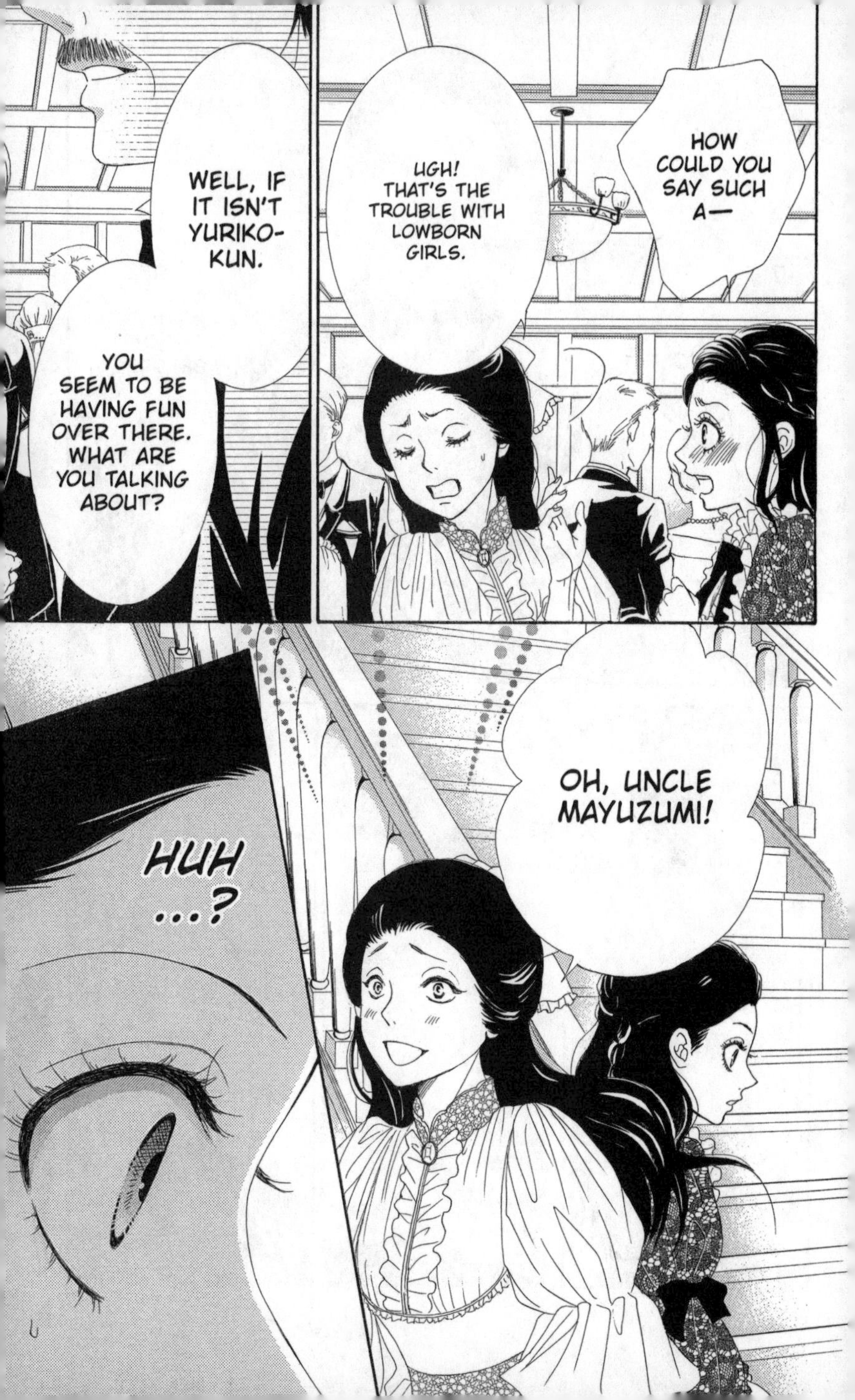
HOW COULD YOU SAY SUCH A—
UGH! THAT'S THE TROUBLE WITH LOWBORN GIRLS.
WELL, IF IT ISN'T YURIKO-KUN.
YOU SEEM TO BE HAVING FUN OVER THERE. WHAT ARE YOU TALKING ABOUT?
OH, UNCLE MAYUZUMI!
HUH ...?

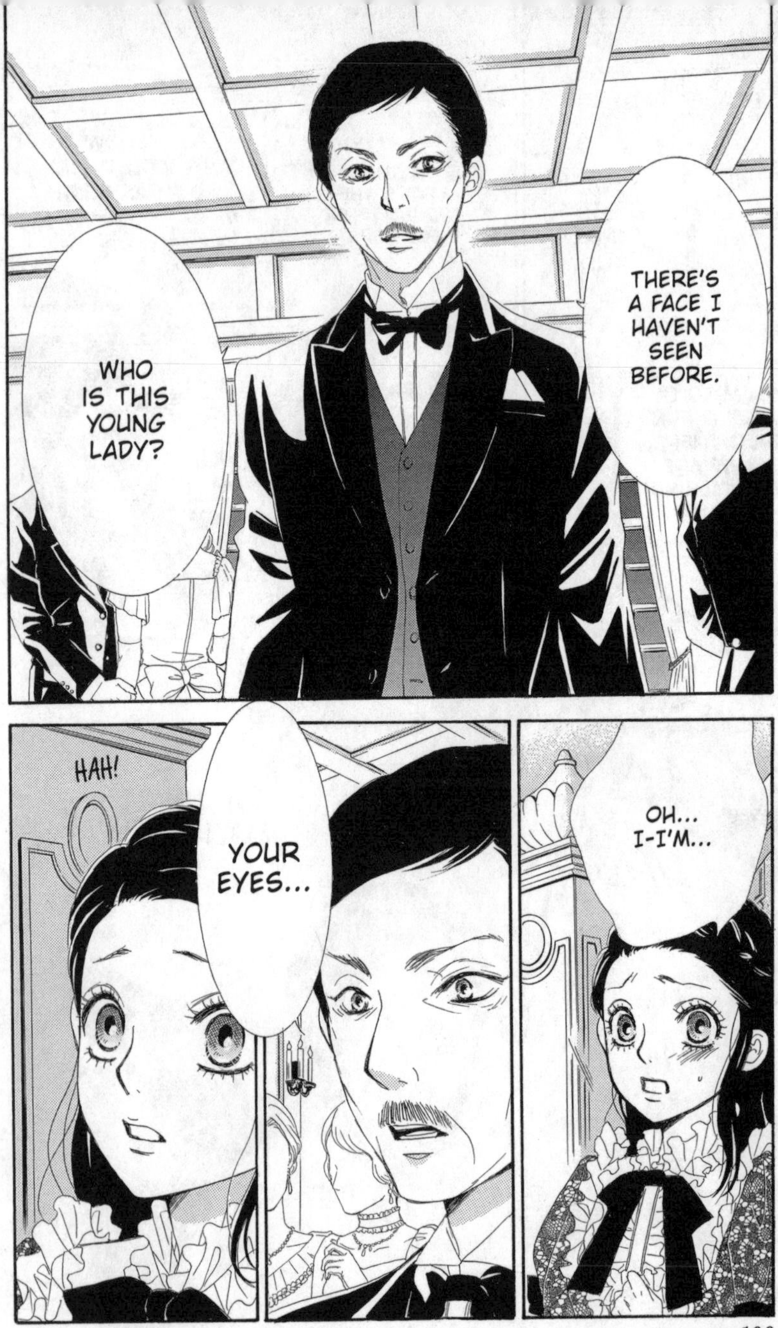
THERE'S A FACE I HAVEN'T SEEN BEFORE.
WHO IS THIS YOUNG LADY?
OH... I-I'M...
YOUR EYES...
HAH!

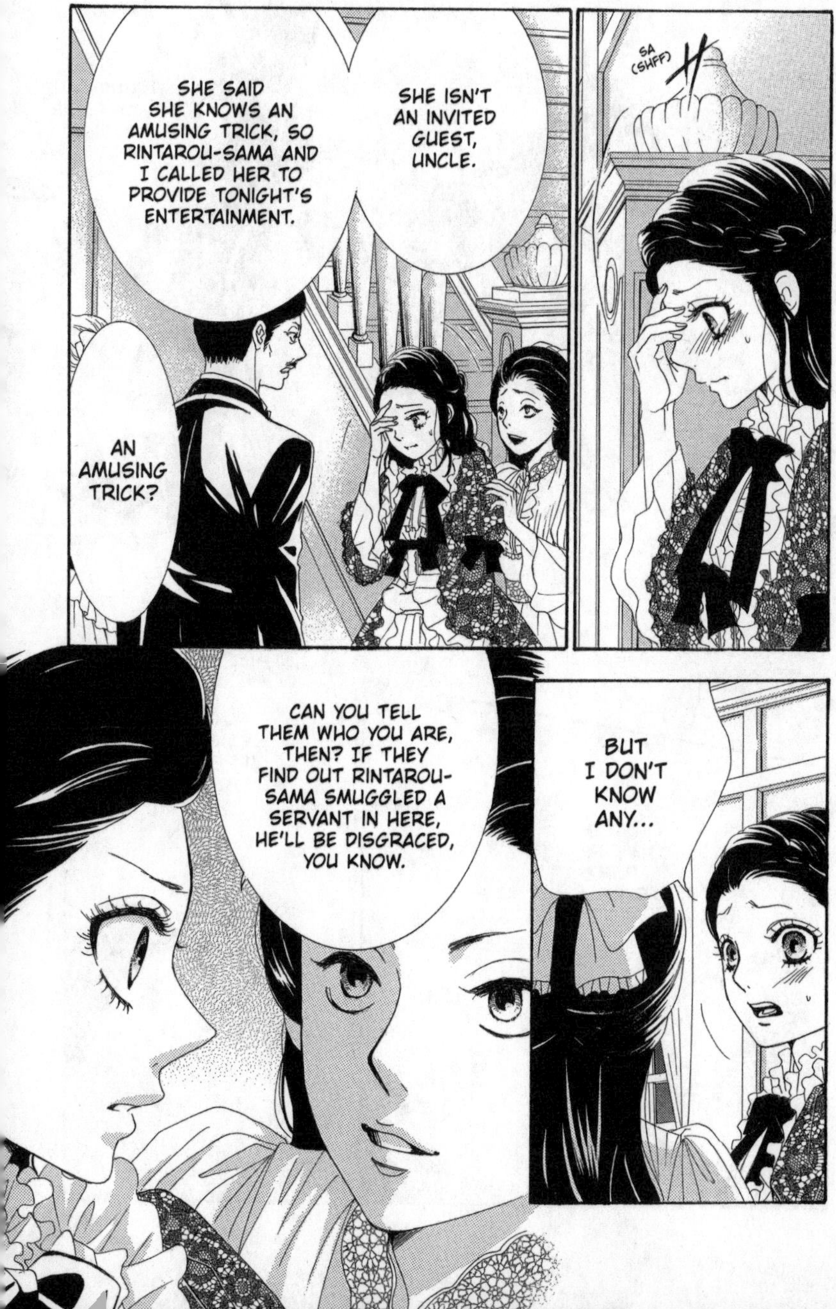
SA (SHFF)
SHE ISN'T AN INVITED GUEST, UNCLE.
SHE SAID SHE KNOWS AN AMUSING TRICK, SO RINTAROU-SAMA AND I CALLED HER TO PROVIDE TONIGHT'S ENTERTAINMENT.
AN AMUSING TRICK?
BUT I DON'T KNOW ANY...
CAN YOU TELL THEM WHO YOU ARE, THEN? IF THEY FIND OUT RINTAROU-SAMA SMUGGLED A SERVANT IN HERE, HE'LL BE DISGRACED, YOU KNOW.

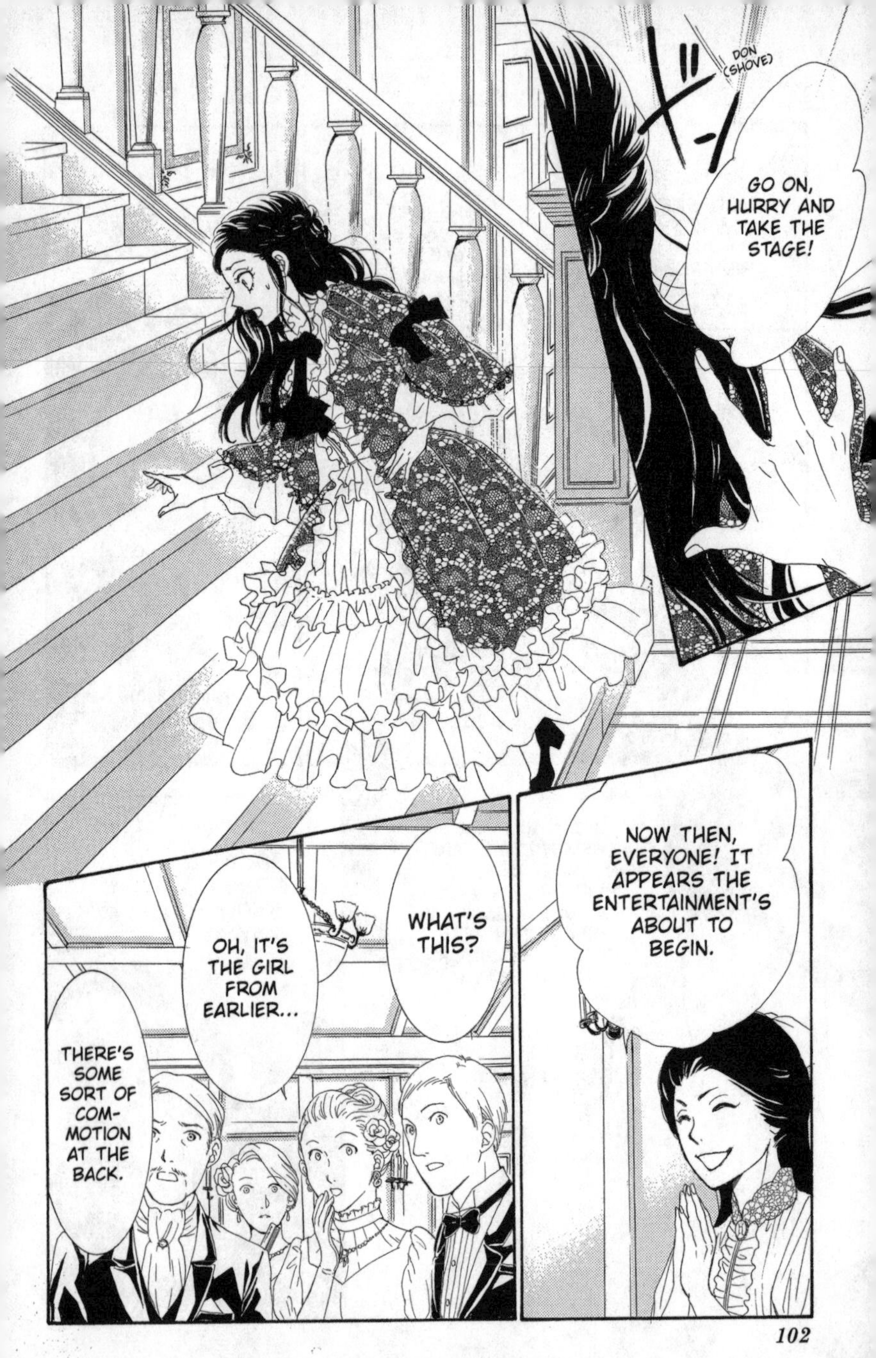
DON (SHOVE)
GO ON, HURRY AND TAKE THE STAGE!
NOW THEN, EVERYONE! IT APPEARS THE ENTERTAINMENT'S ABOUT TO BEGIN.
WHAT'S THIS?
OH, IT'S THE GIRL FROM EARLIER...
THERE'S SOME SORT OF COM-MOTION AT THE BACK.

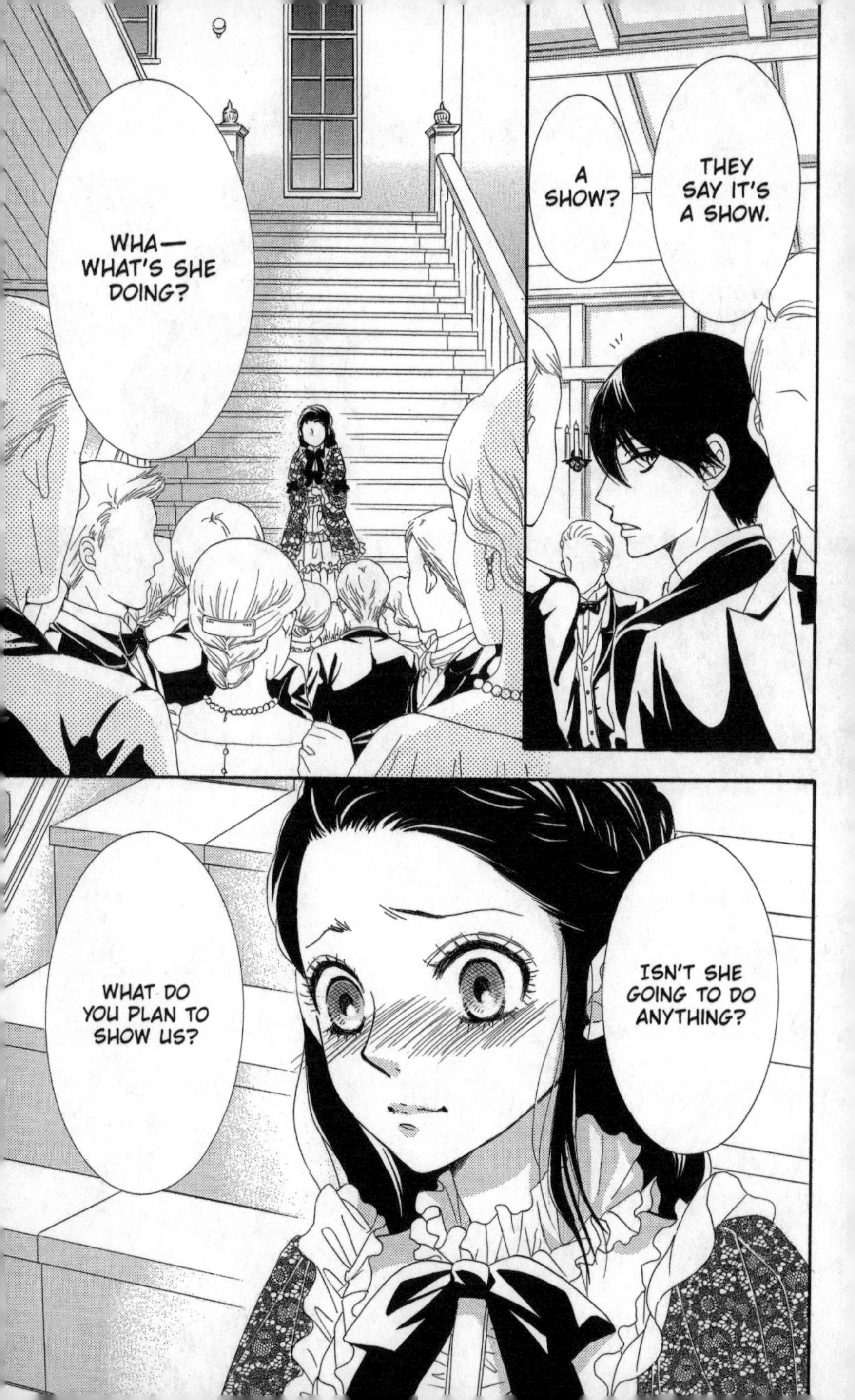
THEY SAY IT'S A SHOW.
A SHOW?
WHA— WHAT'S SHE DOING?
ISN'T SHE GOING TO DO ANYTHING?
WHAT DO YOU PLAN TO SHOW US?

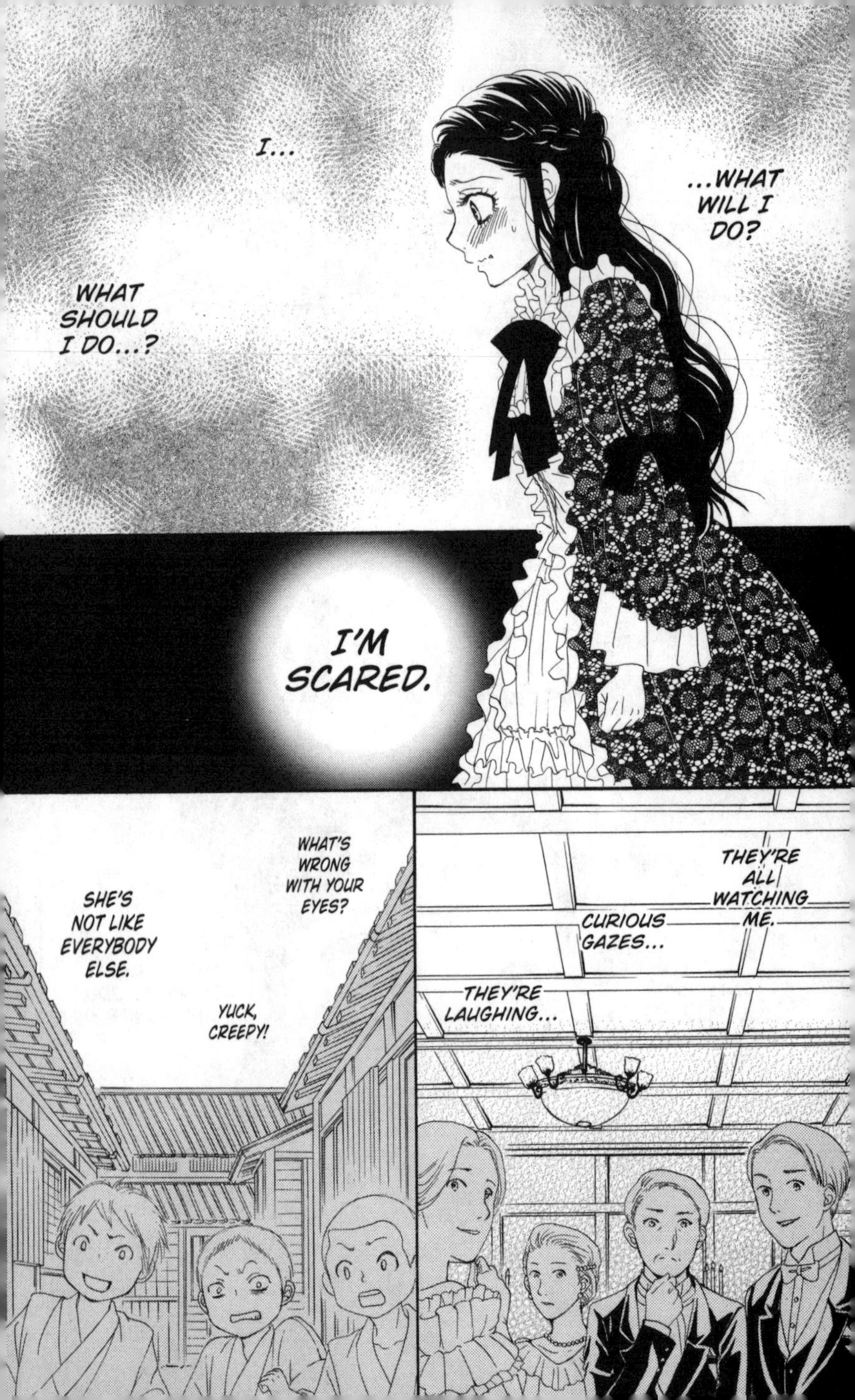
...WHAT WILL I DO?
I...
WHAT SHOULD I DO...?
I'M SCARED.
THEY'RE ALL WATCHING ME.
CURIOUS GAZES...
THEY'RE LAUGHING...
WHAT'S WRONG WITH YOUR EYES?
SHE'S NOT LIKE EVERYBODY ELSE.
YUCK, CREEPY!

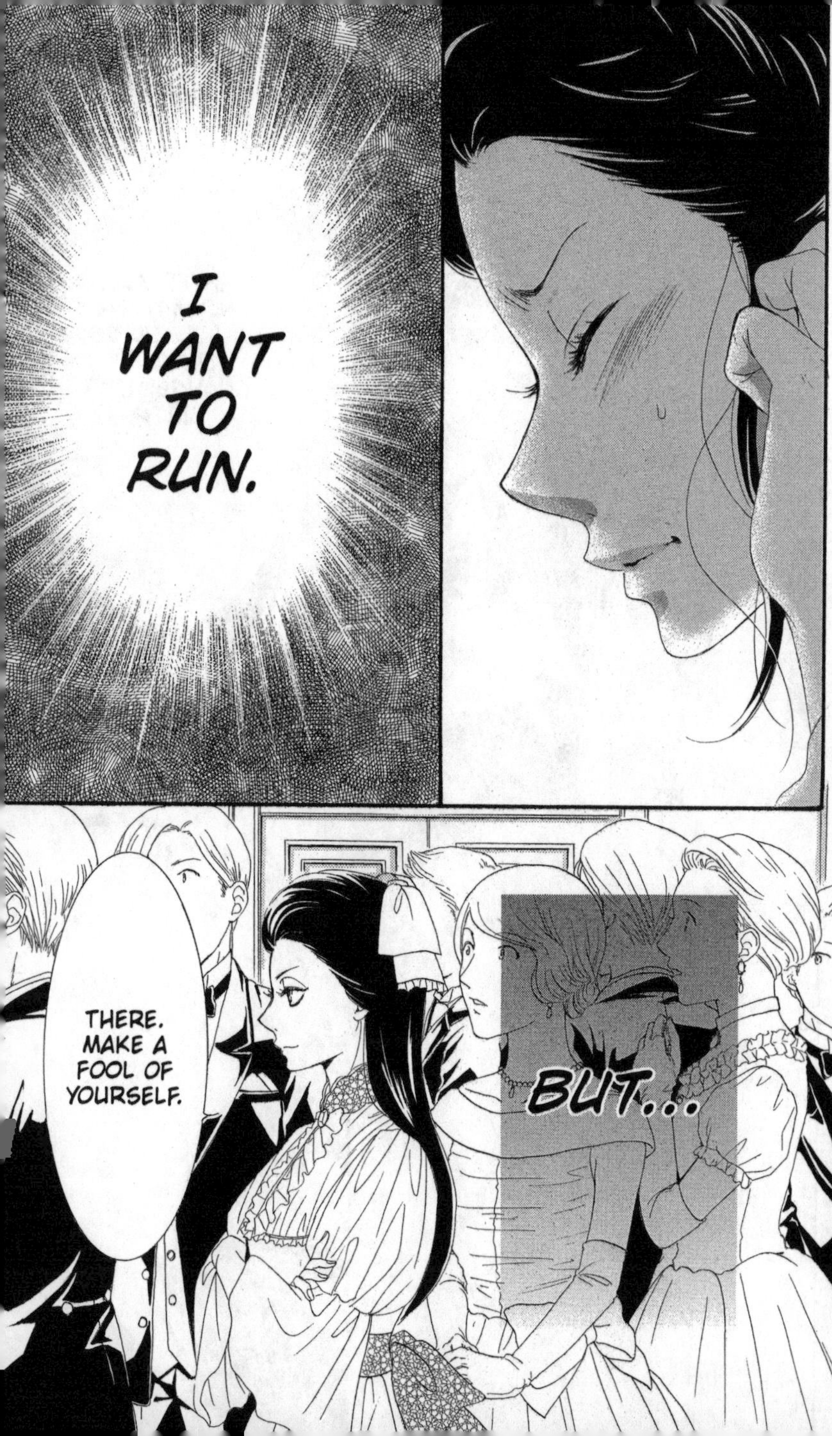
I WANT TO RUN.
BUT...
THERE. MAKE A FOOL OF YOURSELF.

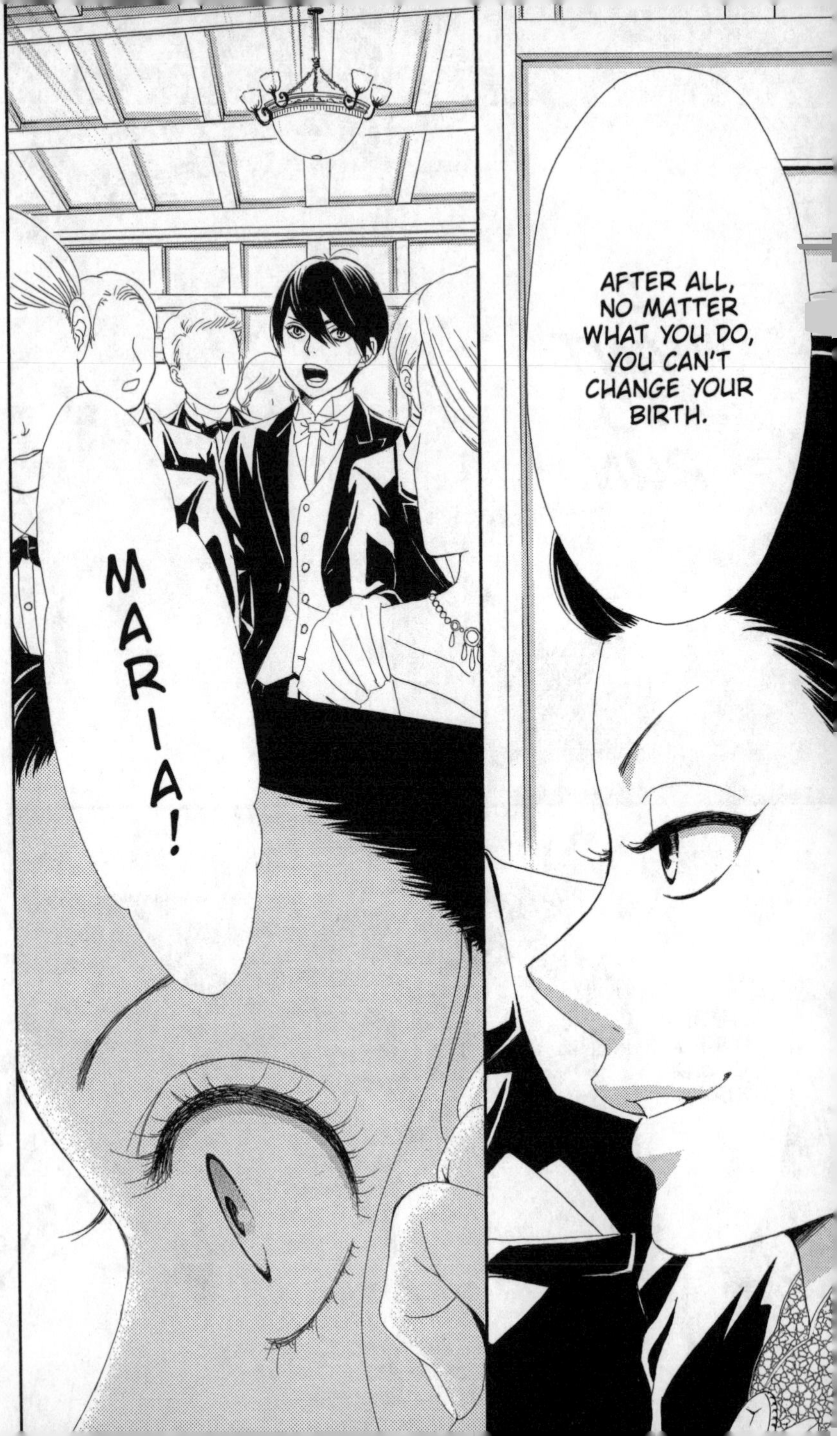
AFTER ALL, NO MATTER WHAT YOU DO, YOU CAN'T CHANGE YOUR BIRTH.
MARIA!

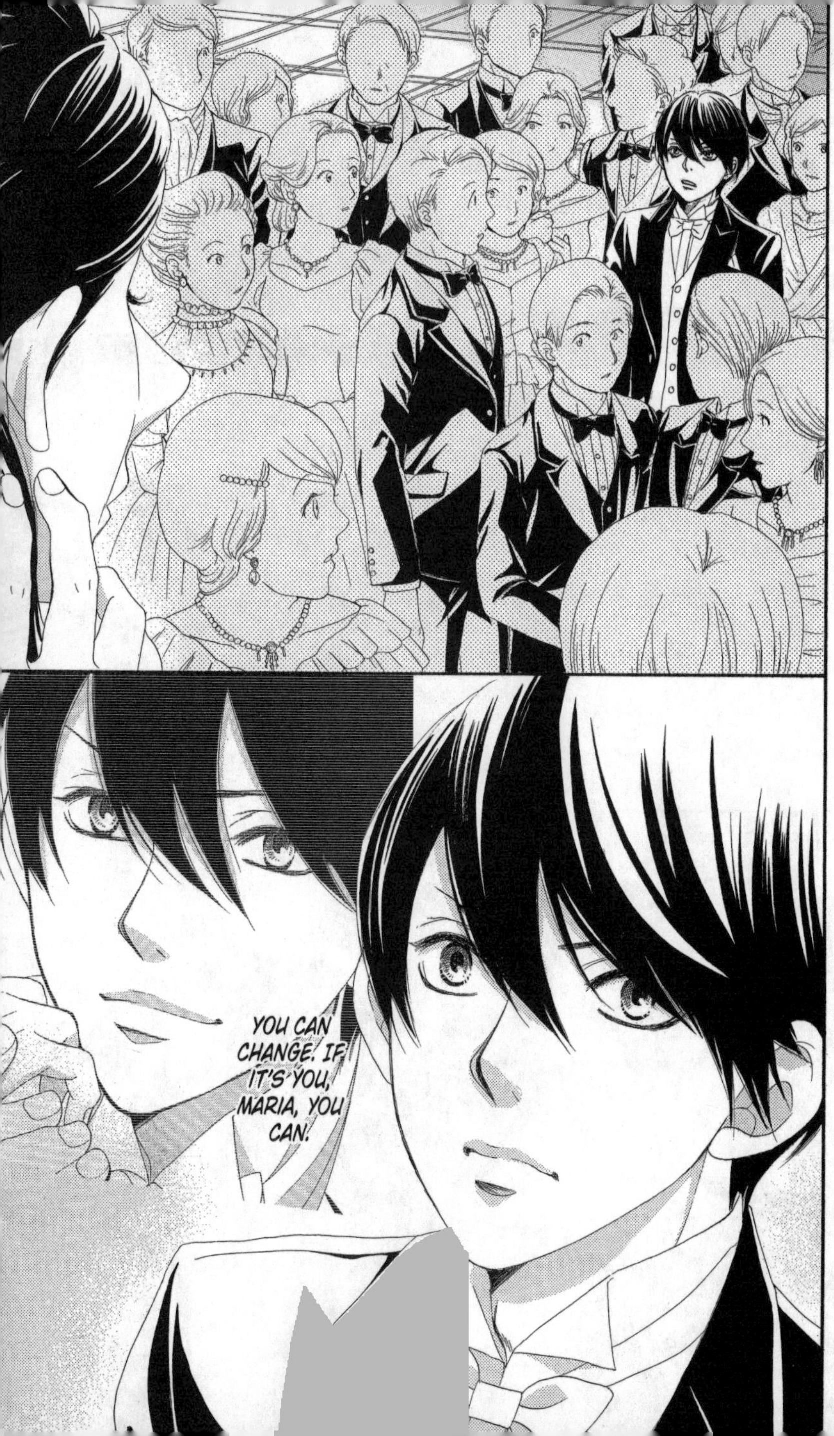
YOU CAN CHANGE. IF IT'S YOU, MARIA, YOU CAN.

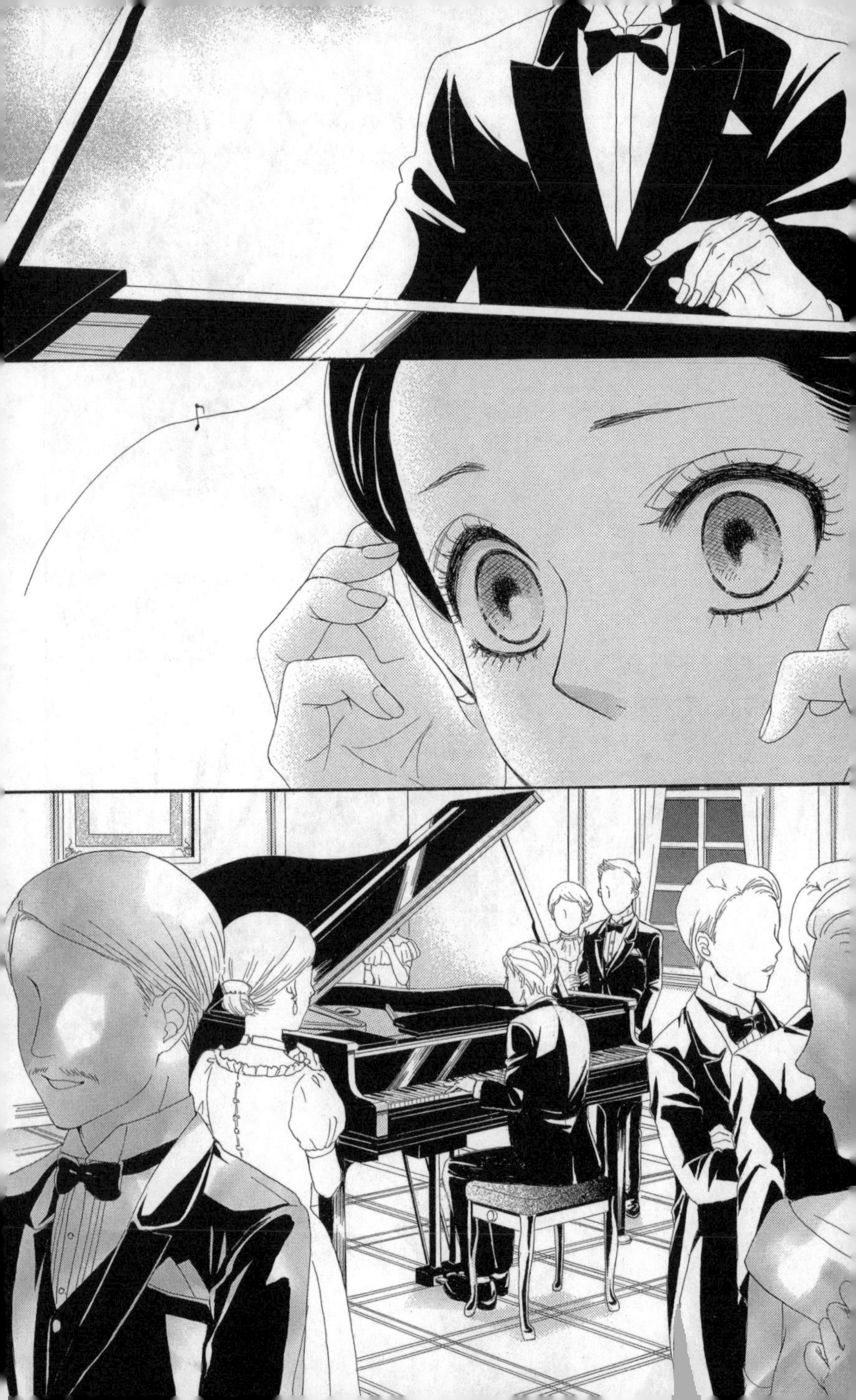

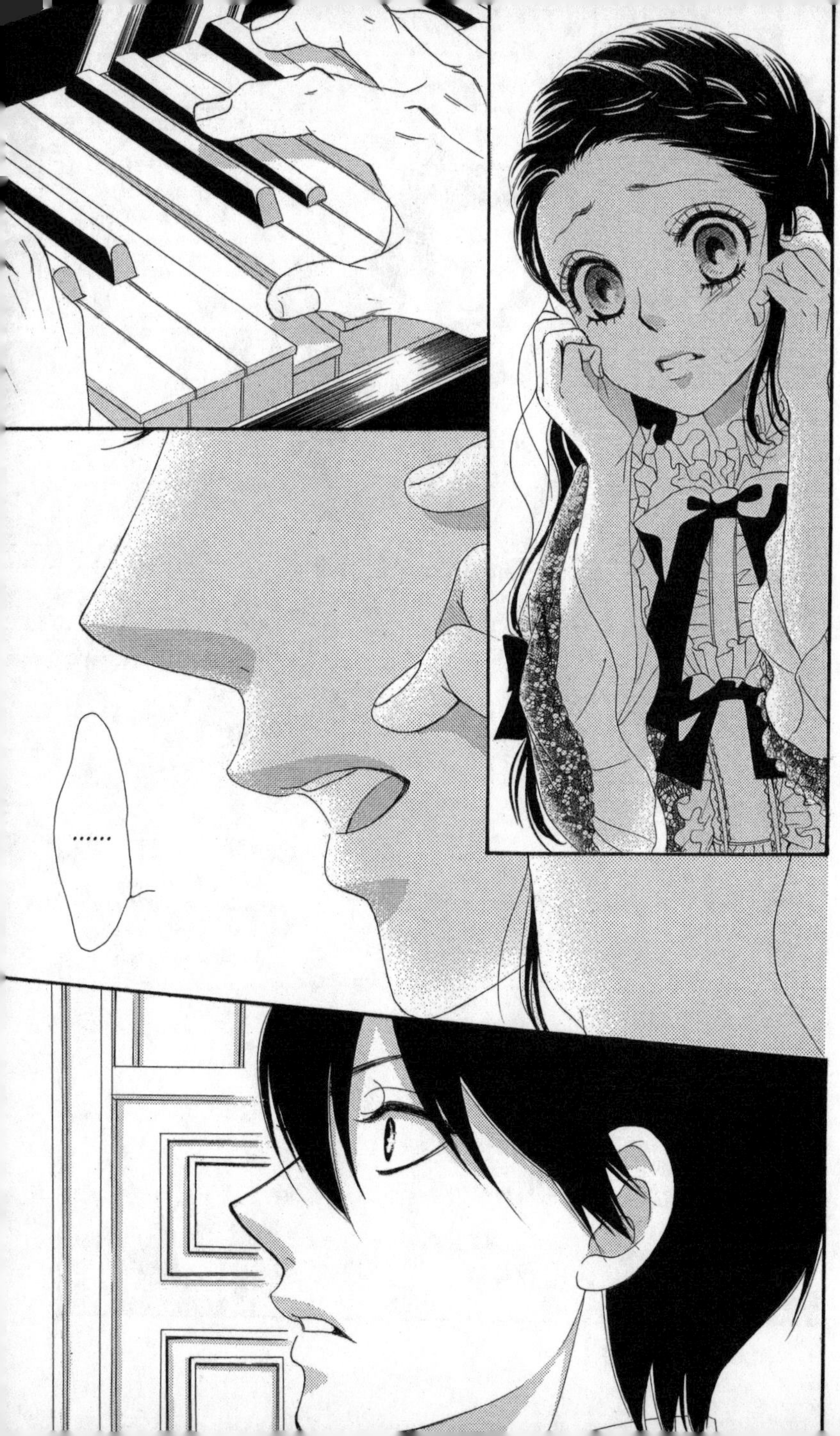
......

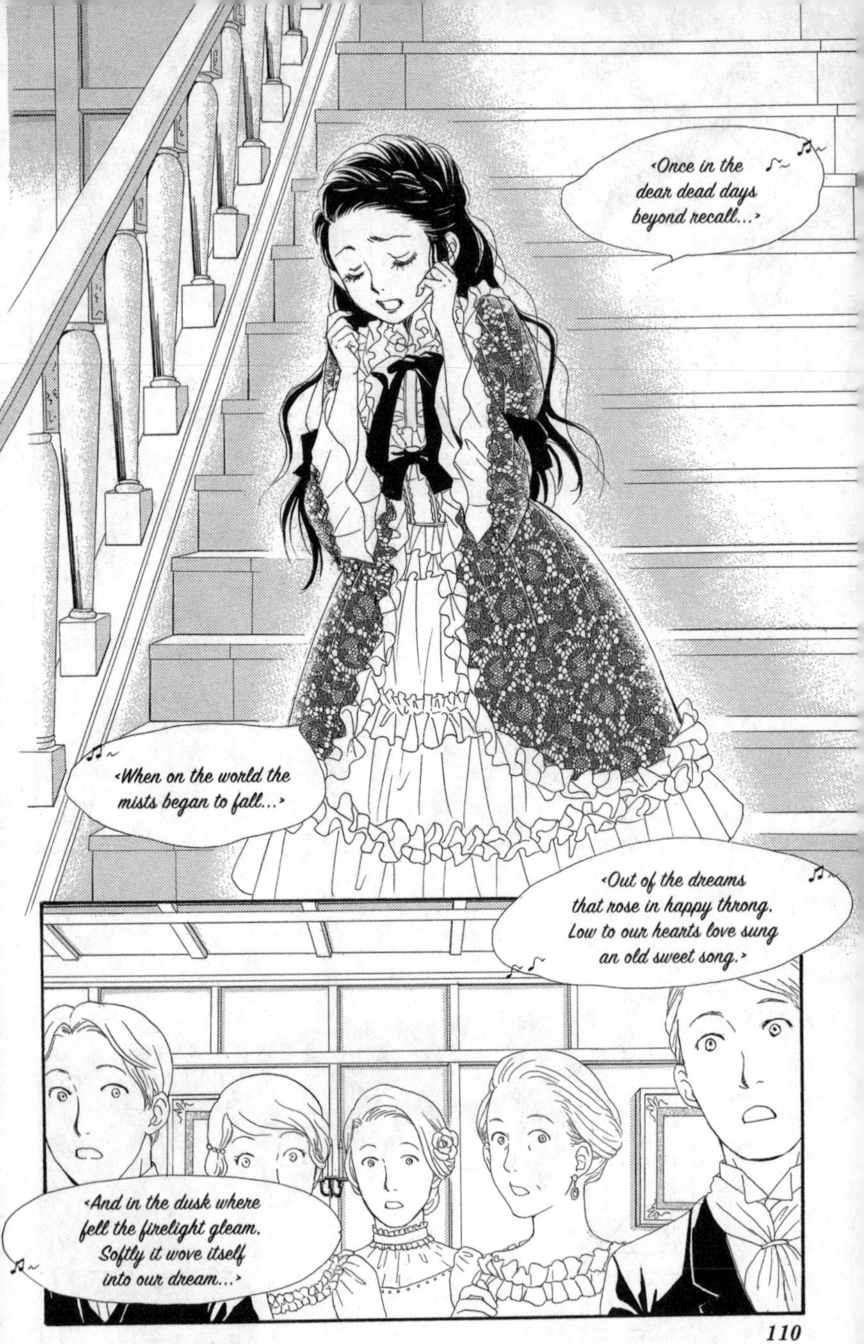
‹Once in the dear dead days beyond recall...›
‹When on the world the mists began to fall...›
‹Out of the dreams that rose in happy throng. Low to our hearts love sung an old sweet song.›
‹And in the dusk where fell the firelight gleam. Softly it wove itself into our dream...›

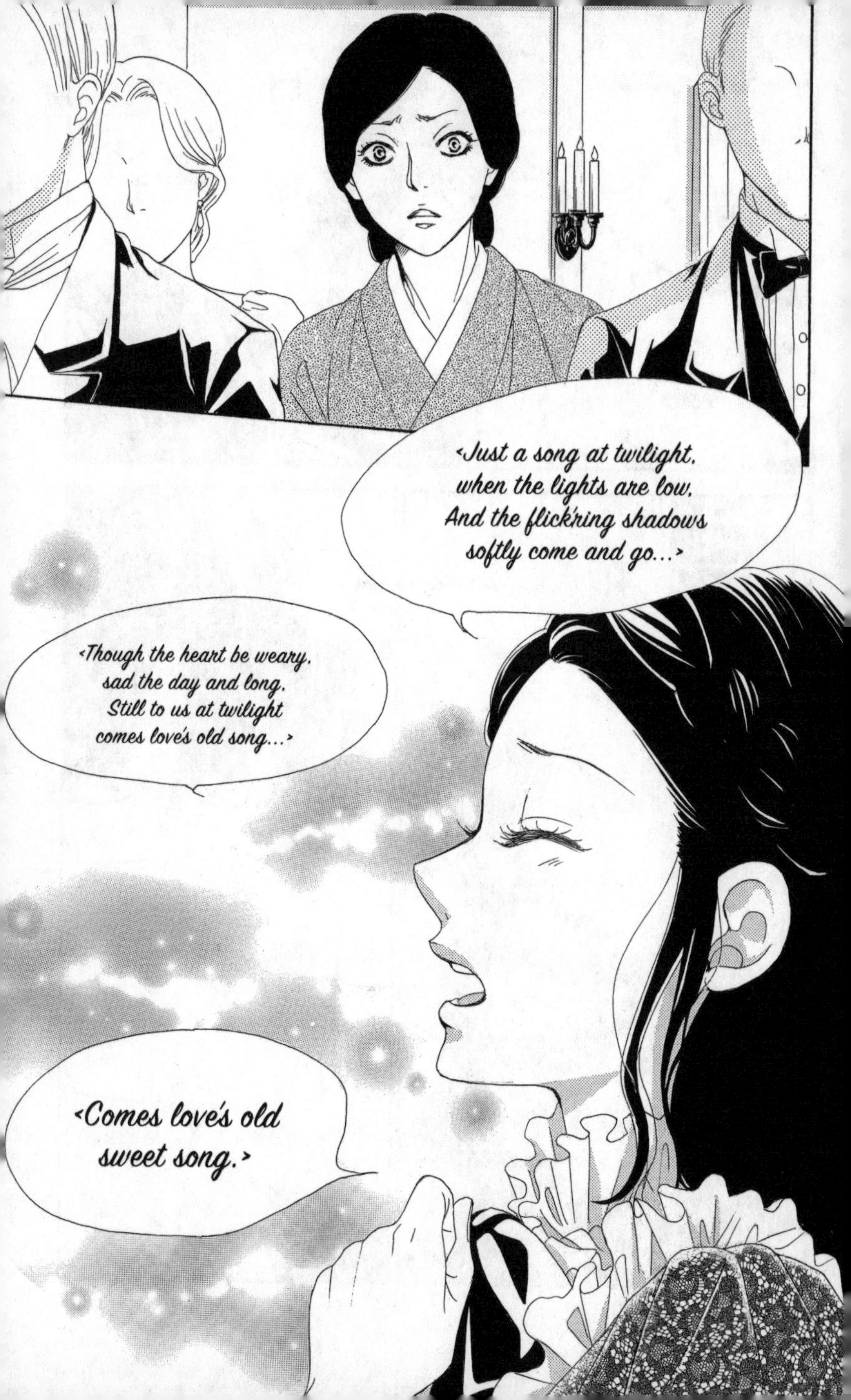
‹Just a song at twilight, when the lights are low, And the flick'ring shadows softly come and go...›
‹Though the heart be weary, sad the day and long, Still to us at twilight comes love's old song...›
‹Comes love's old sweet song.›

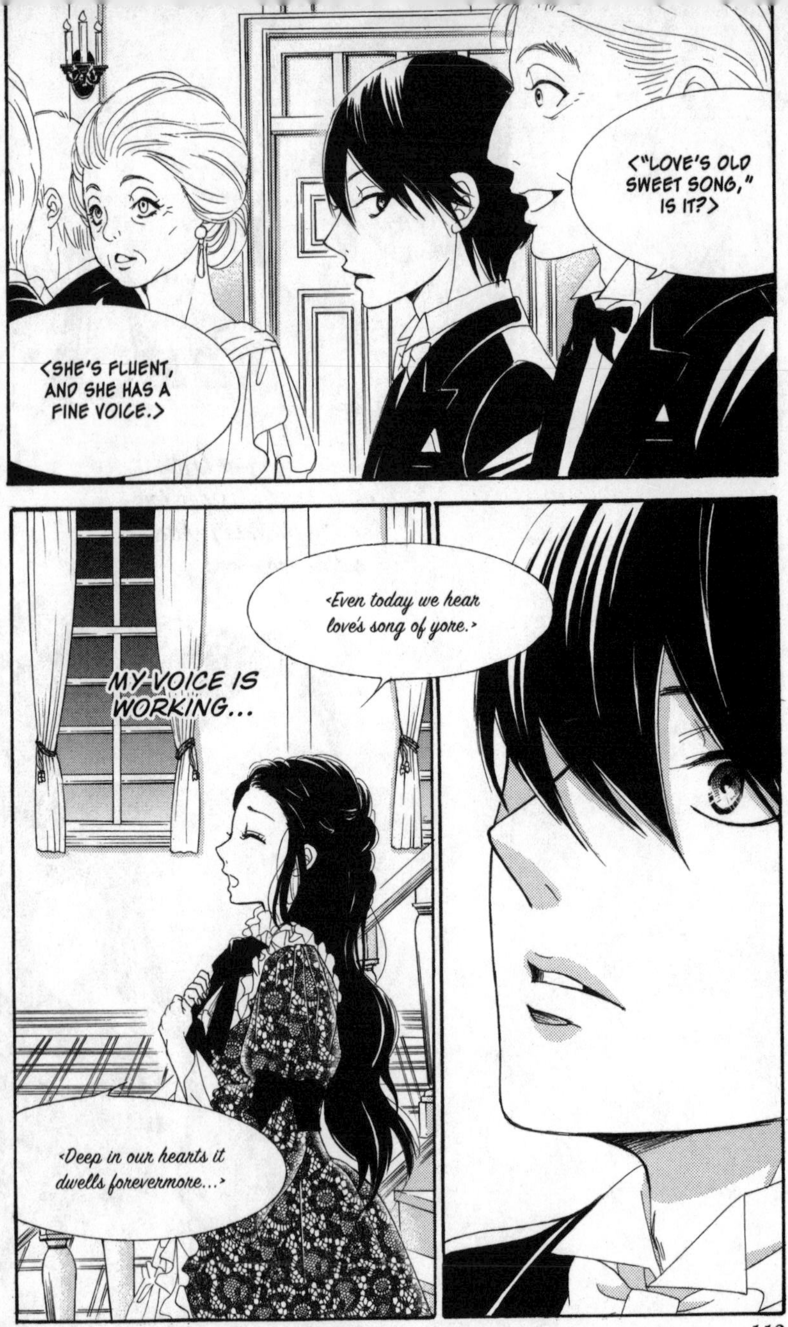
<"LOVE'S OLD SWEET SONG," IS IT?>
<SHE'S FLUENT, AND SHE HAS A FINE VOICE.>
‹Even today we hear love's song of yore.›
MY VOICE IS WORKING...
‹Deep in our hearts it dwells forevermore...›

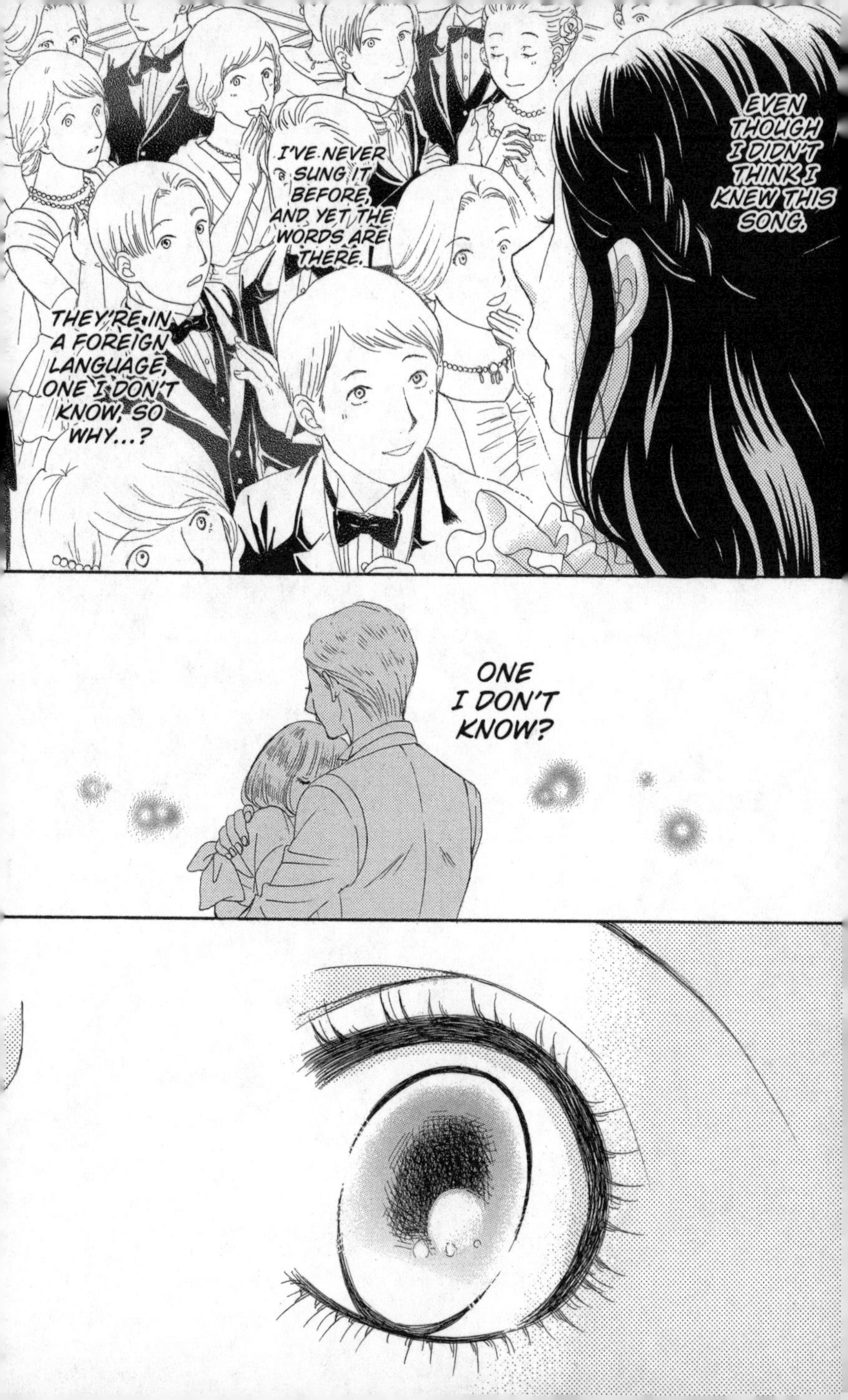
EVEN THOUGH I DIDN'T THINK I KNEW THIS SONG.
I'VE NEVER SUNG IT BEFORE, AND YET THE WORDS ARE THERE.
THEY'RE IN A FOREIGN LANGUAGE, ONE I DON'T KNOW, SO WHY...?
ONE I DON'T KNOW?

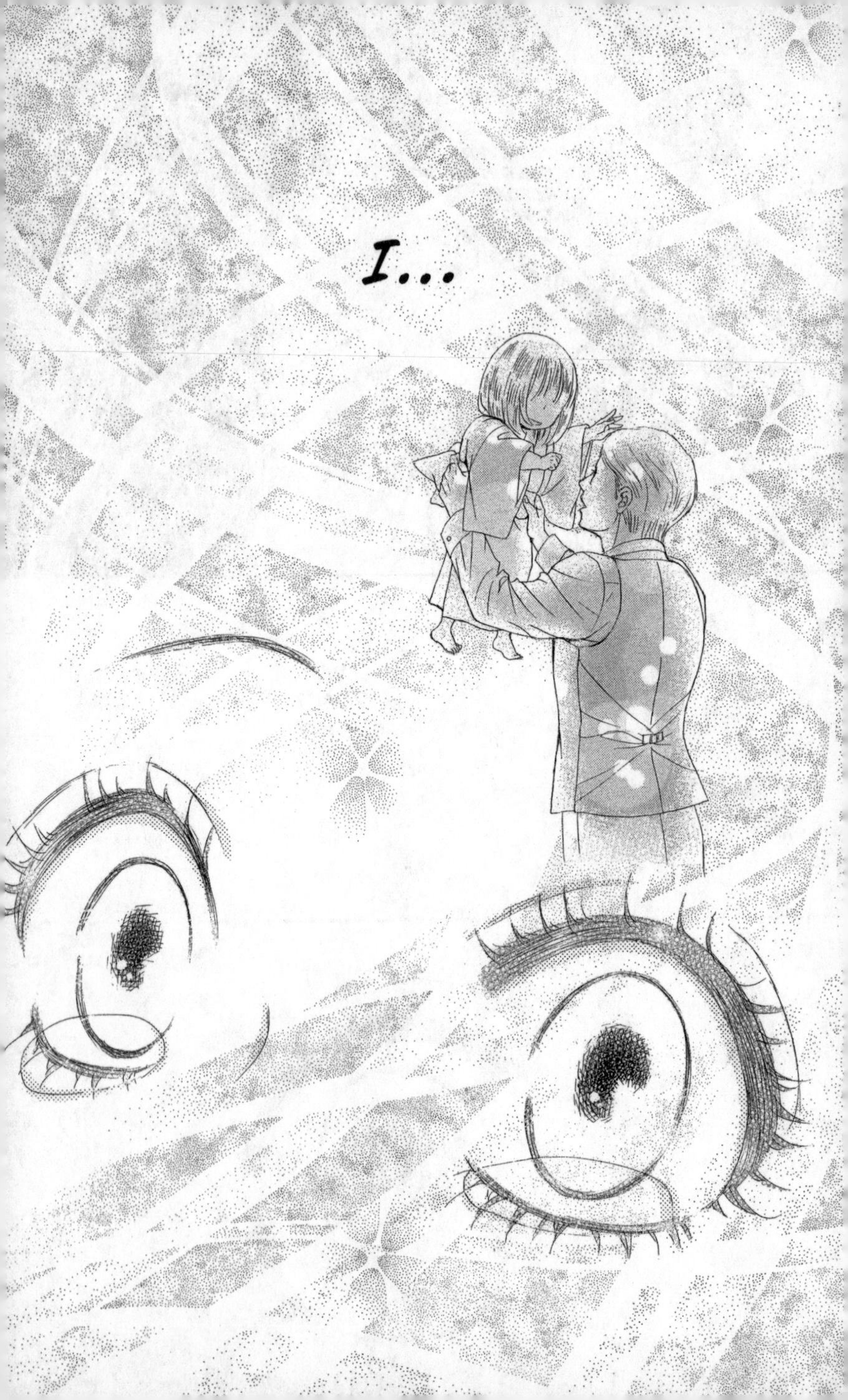
I...

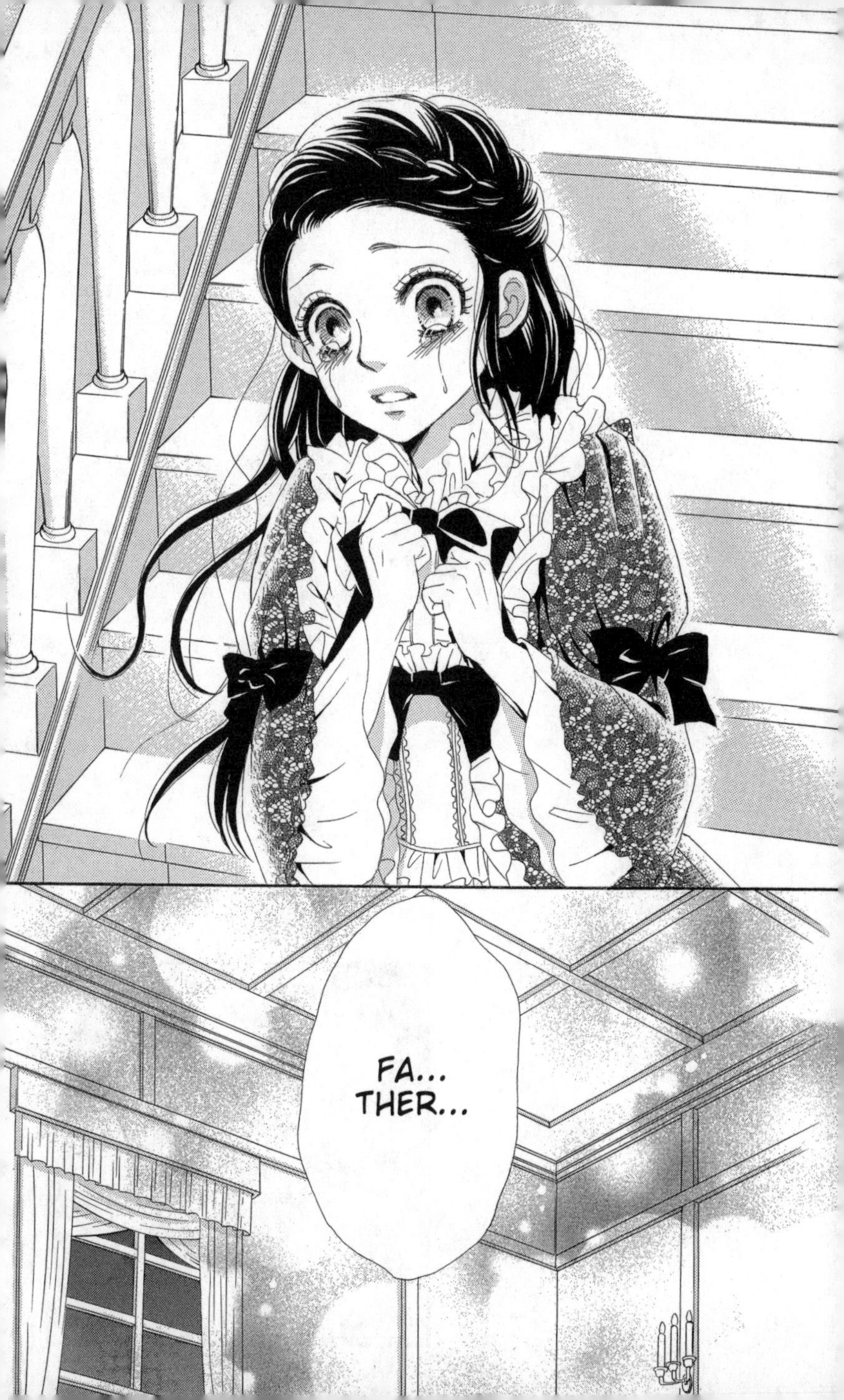
FA... THER...

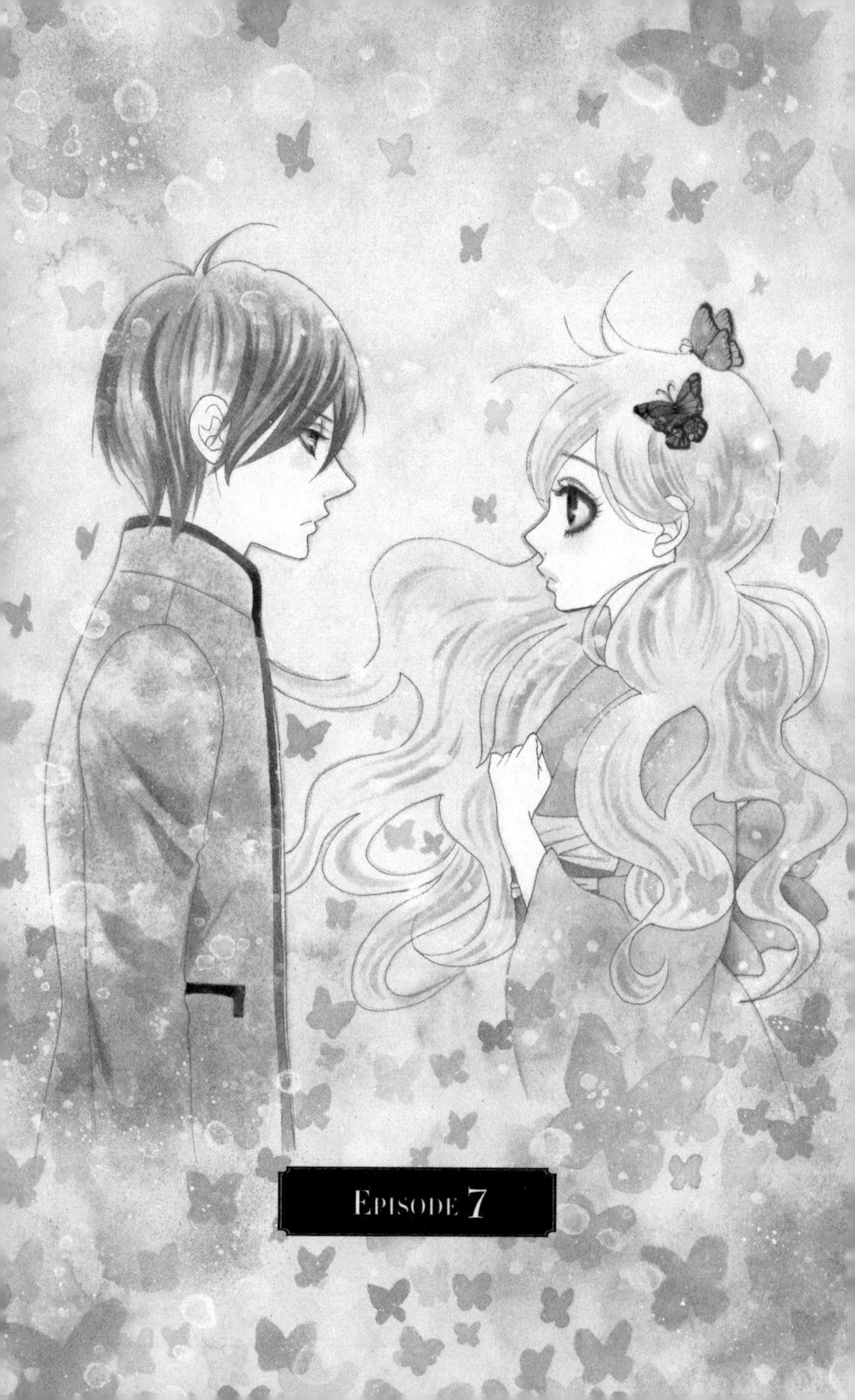
Episode 7

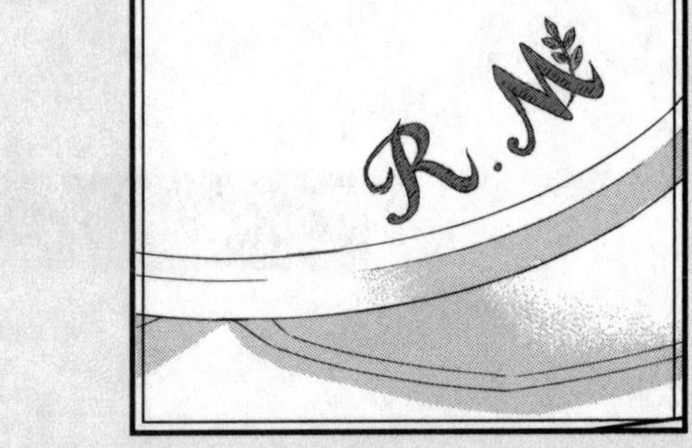
R.M

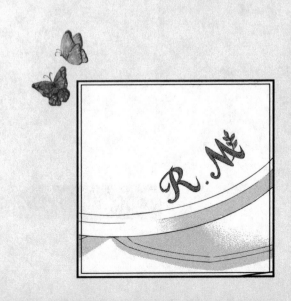

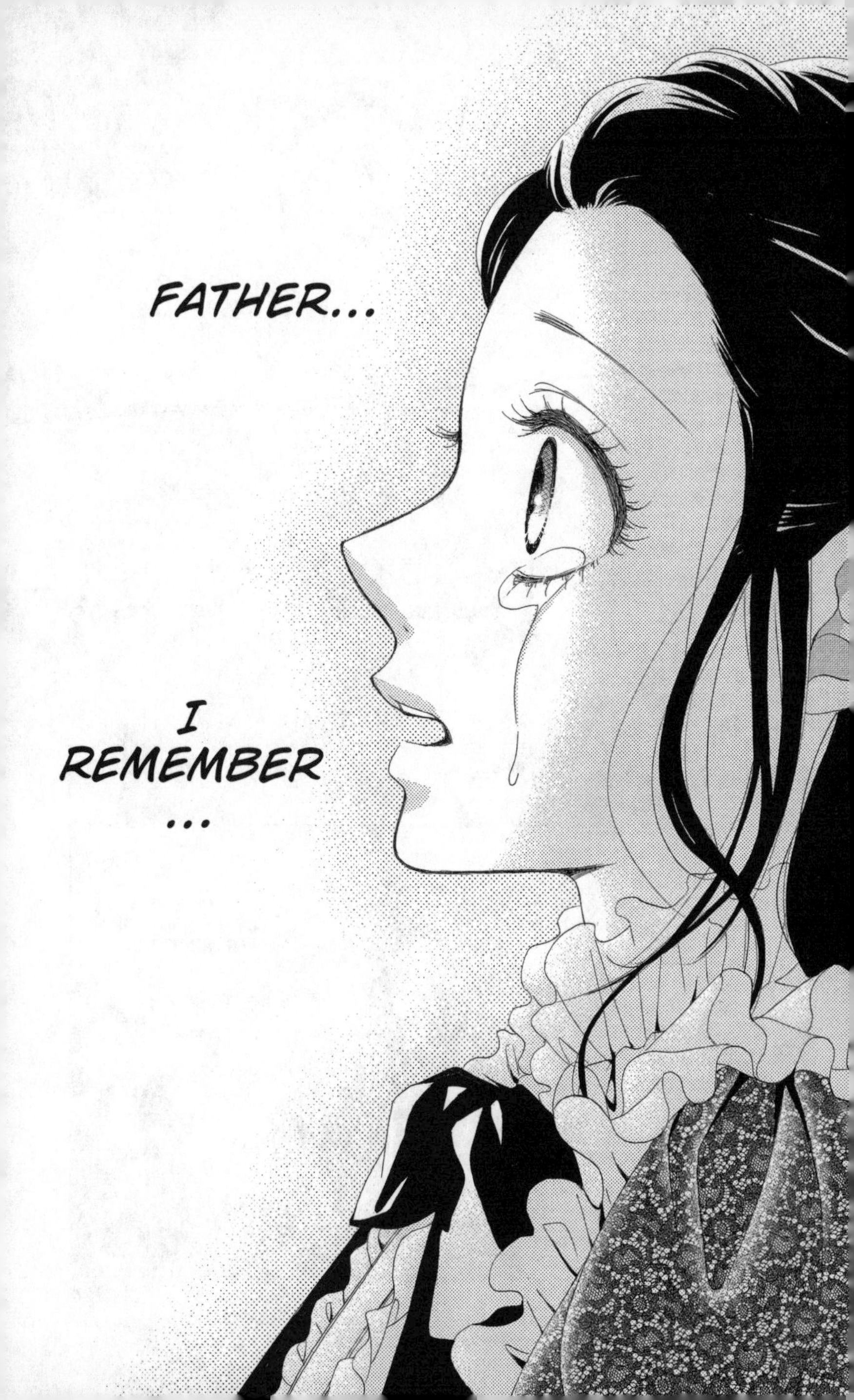
FATHER...
I REMEMBER ...

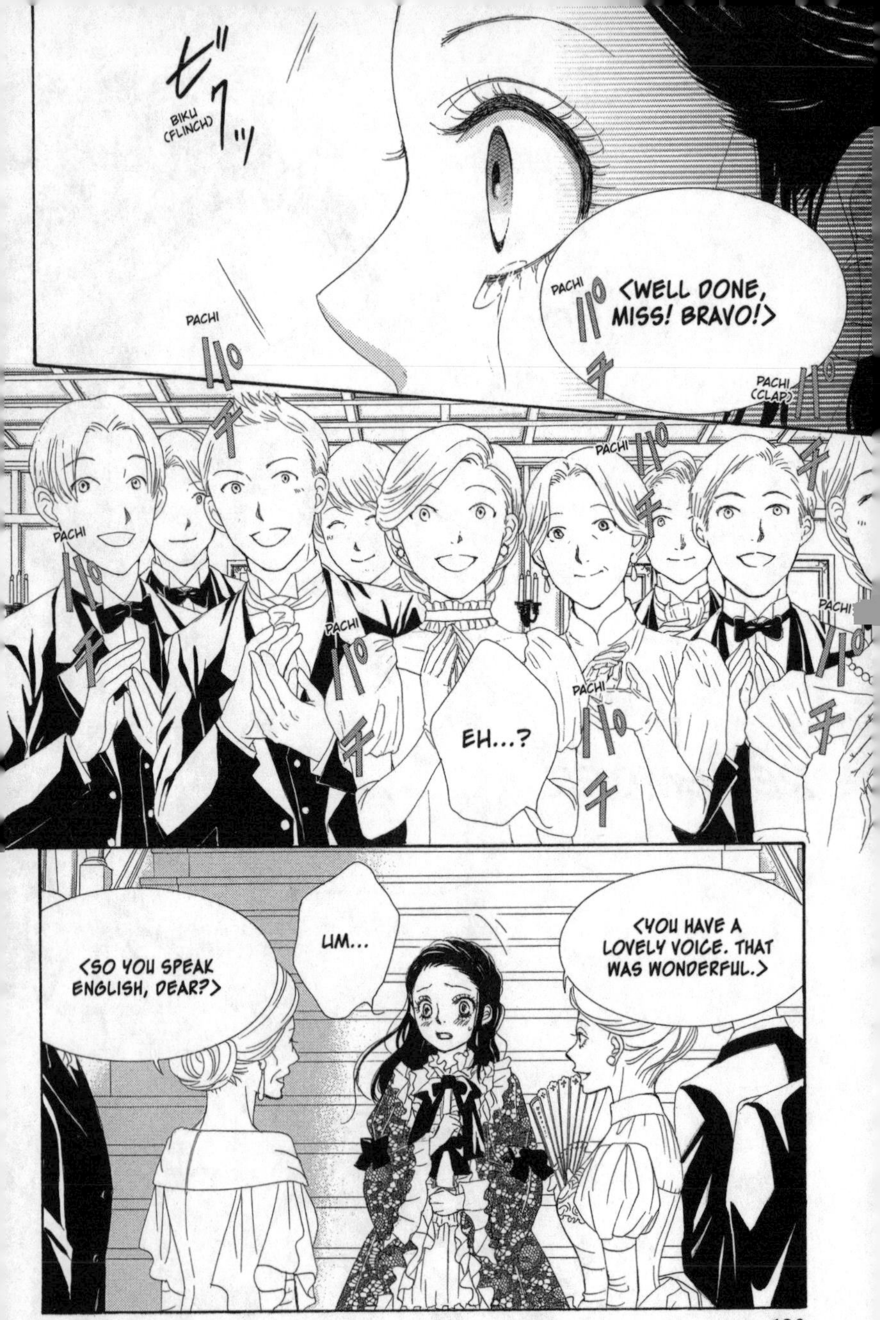
BIKU (FLINCH)
PACHI
<WELL DONE, MISS! BRAVO!>
PACHI
PACHI (CLAP)
PACHI
PACHI
PACHI
PACHI
PACHI
EH...?
<YOU HAVE A LOVELY VOICE. THAT WAS WONDERFUL.>
UM...
<SO YOU SPEAK ENGLISH, DEAR?>

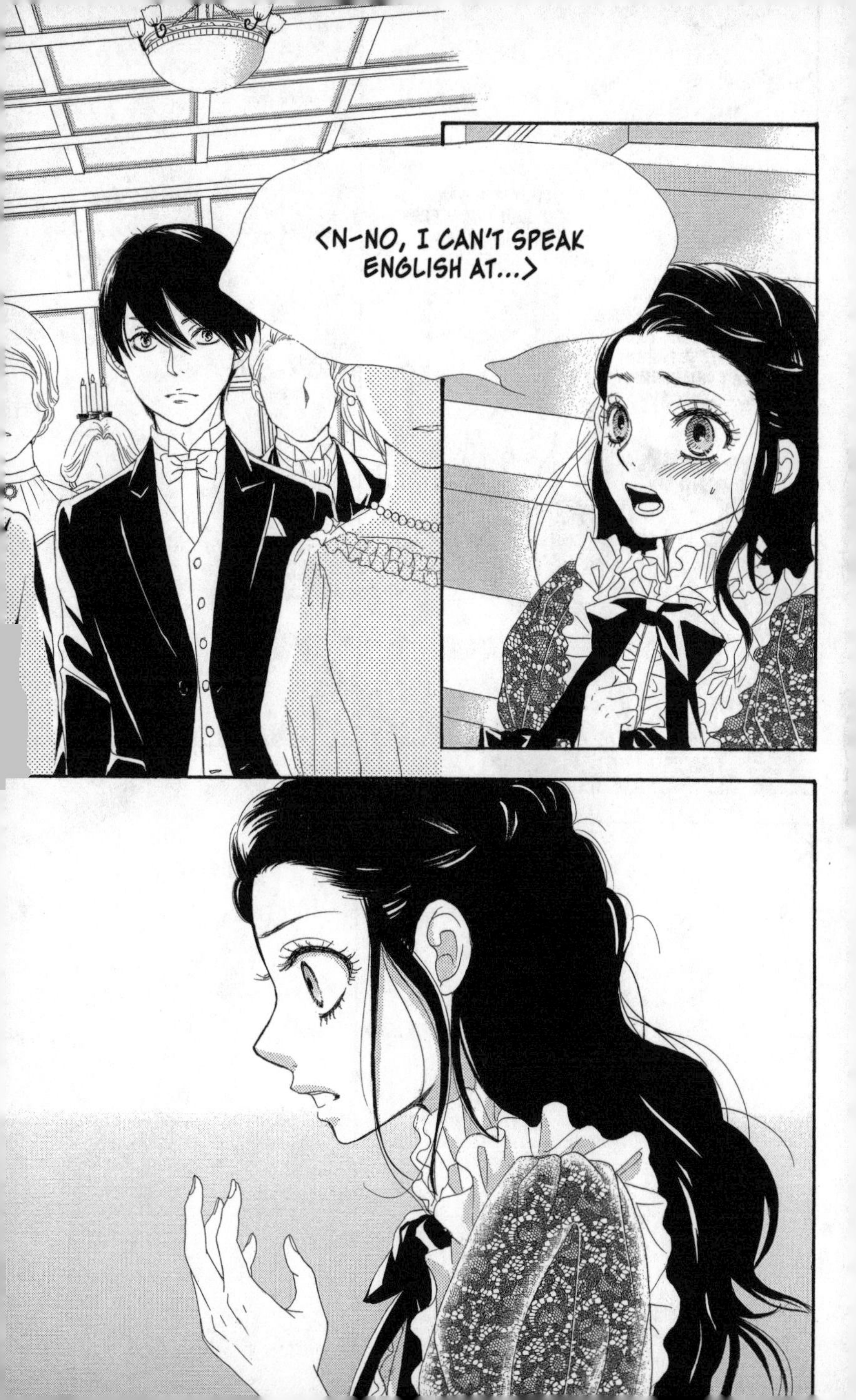
<N-NO, I CAN'T SPEAK ENGLISH AT...>

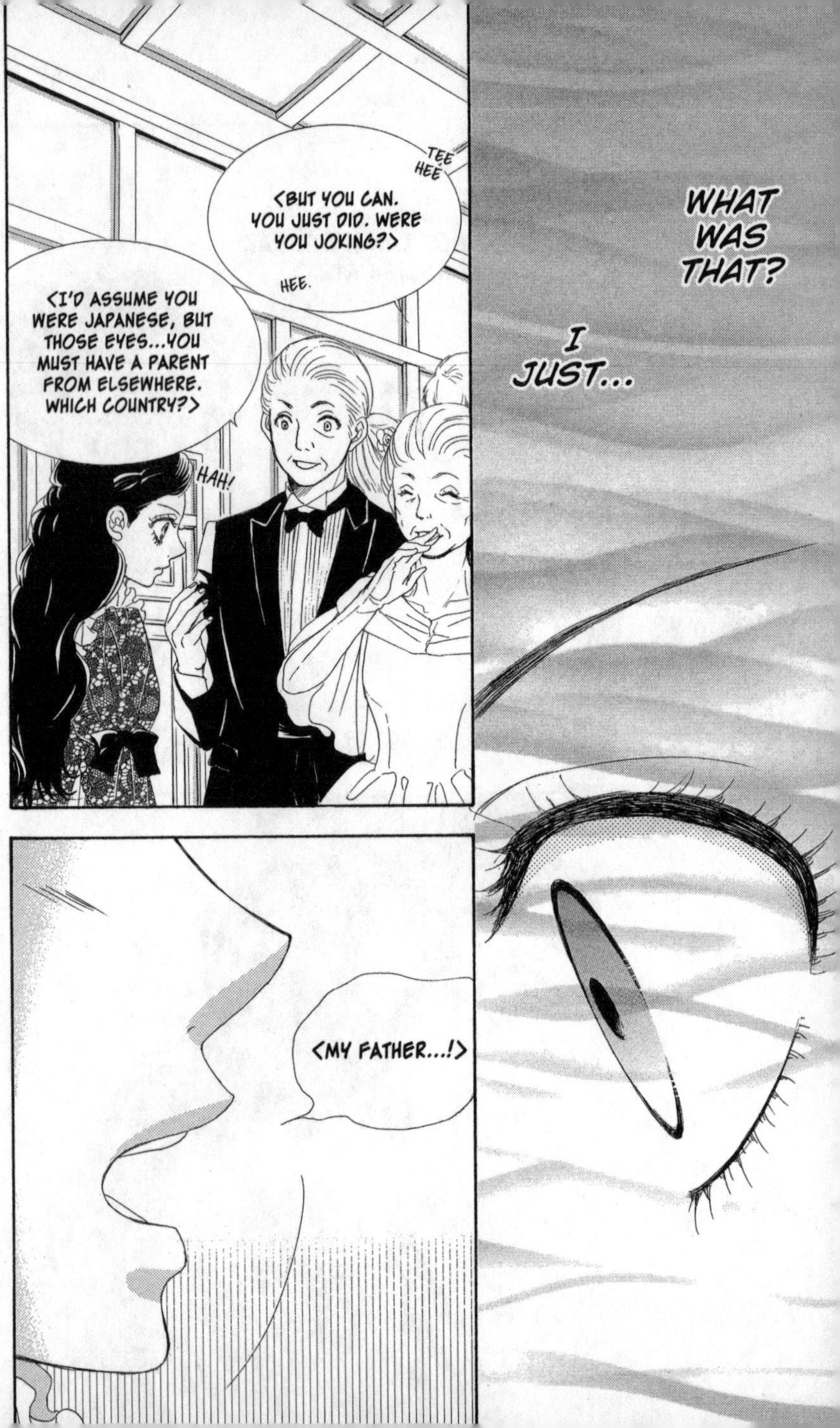
WHAT WAS THAT?
I JUST...
TEE HEE
<BUT YOU CAN. YOU JUST DID. WERE YOU JOKING?>
HEE.
<I'D ASSUME YOU WERE JAPANESE, BUT THOSE EYES...YOU MUST HAVE A PARENT FROM ELSEWHERE. WHICH COUNTRY?>
HAH!
<MY FATHER...!>

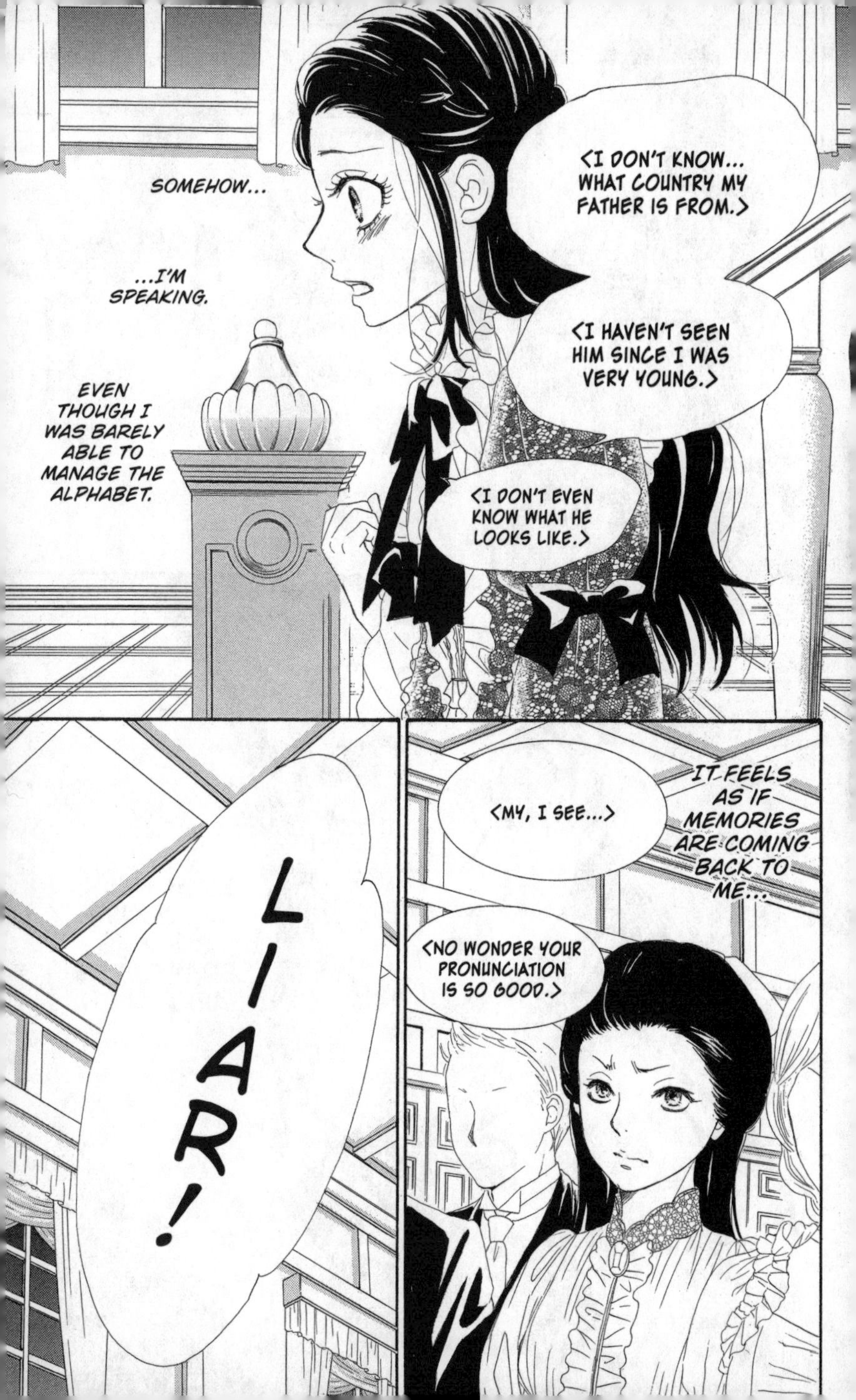
<I DON'T KNOW... WHAT COUNTRY MY FATHER IS FROM.>
SOMEHOW...
...I'M SPEAKING.
<I HAVEN'T SEEN HIM SINCE I WAS VERY YOUNG.>
EVEN THOUGH I WAS BARELY ABLE TO MANAGE THE ALPHABET.
<I DON'T EVEN KNOW WHAT HE LOOKS LIKE.>
IT FEELS AS IF MEMORIES ARE COMING BACK TO ME...
<MY, I SEE...>
<NO WONDER YOUR PRONUNCIATION IS SO GOOD.>
LIAR!

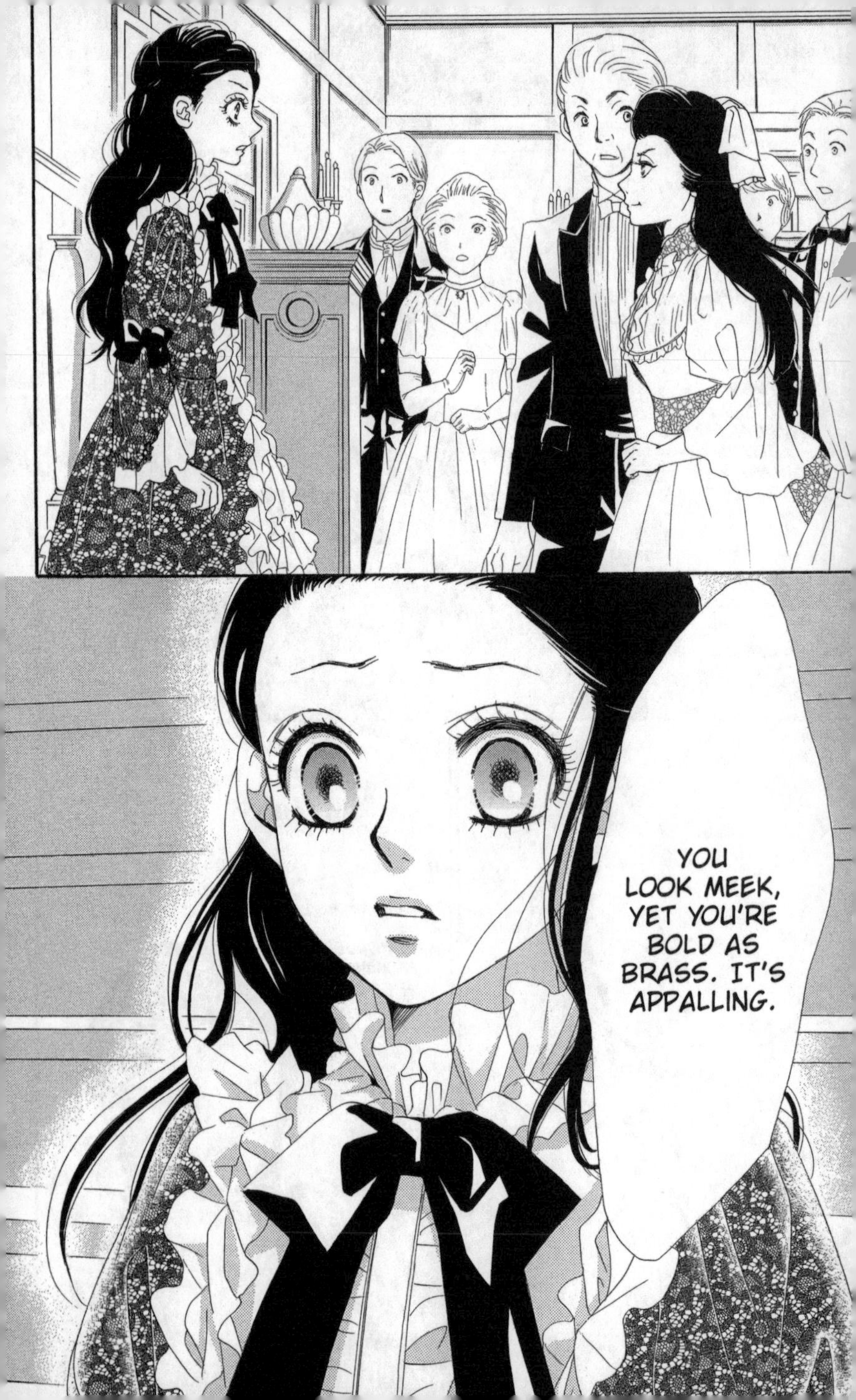
YOU LOOK MEEK, YET YOU'RE BOLD AS BRASS. IT'S APPALLING.

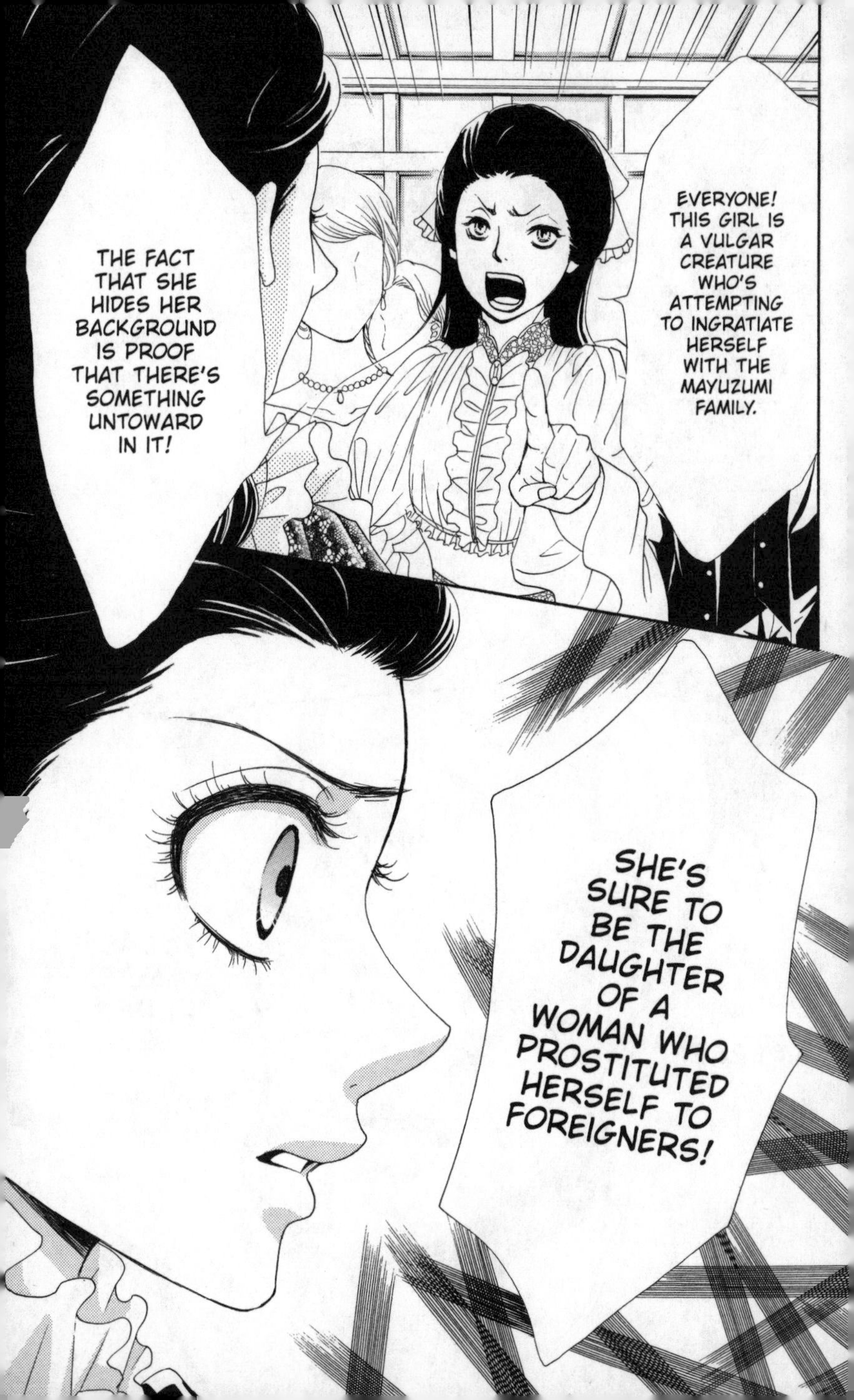
EVERYONE! THIS GIRL IS A VULGAR CREATURE WHO'S ATTEMPTING TO INGRATIATE HERSELF WITH THE MAYUZUMI FAMILY.
THE FACT THAT SHE HIDES HER BACKGROUND IS PROOF THAT THERE'S SOMETHING UNTOWARD IN IT!
SHE'S SURE TO BE THE DAUGHTER OF A WOMAN WHO PROSTITUTED HERSELF TO FOREIGNERS!

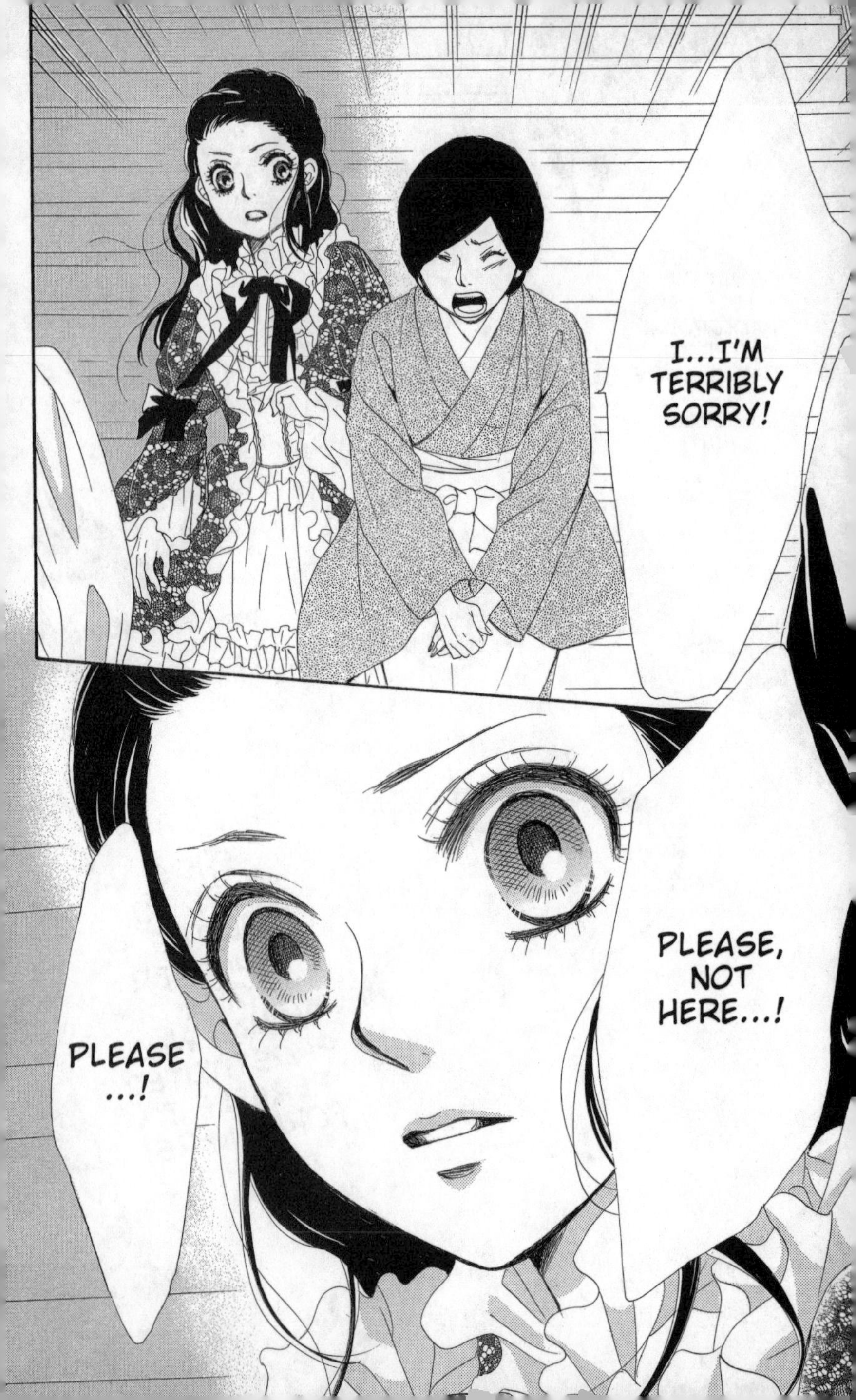
I...I'M TERRIBLY SORRY!
PLEASE, NOT HERE...!
PLEASE ...!

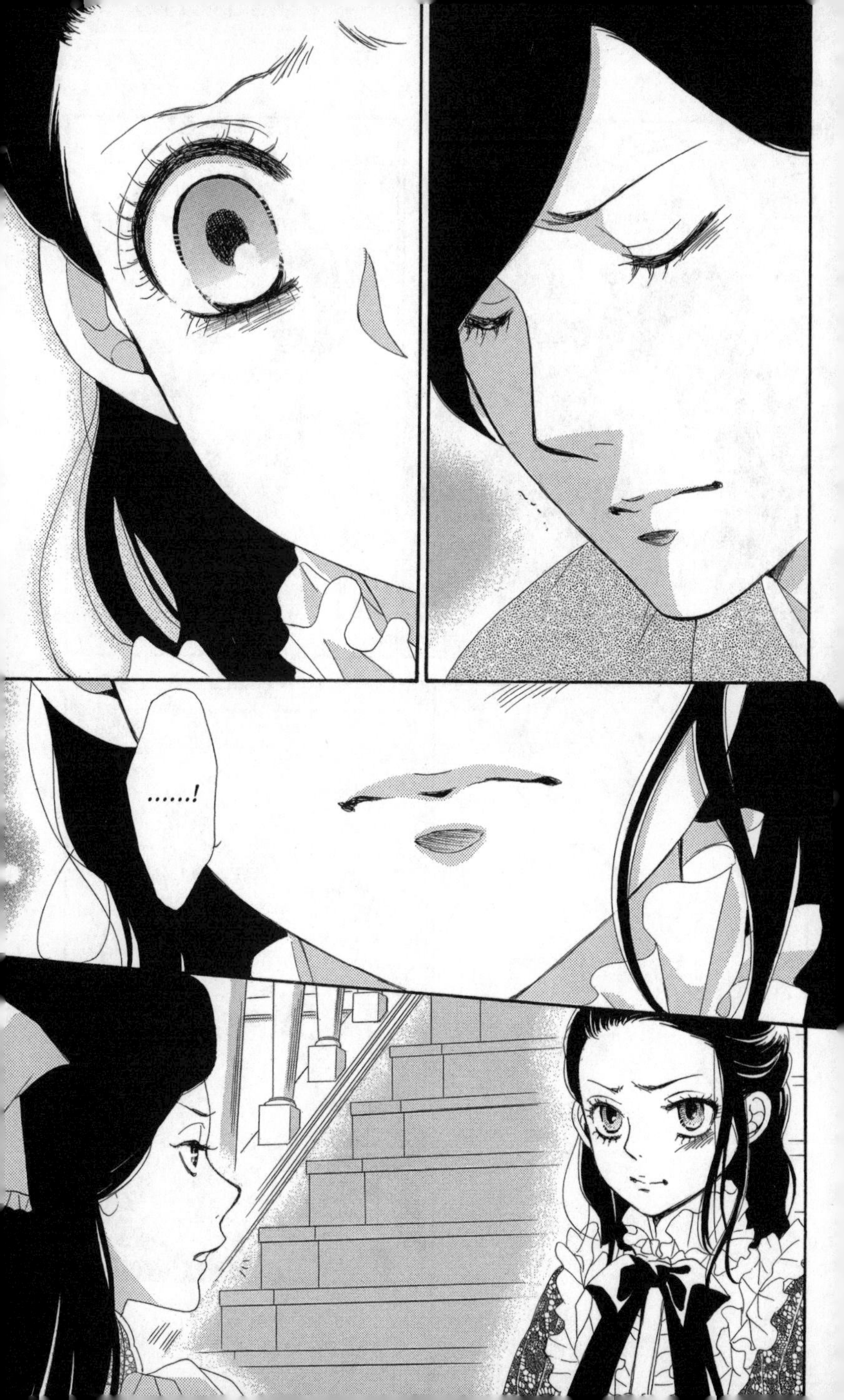
......!

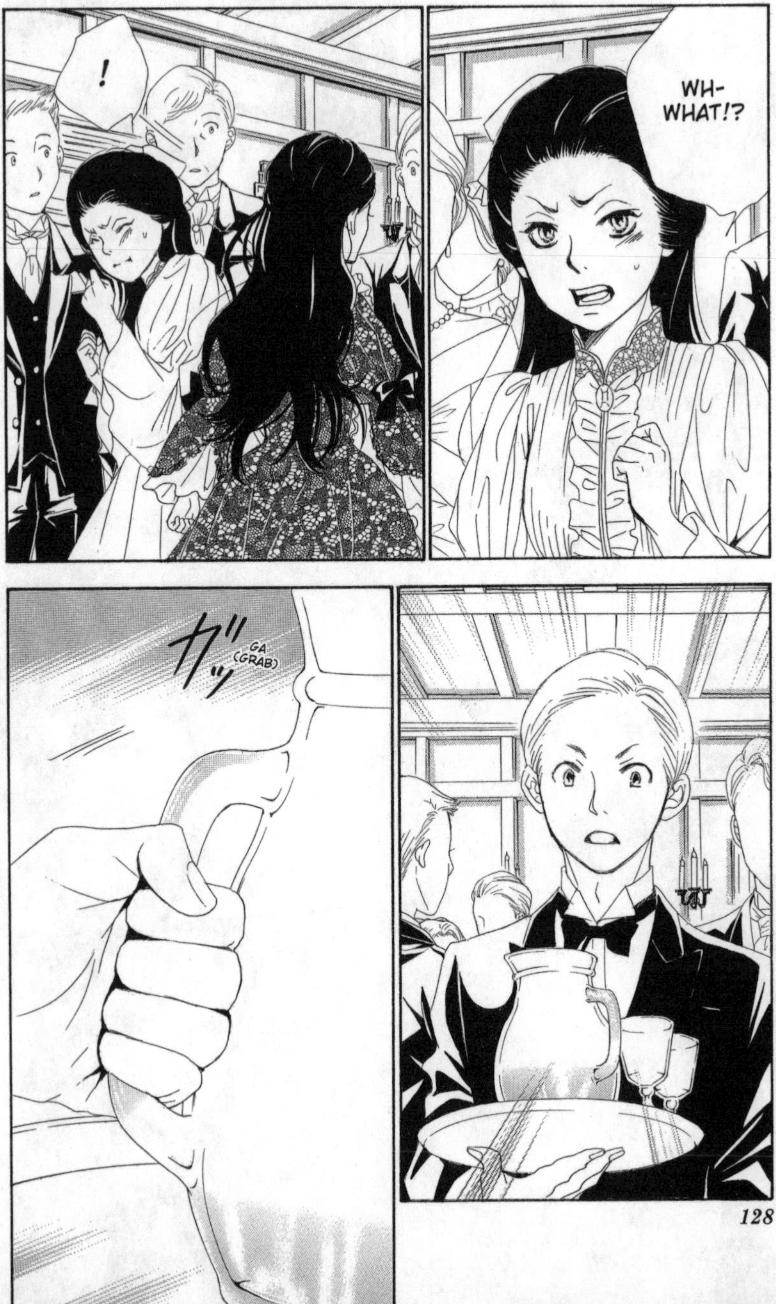
WH-
WHAT!?
!
GA
(GRAB)

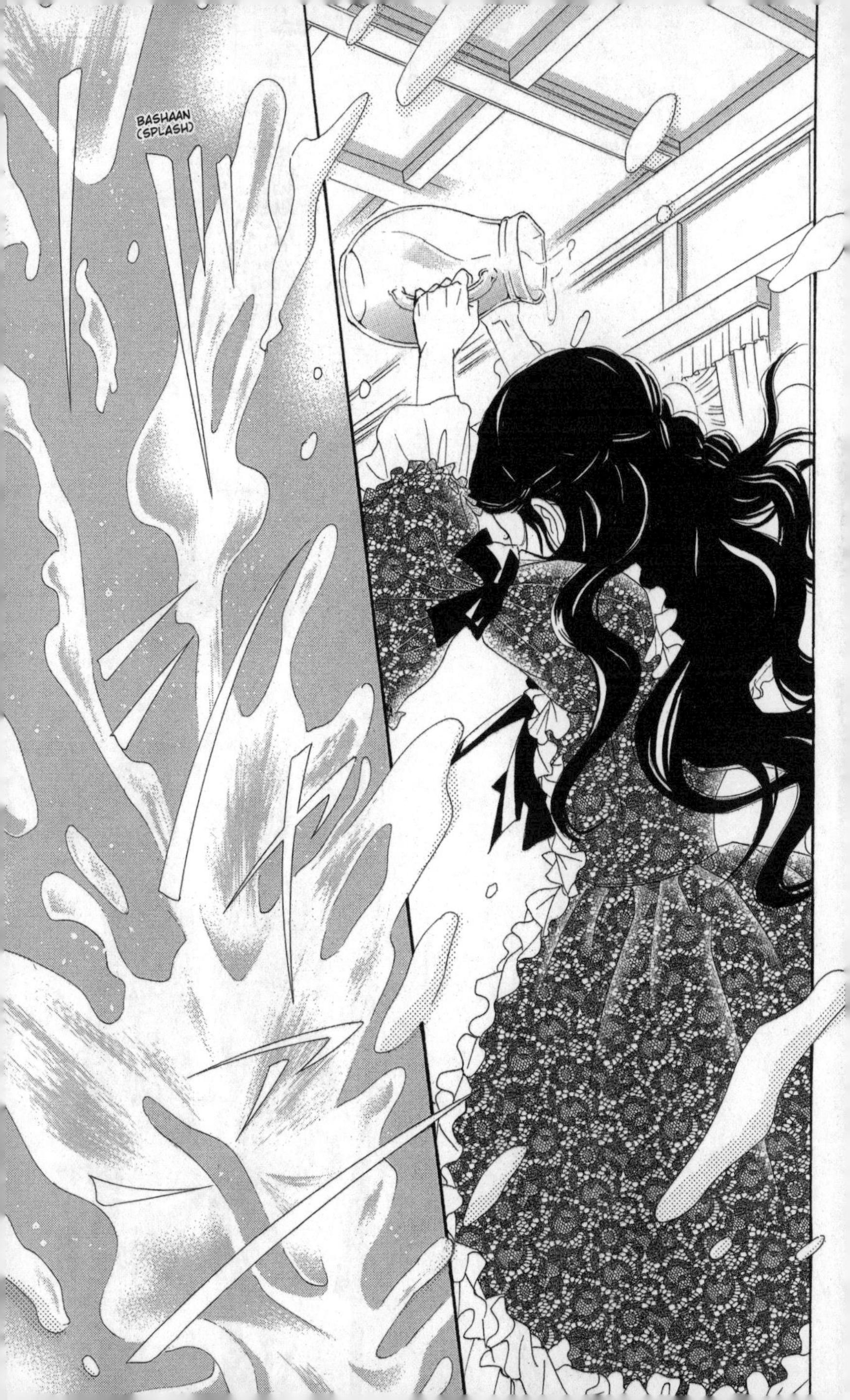
BASHAAN
(SPLASH)

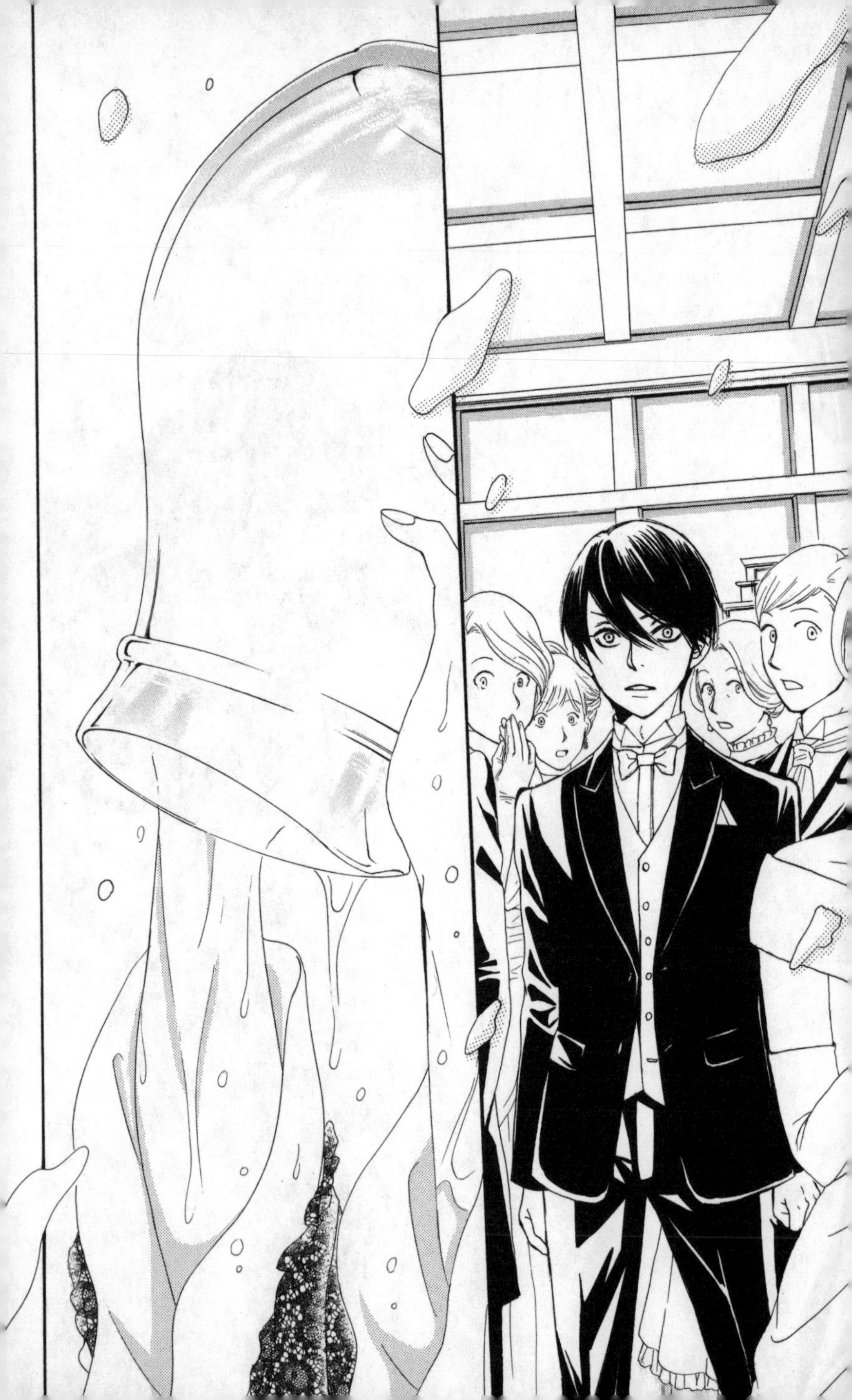

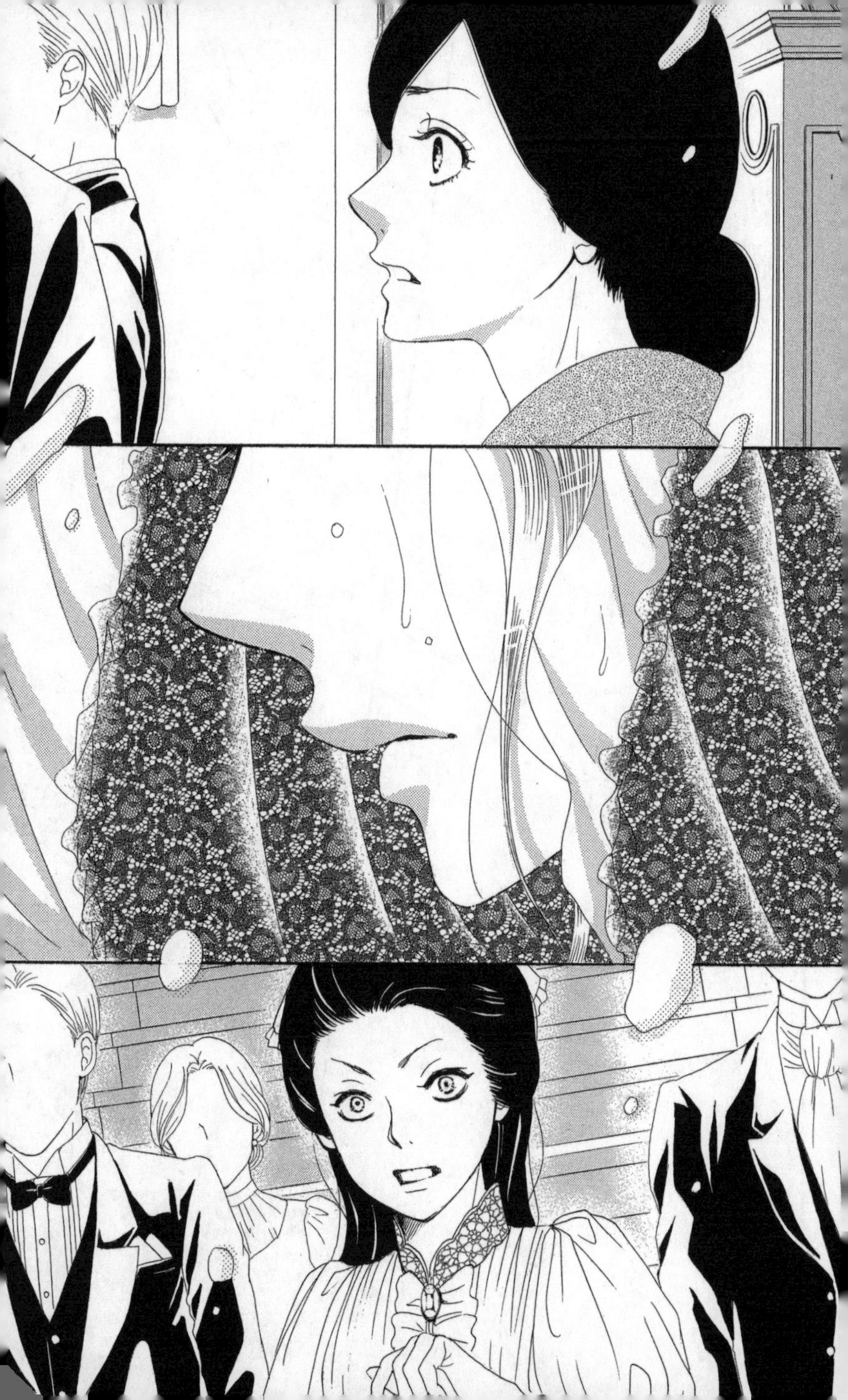

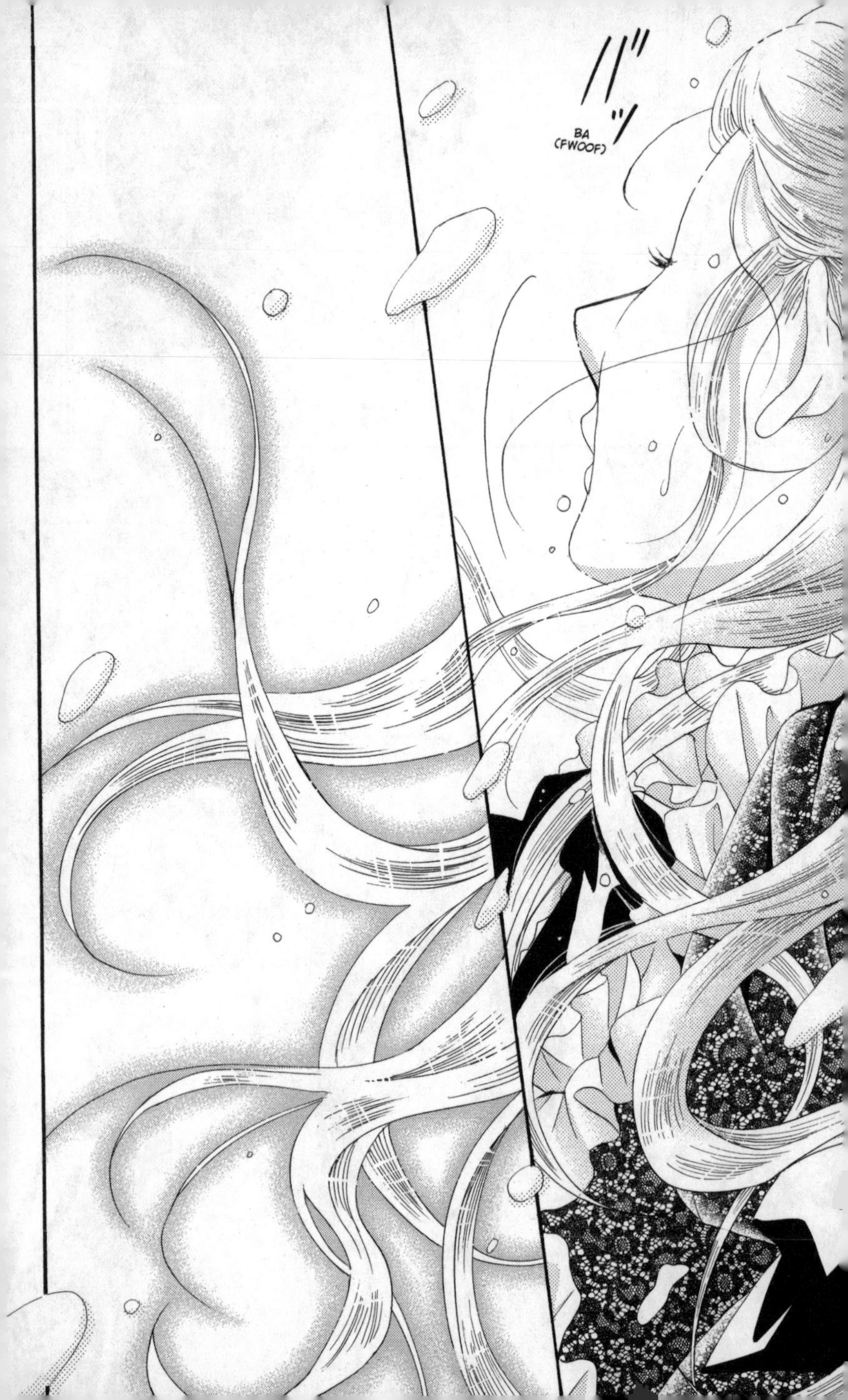
BA
(FWOOF)

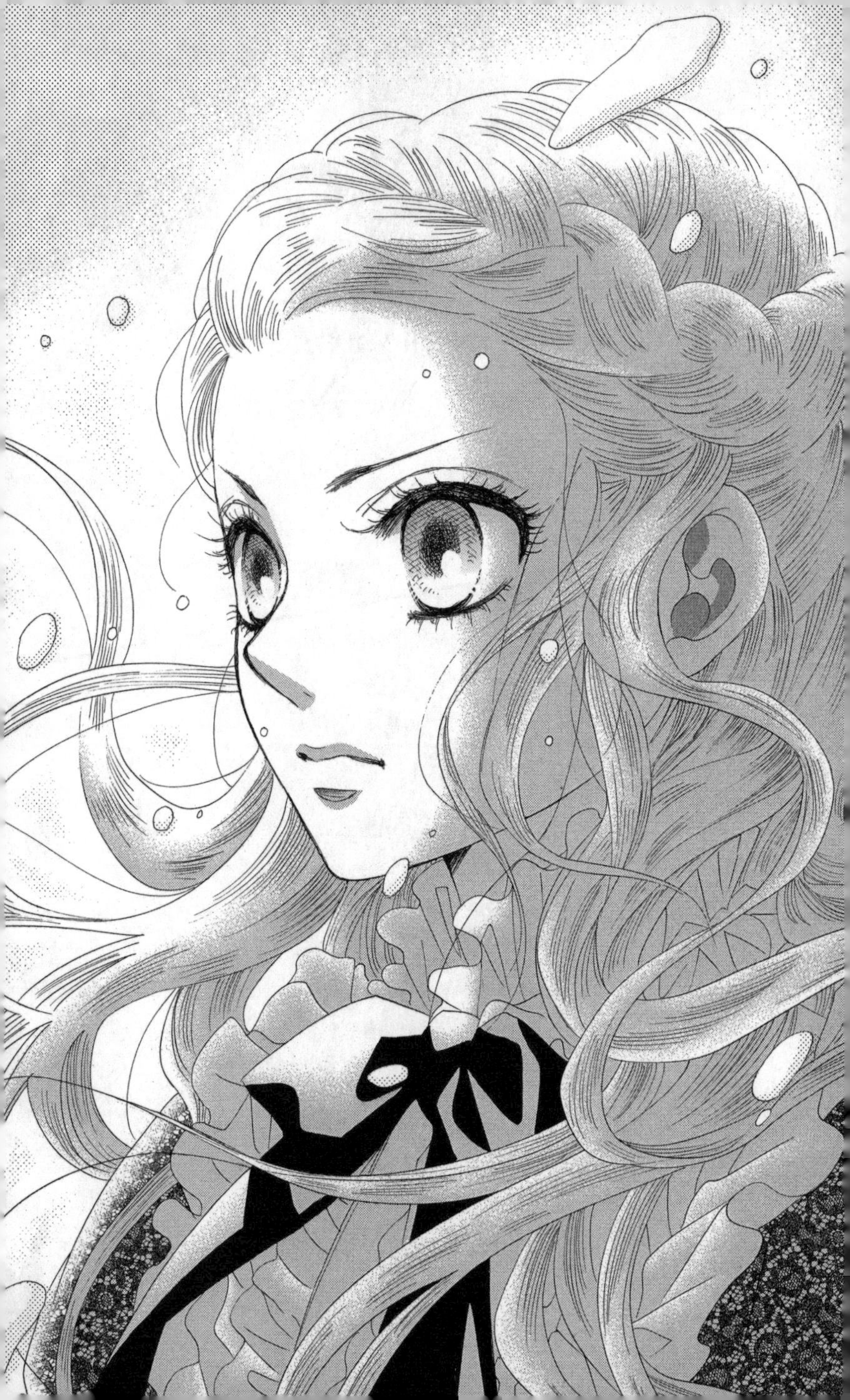

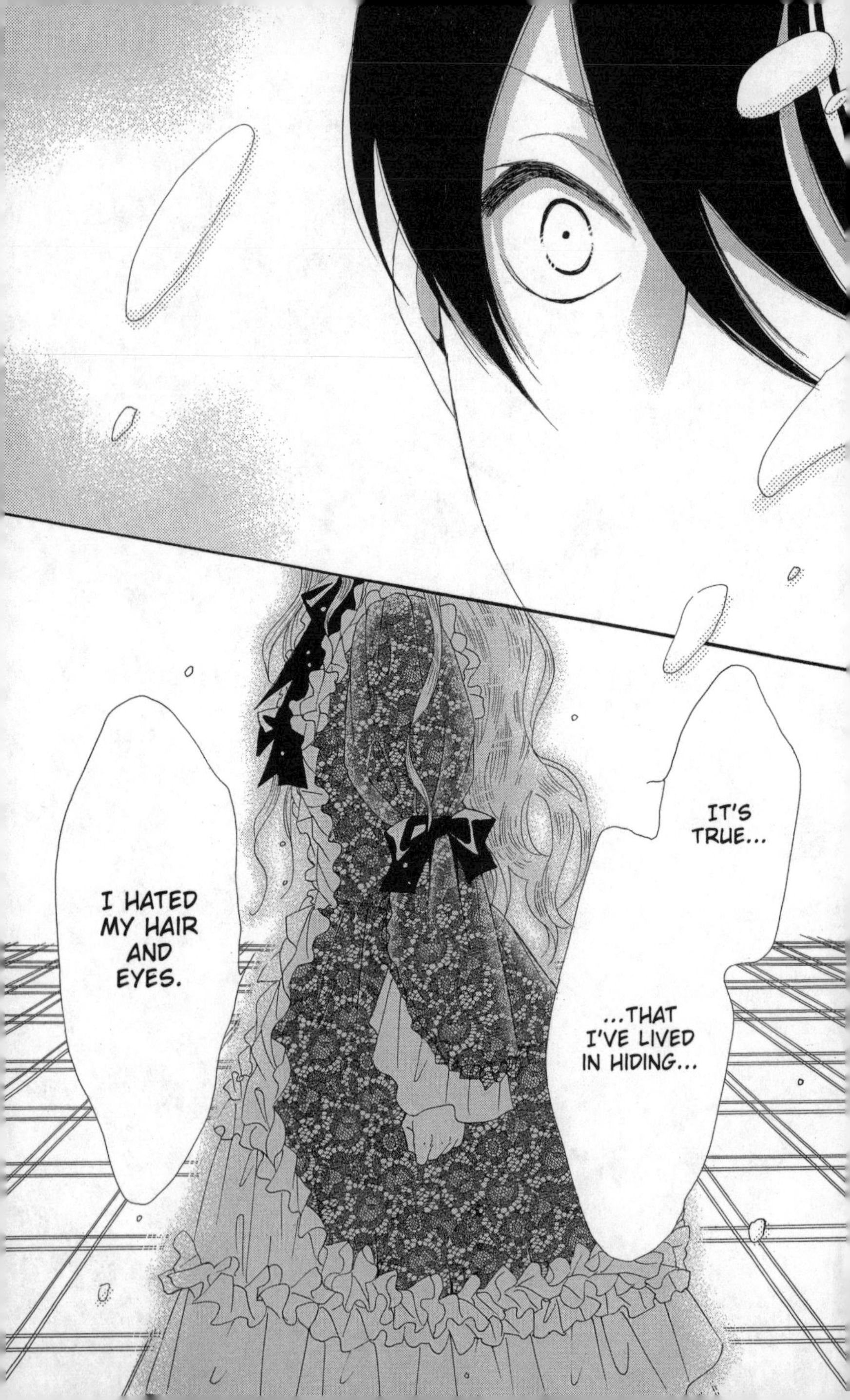
IT'S TRUE...
...THAT I'VE LIVED IN HIDING...
I HATED MY HAIR AND EYES.

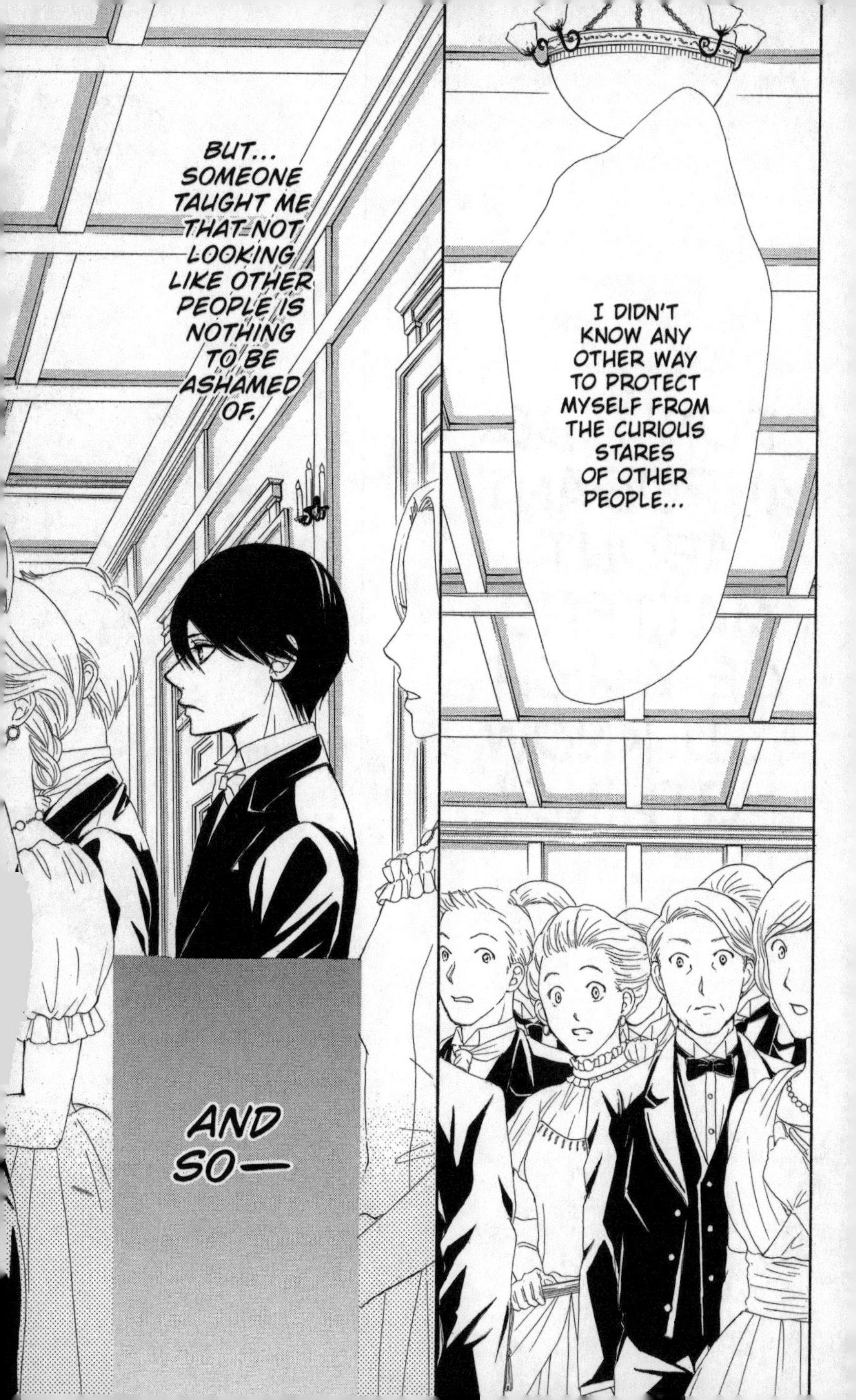
I DIDN'T KNOW ANY OTHER WAY TO PROTECT MYSELF FROM THE CURIOUS STARES OF OTHER PEOPLE...
BUT... SOMEONE TAUGHT ME THAT NOT LOOKING LIKE OTHER PEOPLE IS NOTHING TO BE ASHAMED OF.
AND SO—

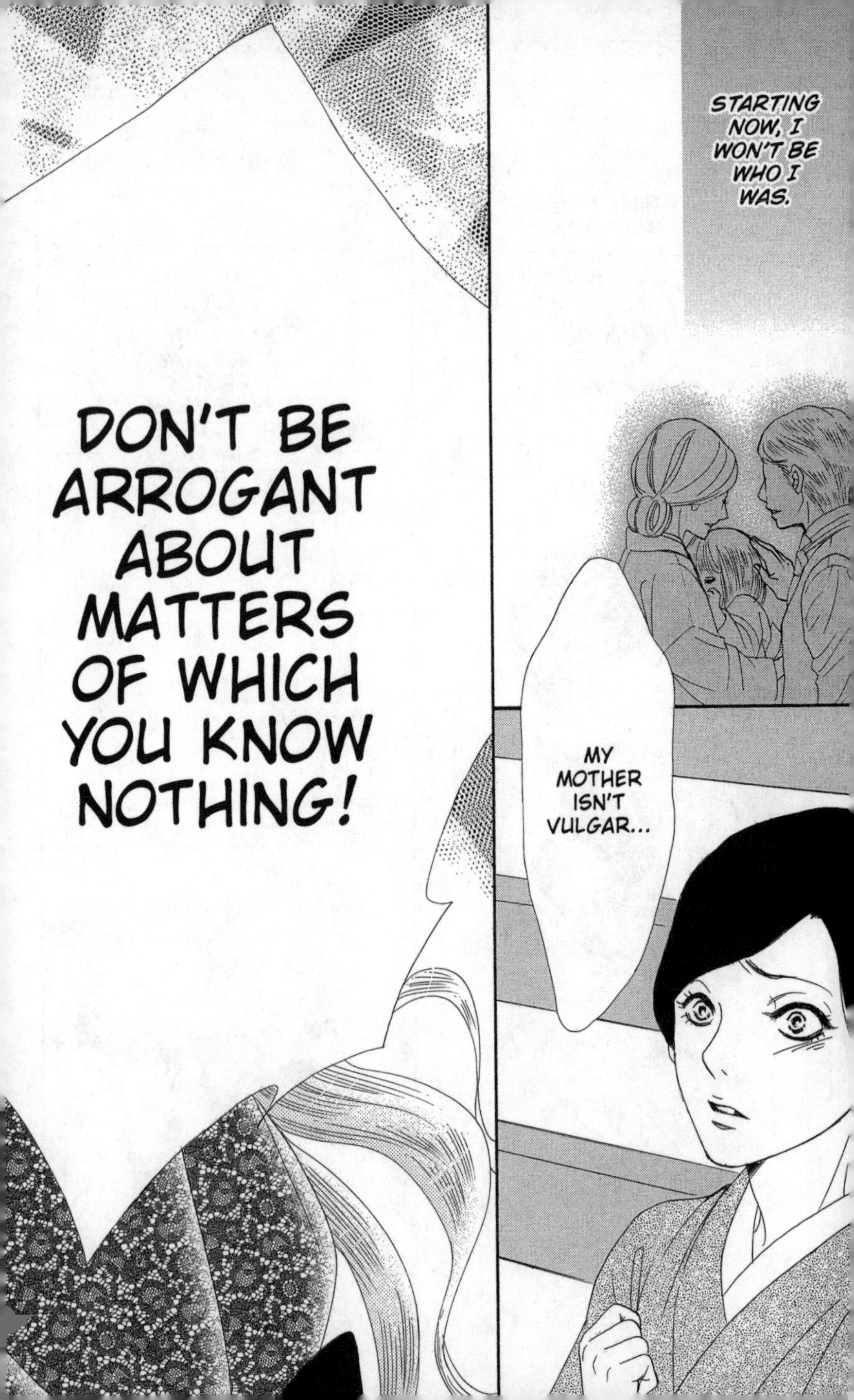
STARTING NOW, I WON'T BE WHO I WAS.
MY MOTHER ISN'T VULGAR...
DON'T BE ARROGANT ABOUT MATTERS OF WHICH YOU KNOW NOTHING!

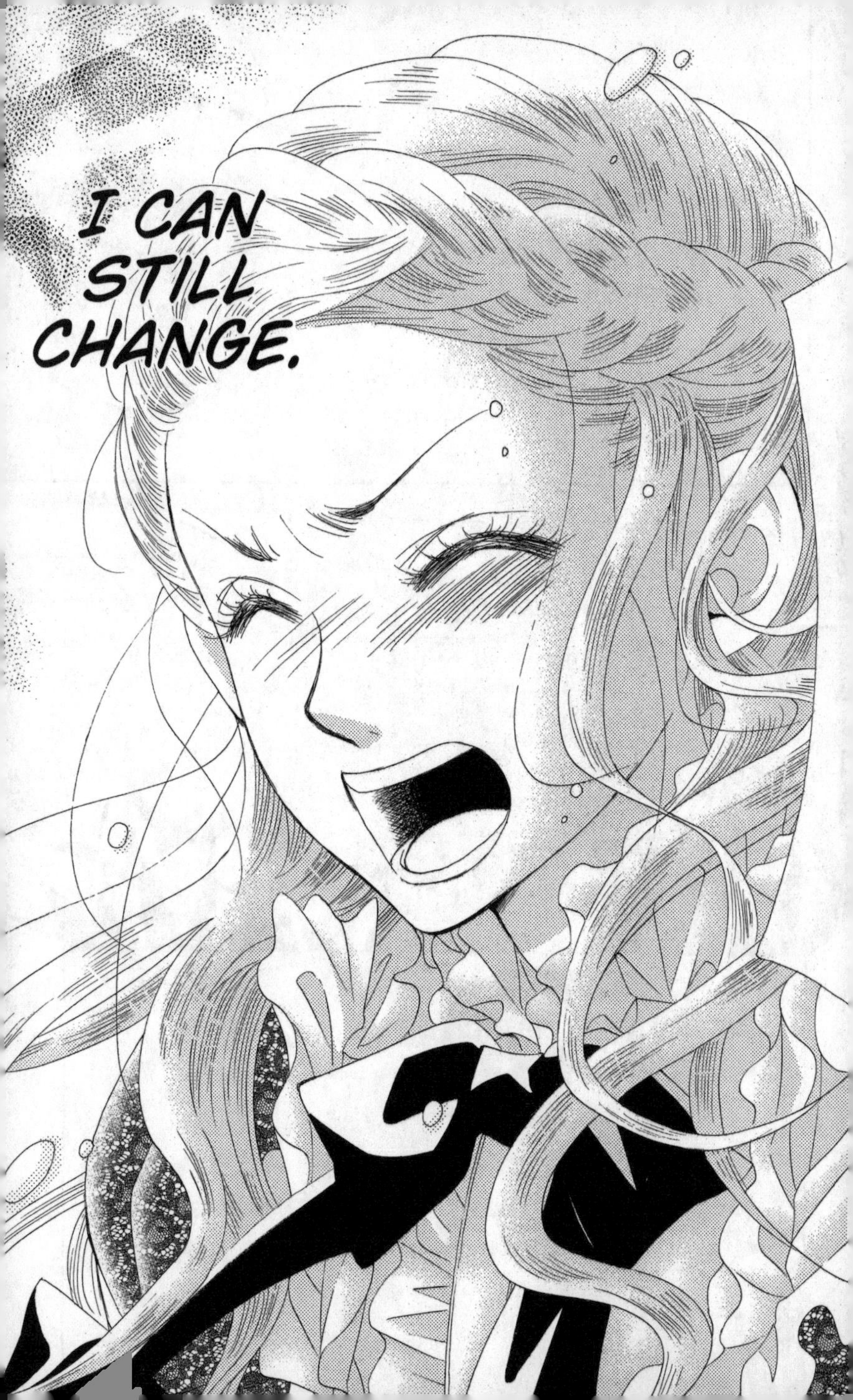
I CAN STILL CHANGE.

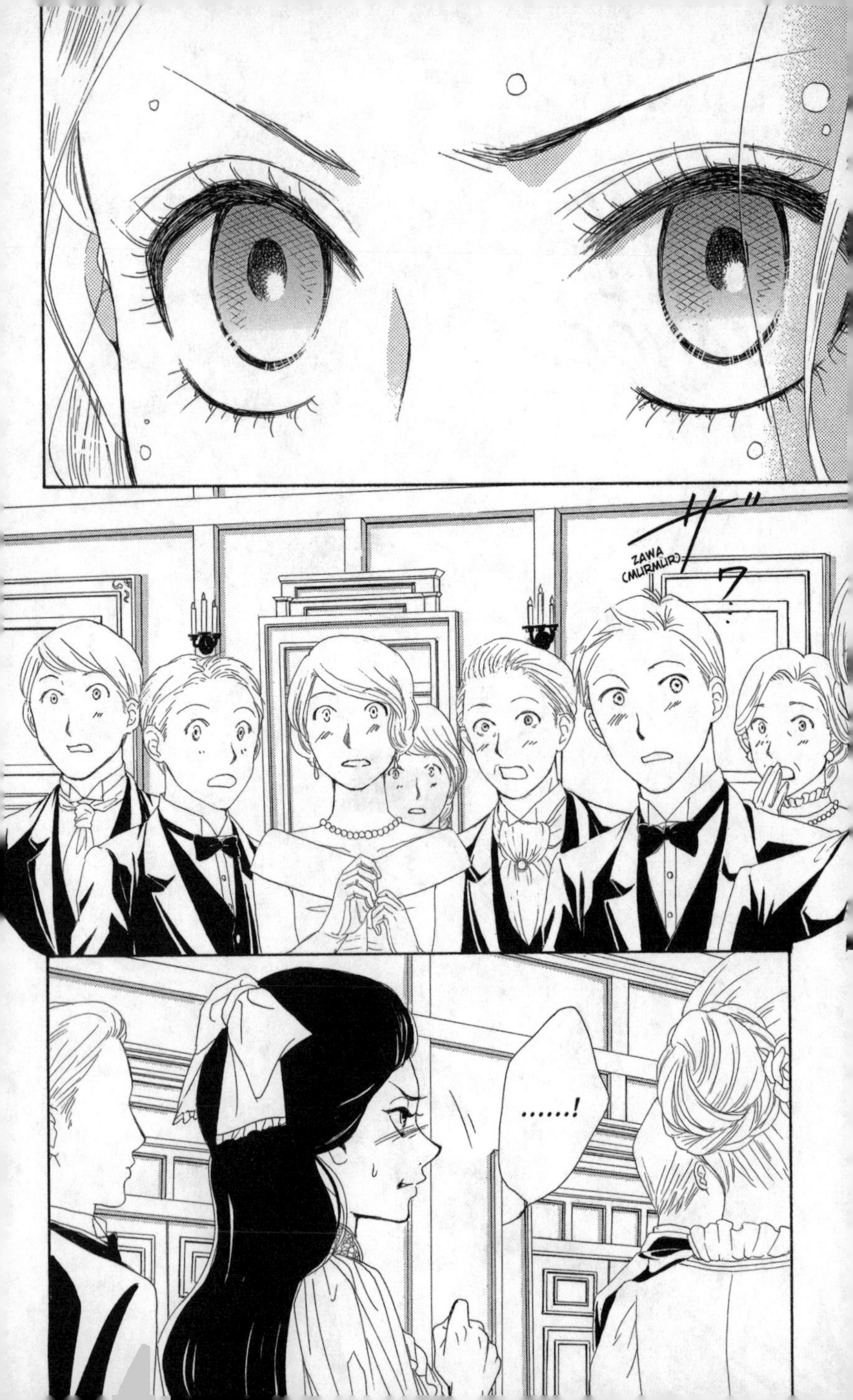
ザワ
ZAWA (MURMUR)
......!

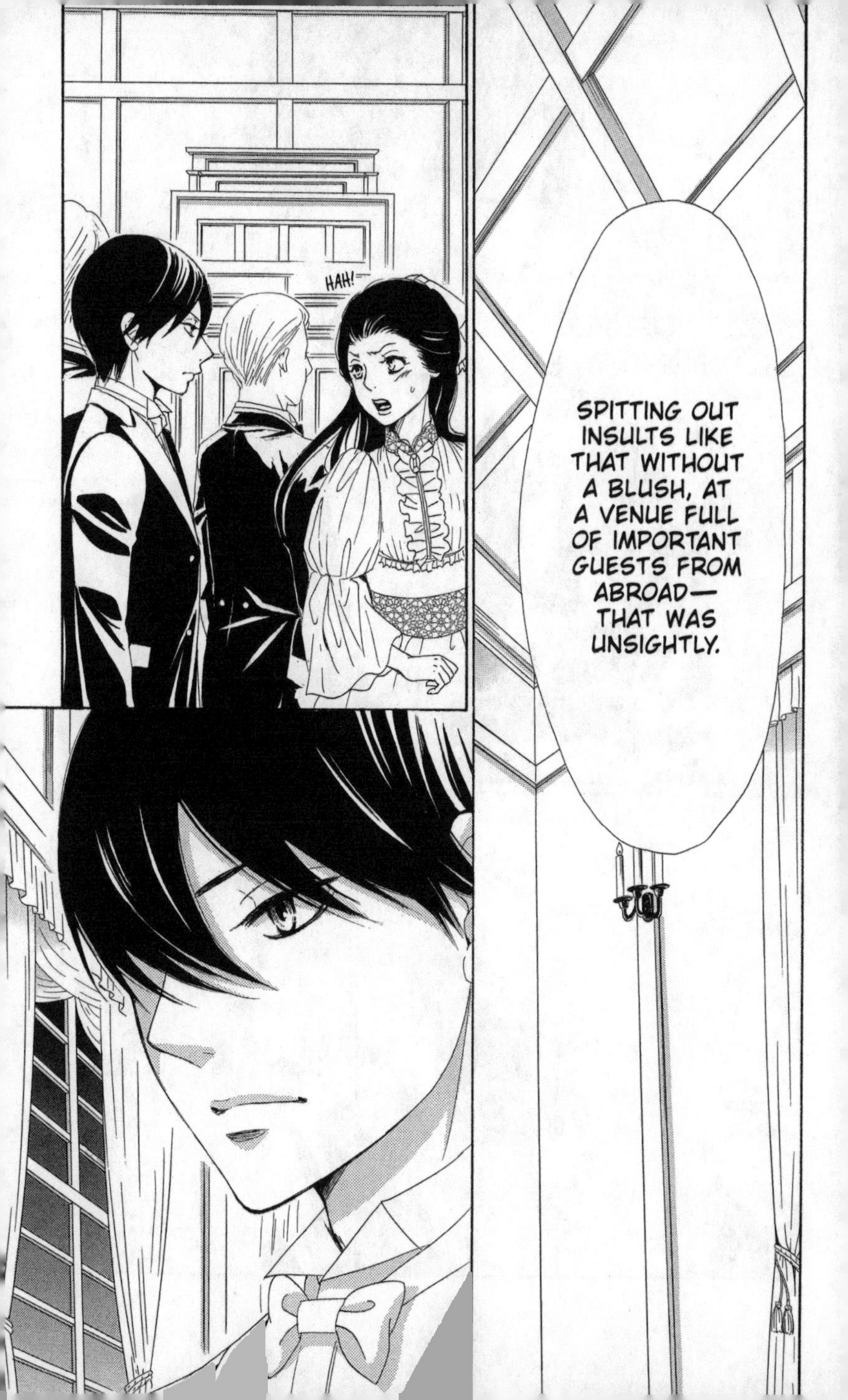
SPITTING OUT INSULTS LIKE THAT WITHOUT A BLUSH, AT A VENUE FULL OF IMPORTANT GUESTS FROM ABROAD— THAT WAS UNSIGHTLY.
HAH!

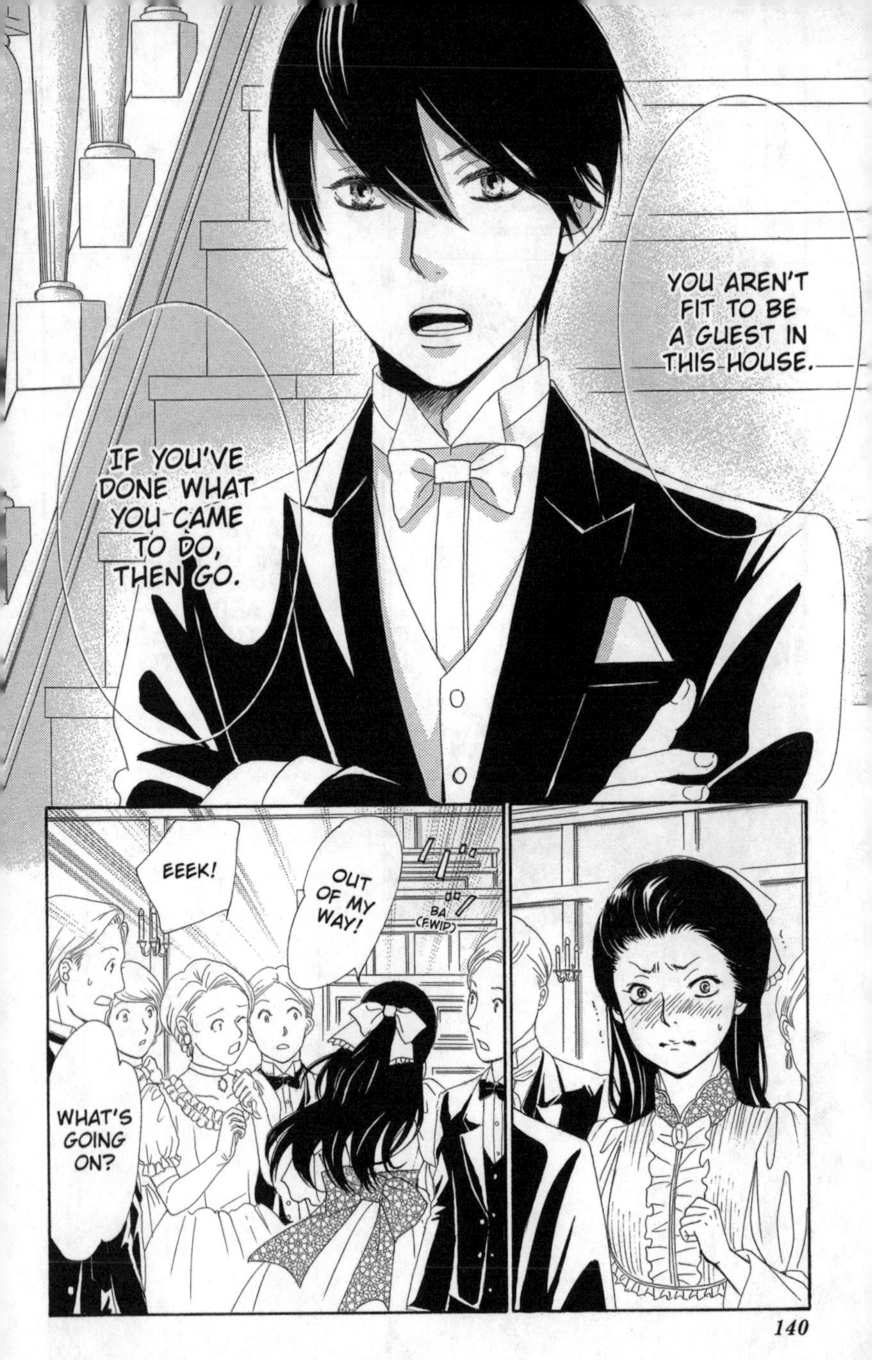
YOU AREN'T FIT TO BE A GUEST IN THIS HOUSE.
IF YOU'VE DONE WHAT YOU CAME TO DO, THEN GO.
BA (FWIP)
OUT OF MY WAY!
EEEK!
WHAT'S GOING ON?

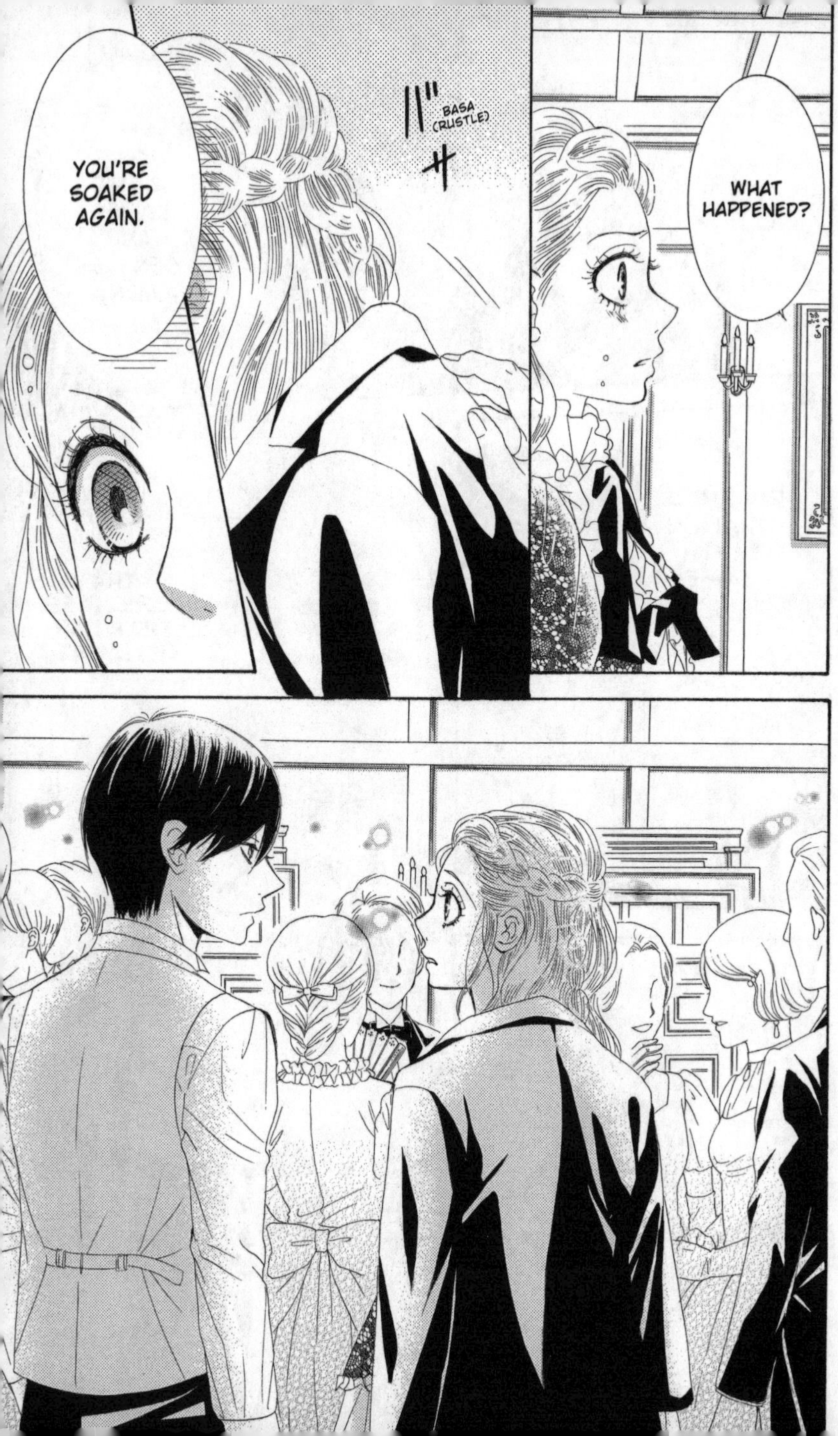
WHAT HAPPENED?
BASA (RUSTLE)
YOU'RE SOAKED AGAIN.

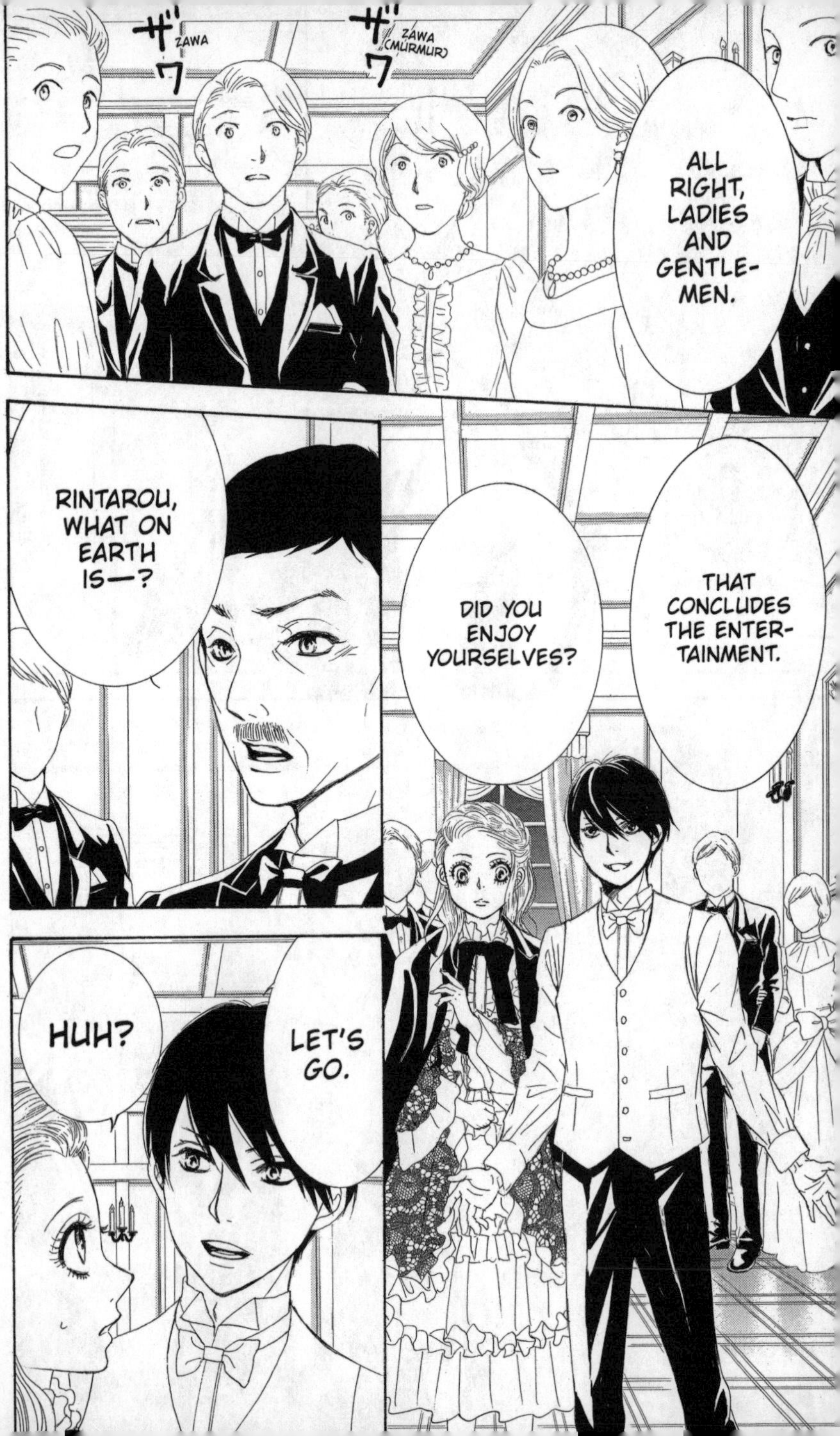
ALL RIGHT, LADIES AND GENTLE-MEN.
ザワ
ZAWA (MURMUR)
ザワ
ZAWA
THAT CONCLUDES THE ENTER-TAINMENT.
DID YOU ENJOY YOURSELVES?
RINTAROU, WHAT ON EARTH IS—?
LET'S GO.
HUH?

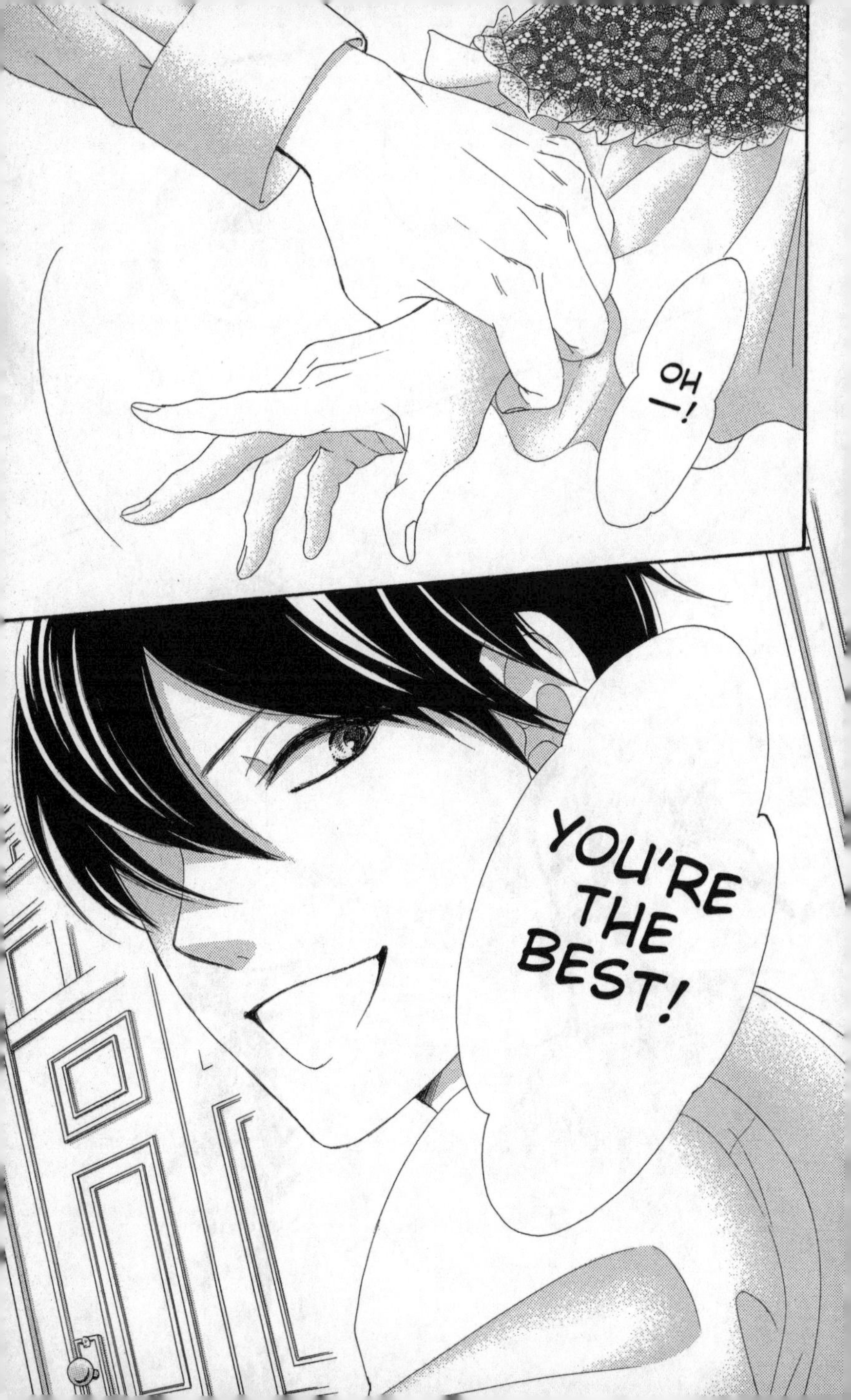
OH—!
YOU'RE THE BEST!

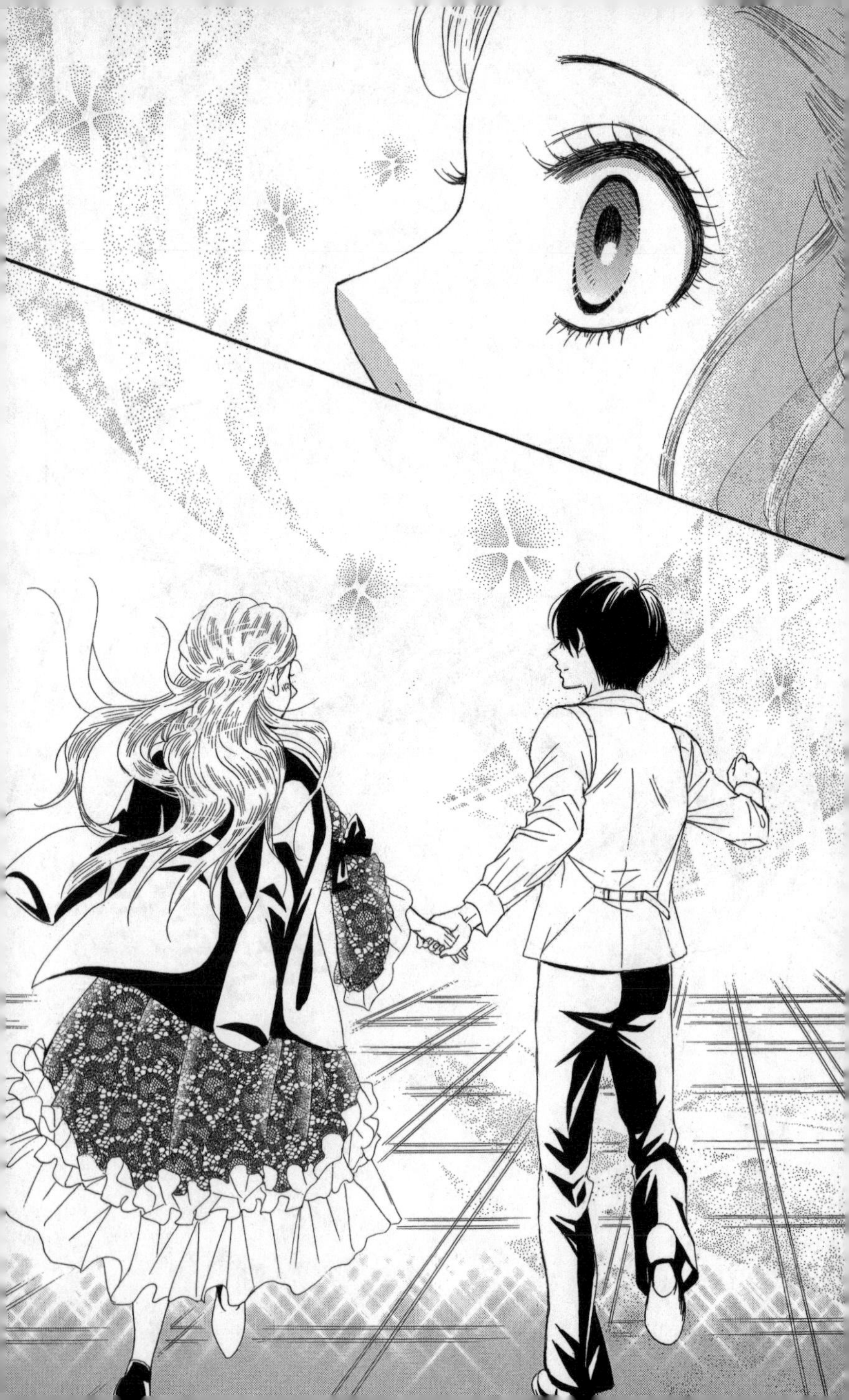

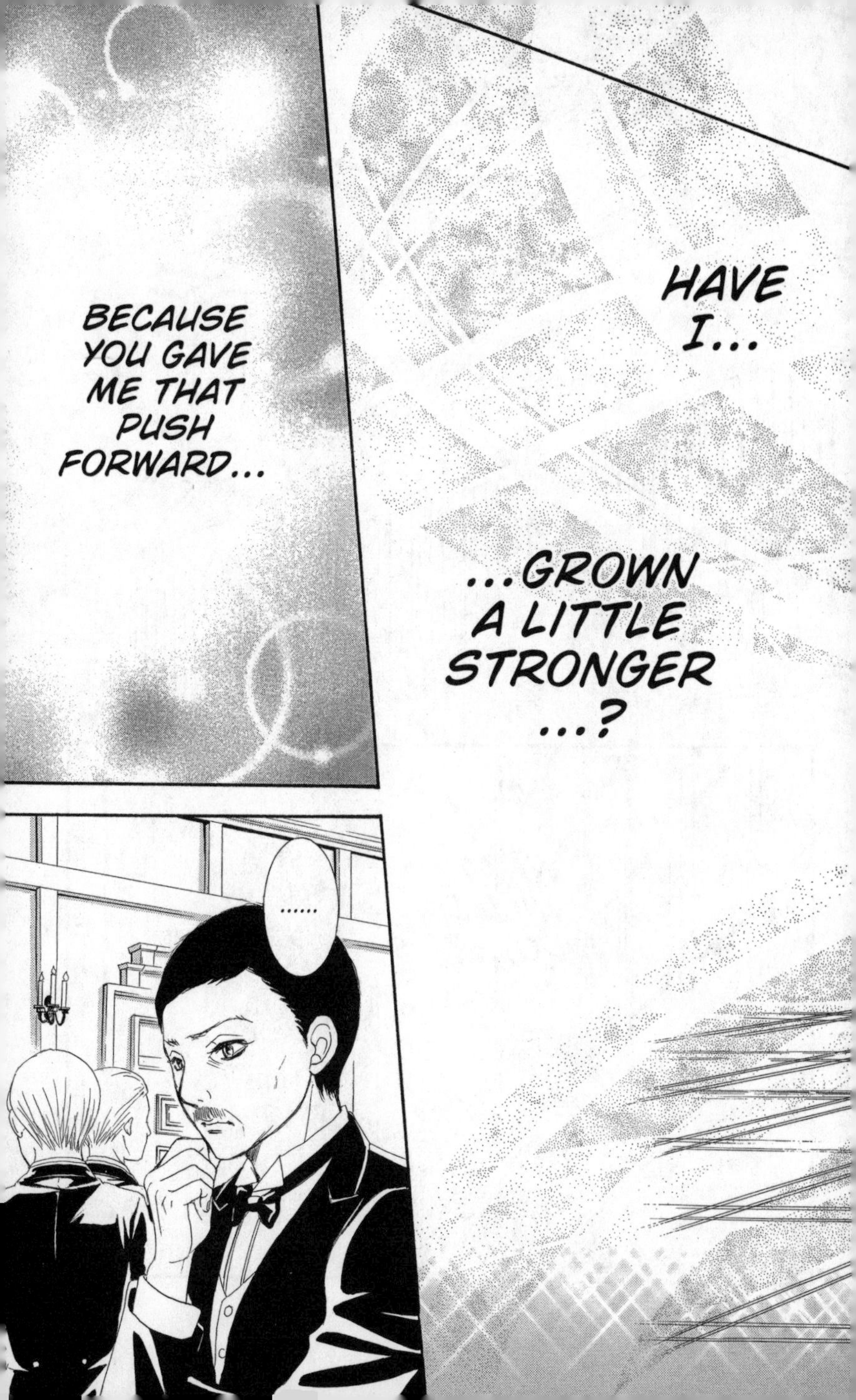
HAVE I...
...GROWN A LITTLE STRONGER ...?
BECAUSE YOU GAVE ME THAT PUSH FORWARD...
......

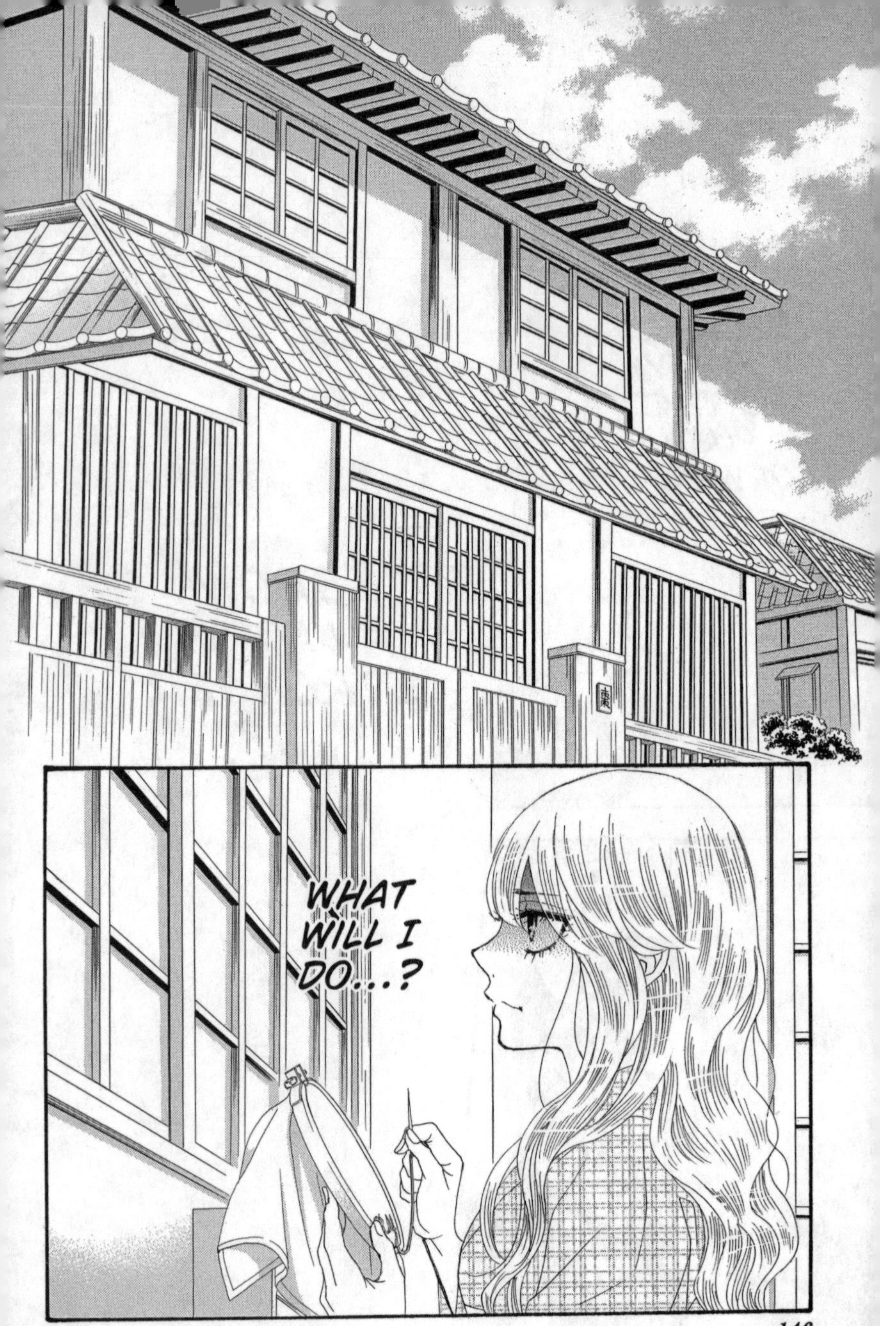
WHAT WILL I DO...?

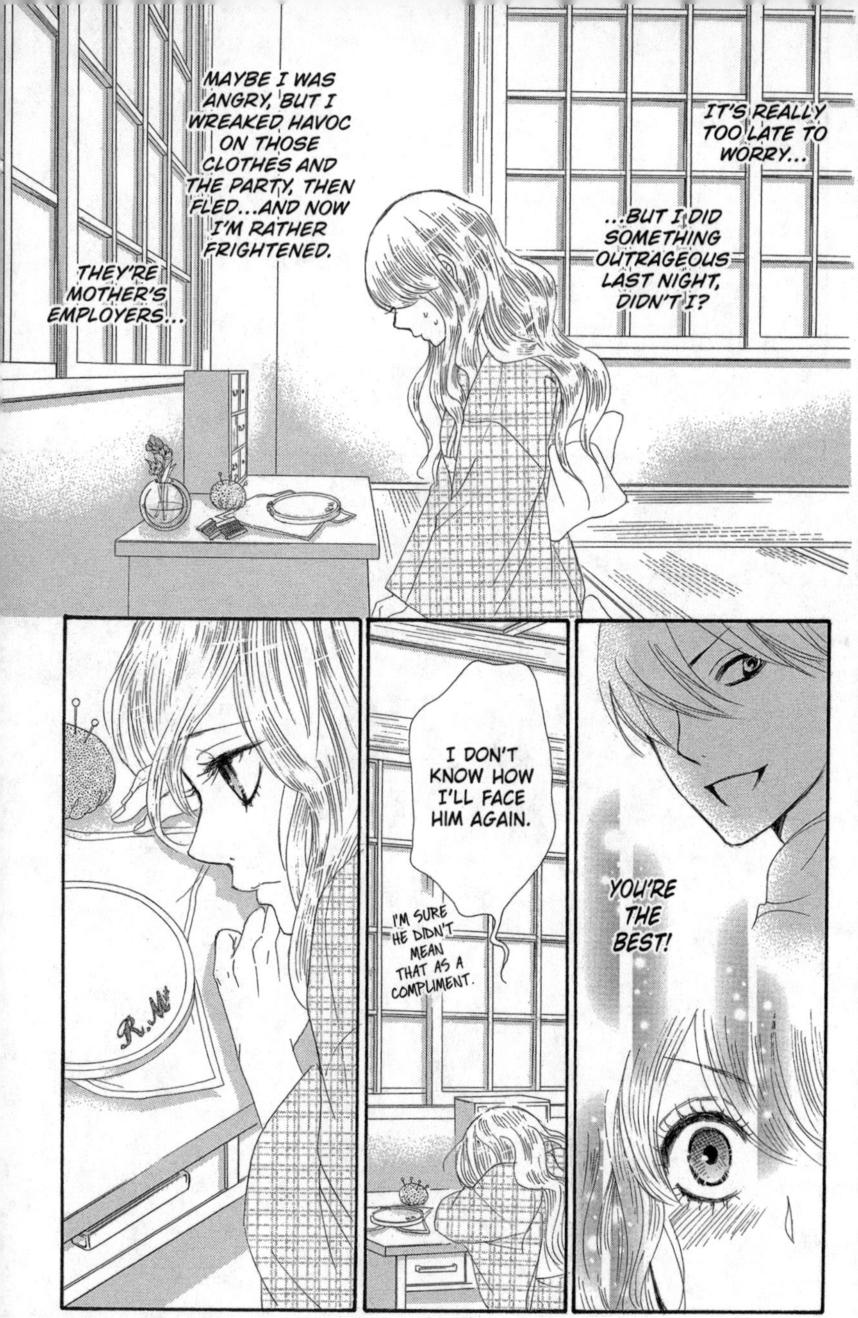
IT'S REALLY TOO LATE TO WORRY...
...BUT I DID SOMETHING OUTRAGEOUS LAST NIGHT, DIDN'T I?
MAYBE I WAS ANGRY, BUT I WREAKED HAVOC ON THOSE CLOTHES AND THE PARTY, THEN FLED...AND NOW I'M RATHER FRIGHTENED.
THEY'RE MOTHER'S EMPLOYERS...
YOU'RE THE BEST!
I DON'T KNOW HOW I'LL FACE HIM AGAIN.
I'M SURE HE DIDN'T MEAN THAT AS A COMPLIMENT.

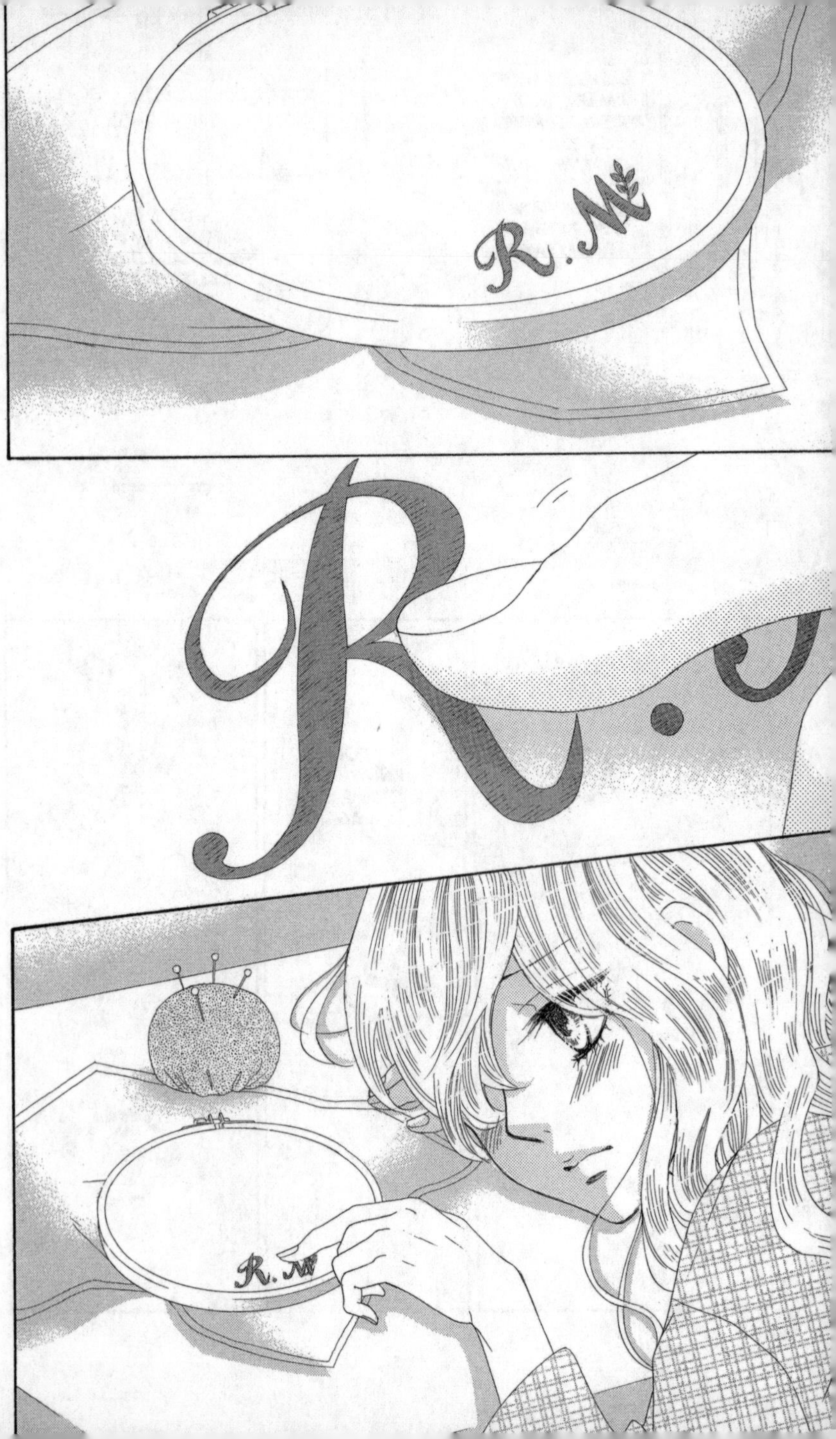
R.M

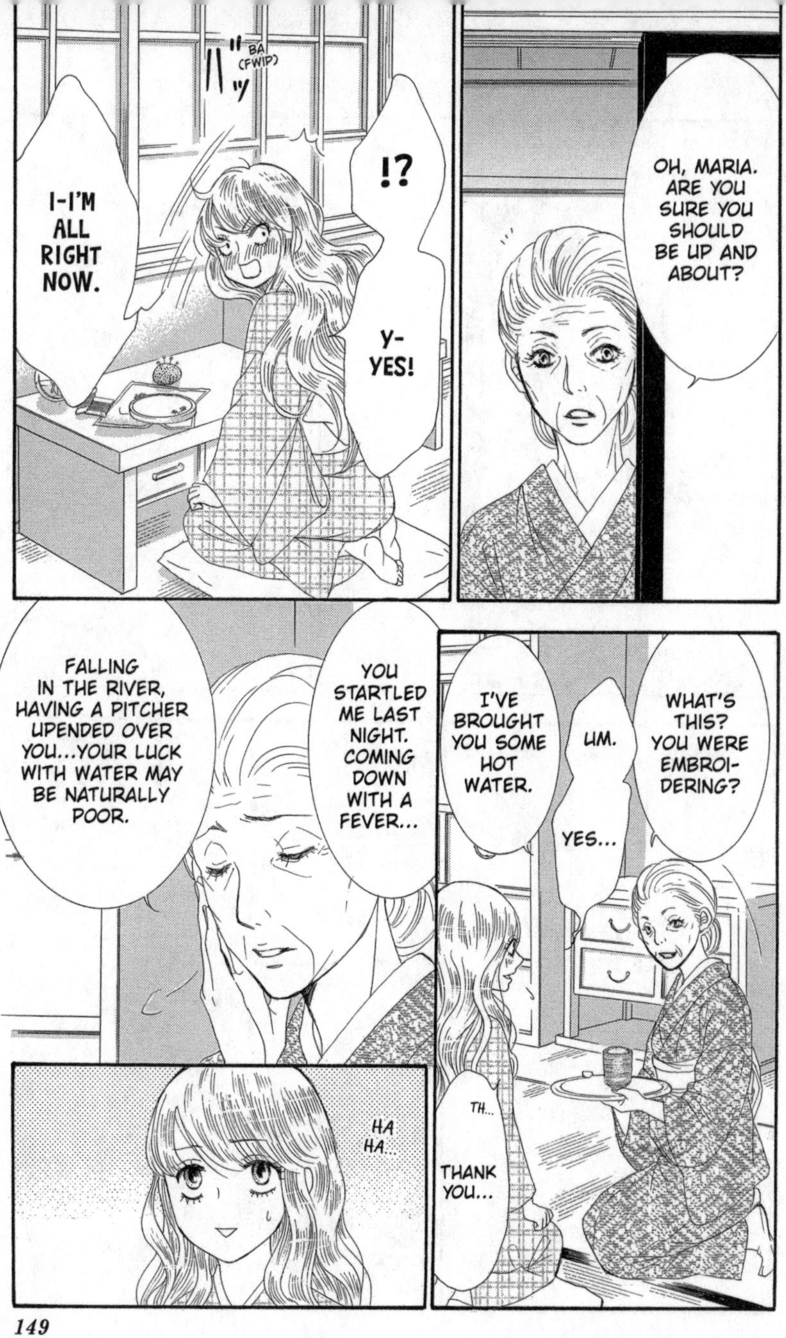
OH, MARIA. ARE YOU SURE YOU SHOULD BE UP AND ABOUT?
BA (FWIP)
!?
Y-YES!
I-I'M ALL RIGHT NOW.
WHAT'S THIS? YOU WERE EMBROIDERING?
UM.
YES...
I'VE BROUGHT YOU SOME HOT WATER.
TH...
THANK YOU...
YOU STARTLED ME LAST NIGHT. COMING DOWN WITH A FEVER...
FALLING IN THE RIVER, HAVING A PITCHER UPENDED OVER YOU...YOUR LUCK WITH WATER MAY BE NATURALLY POOR.
HA HA...

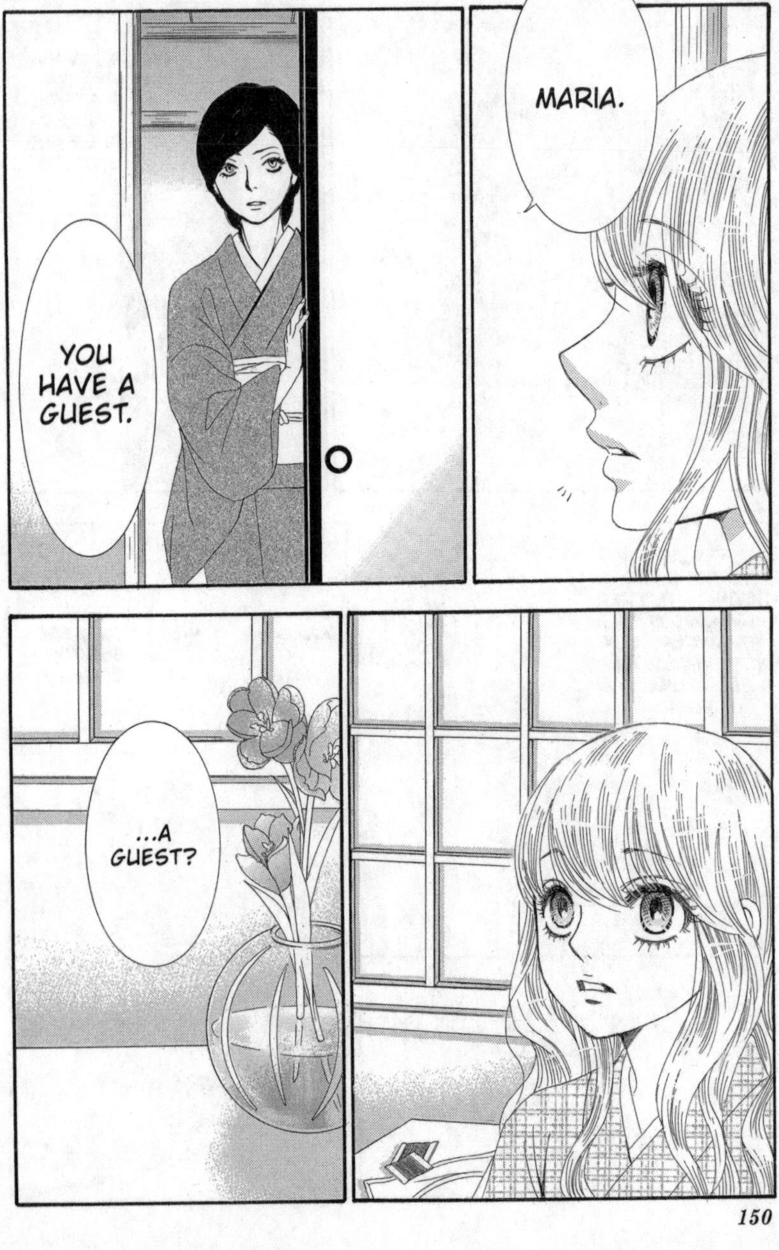
MARIA.
YOU HAVE A GUEST.
...A GUEST?

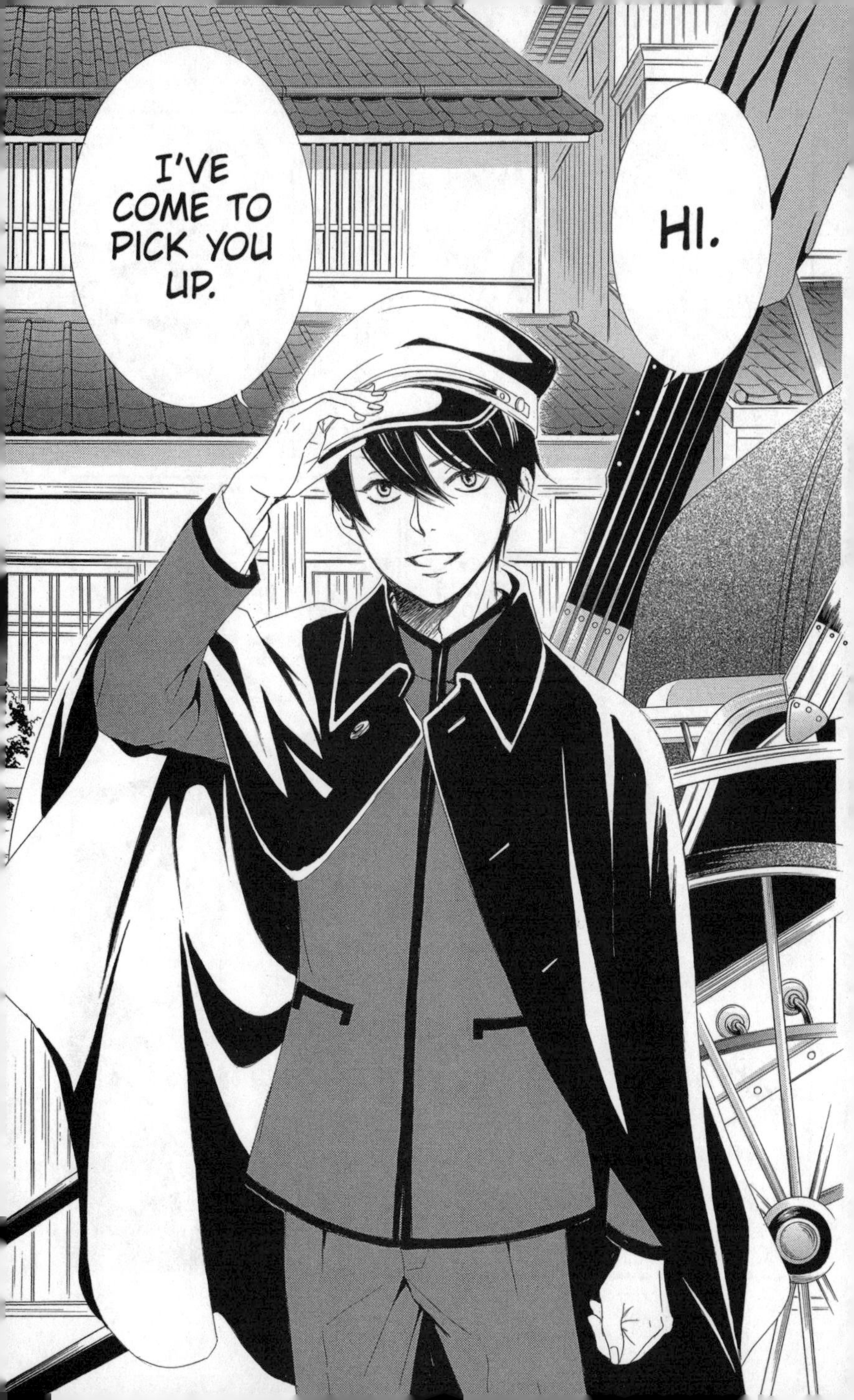
HI.
I'VE COME TO PICK YOU UP.

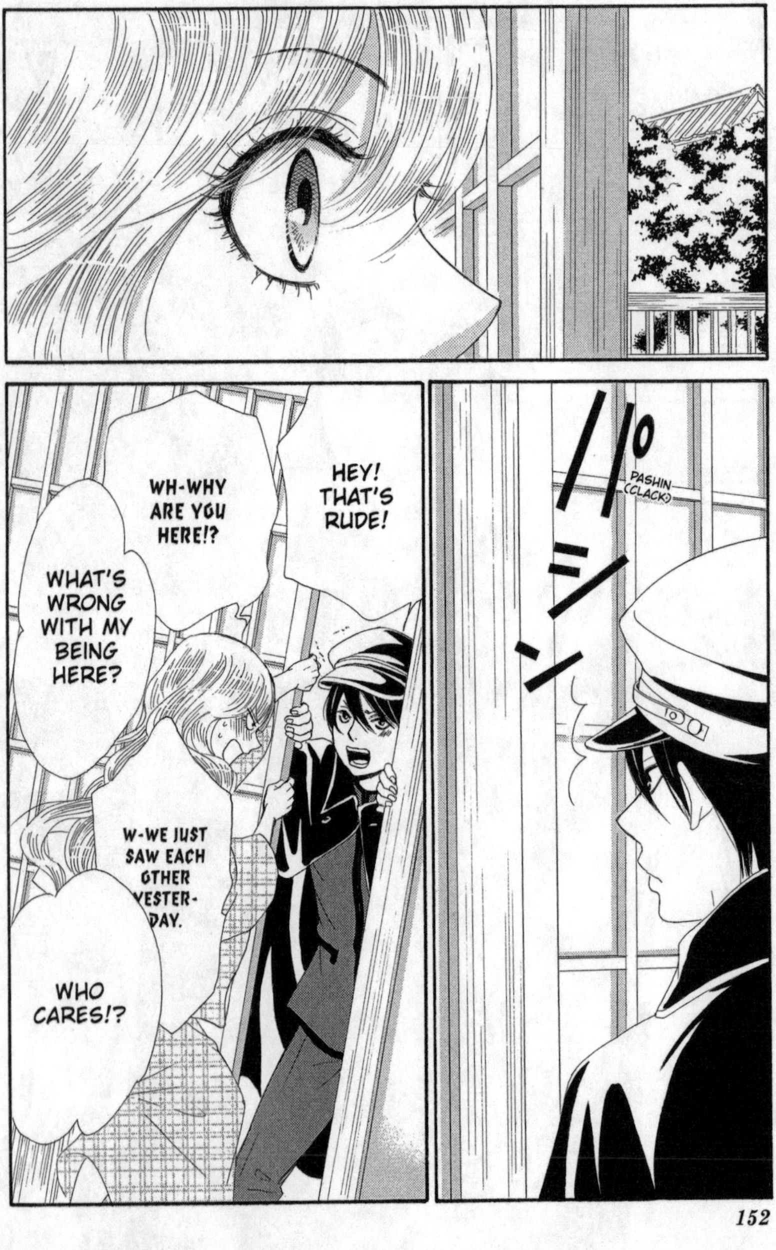
PASHIN (CLACK)
HEY! THAT'S RUDE!
WH-WHY ARE YOU HERE!?
WHAT'S WRONG WITH MY BEING HERE?
W-WE JUST SAW EACH OTHER YESTER-DAY.
WHO CARES!?

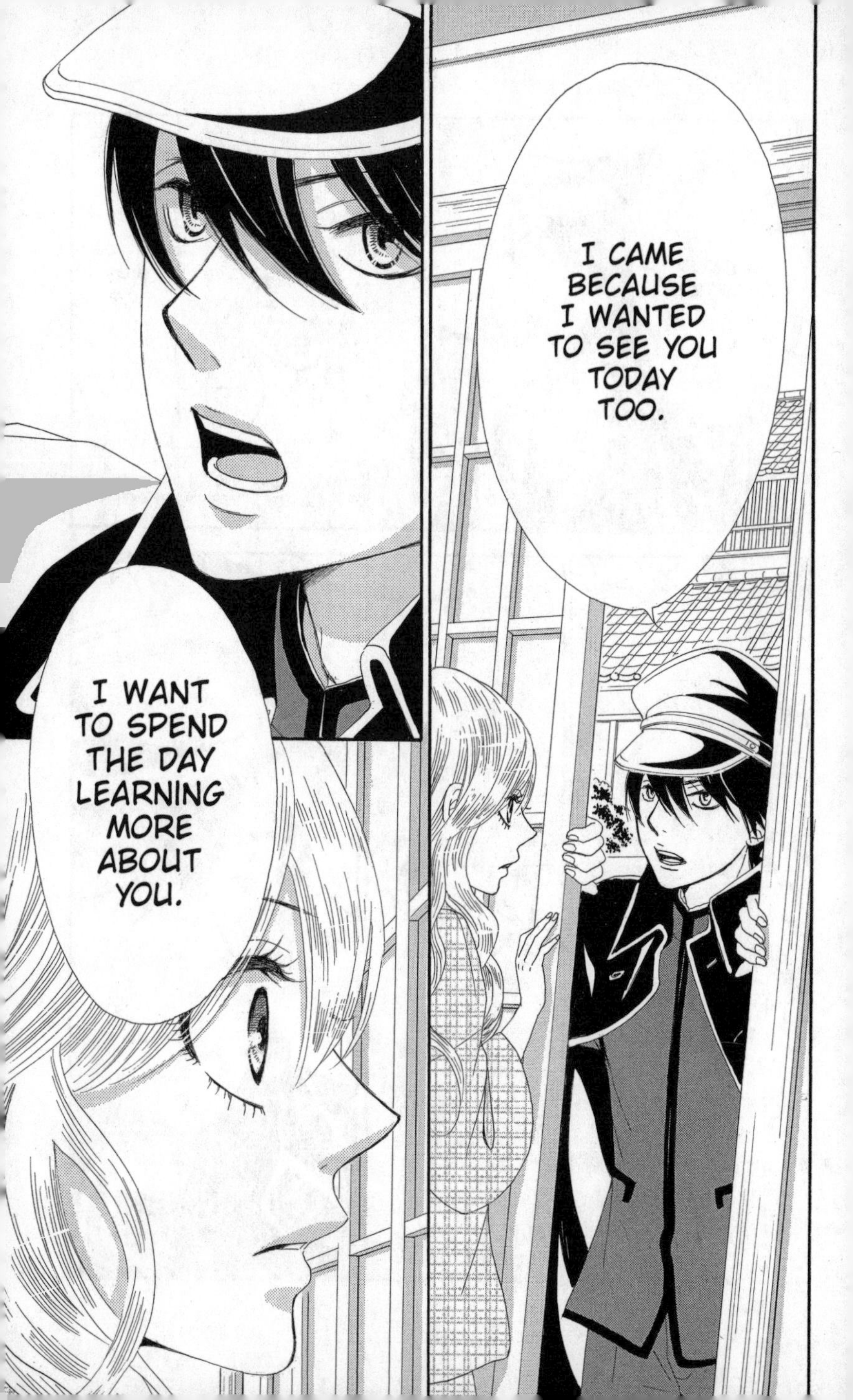
I CAME BECAUSE I WANTED TO SEE YOU TODAY TOO.
I WANT TO SPEND THE DAY LEARNING MORE ABOUT YOU.

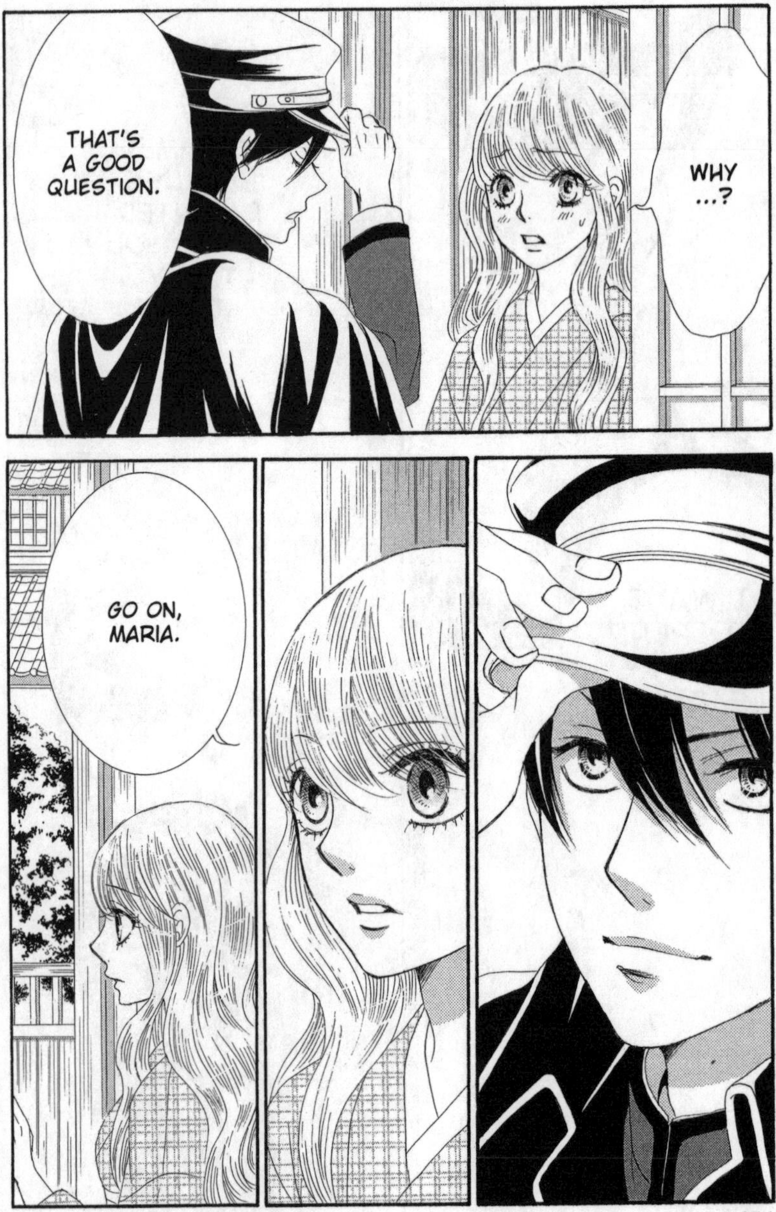
WHY ...?
THAT'S A GOOD QUESTION.
GO ON, MARIA.

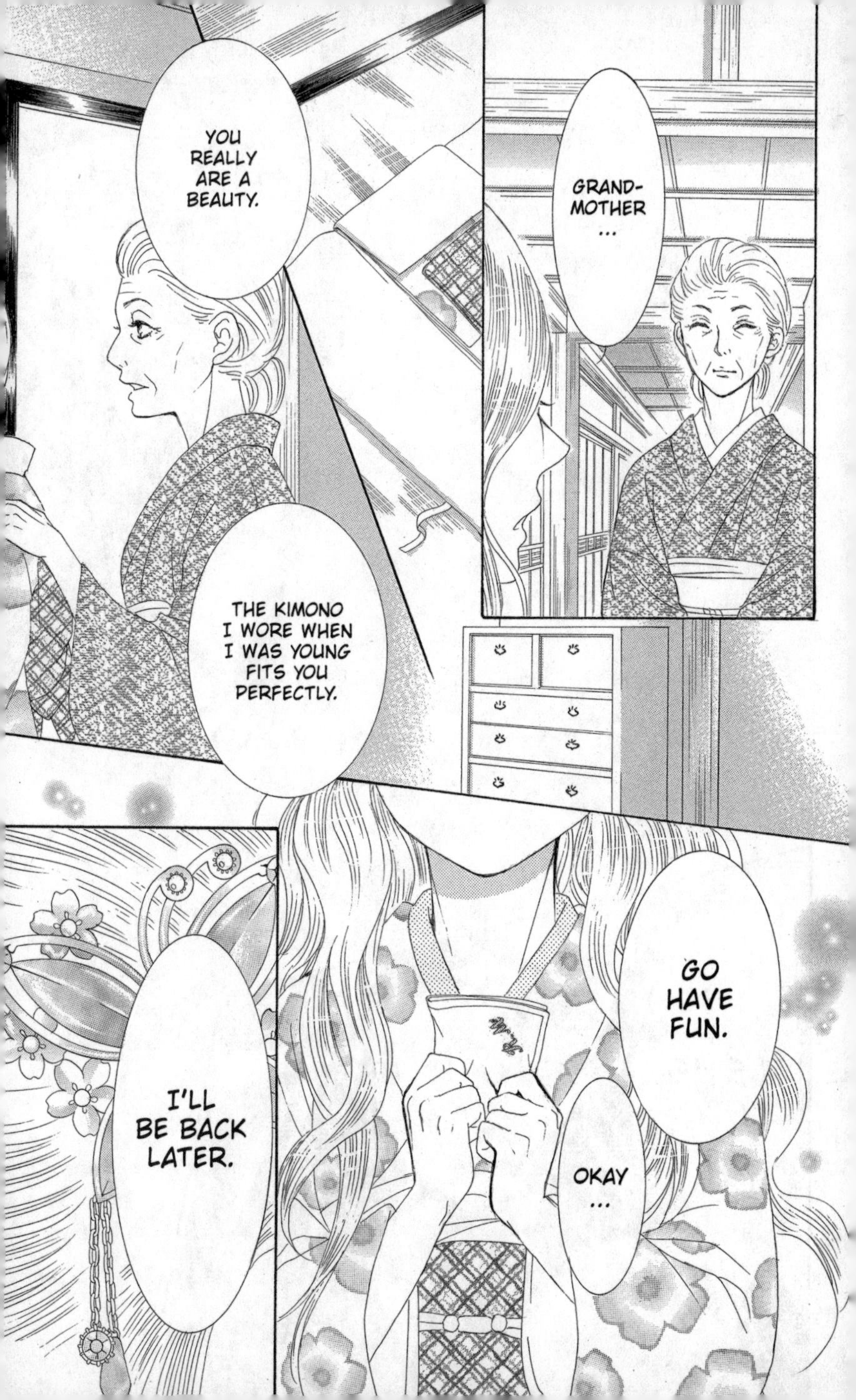
GRAND-MOTHER...
YOU REALLY ARE A BEAUTY.
THE KIMONO I WORE WHEN I WAS YOUNG FITS YOU PERFECTLY.
GO HAVE FUN.
OKAY...
I'LL BE BACK LATER.

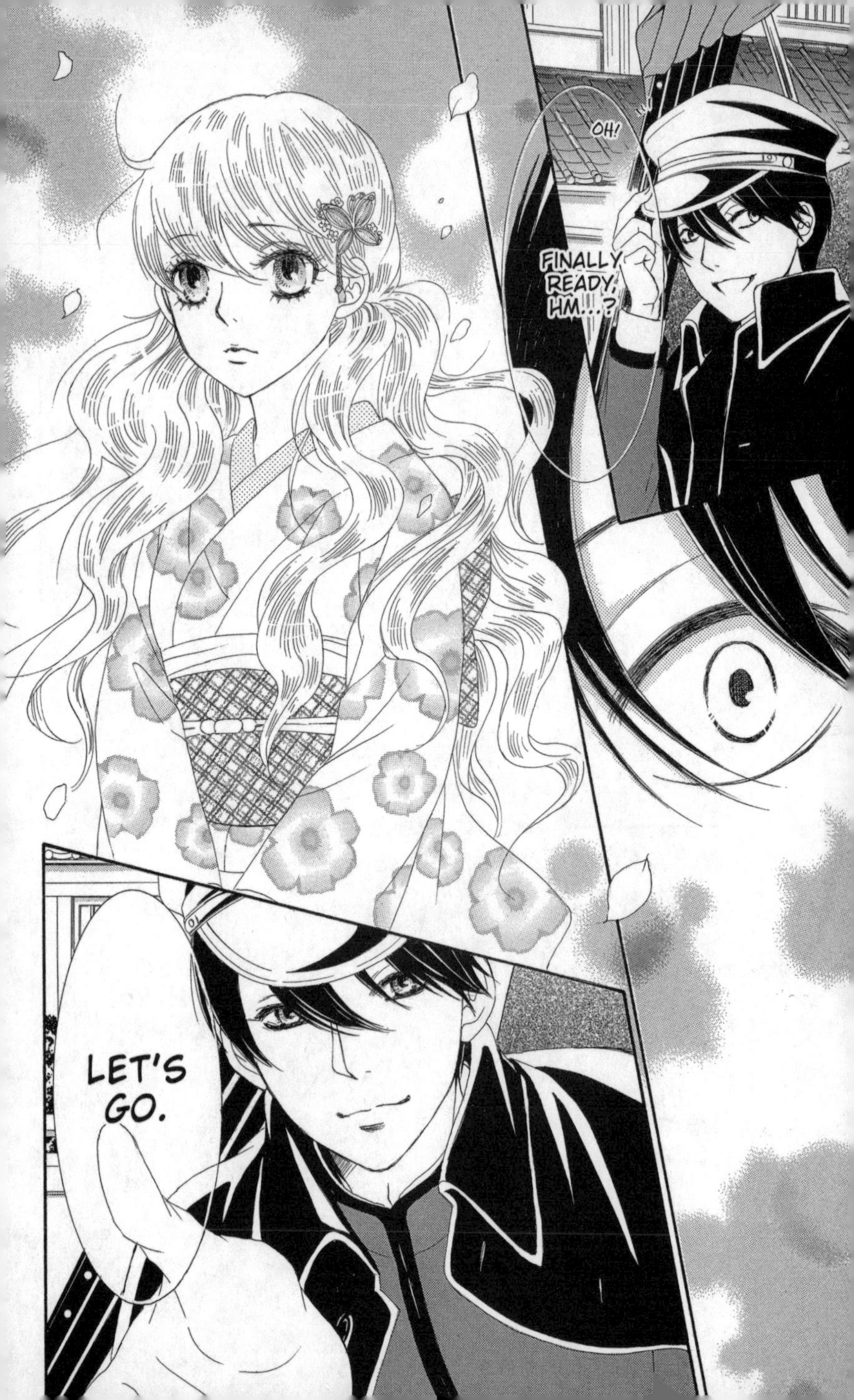
OH!
FINALLY READY, HM...?
LET'S GO.

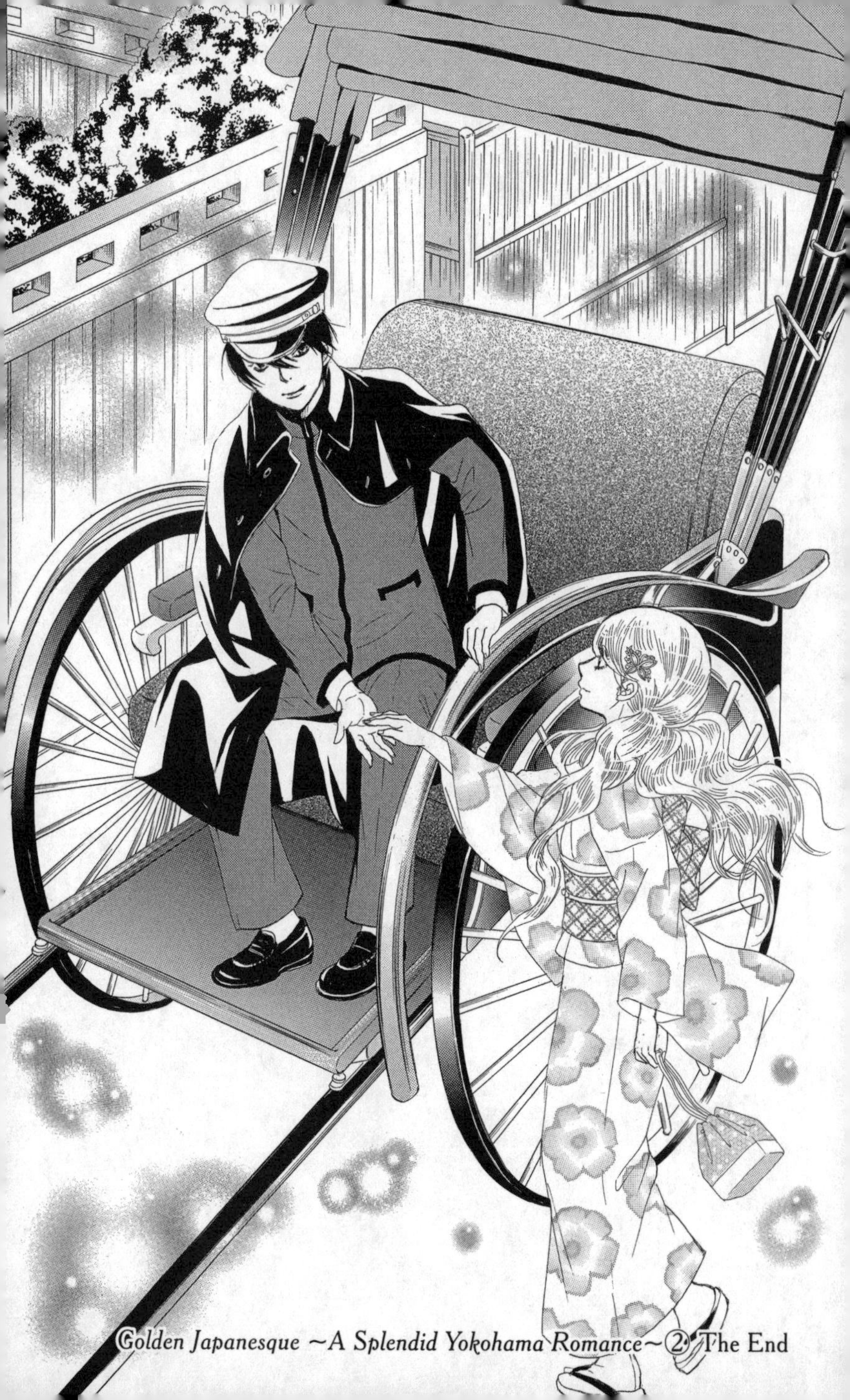
Golden Japanesque ~A Splendid Yokohama Romance~ 2 The End

Special Thanks

■Assistants■

Alice Tsukada
Nozomi Hirama
Ikuko Shiroya
Yuri Sato
T. Sato
R. Nishida

■Editor■
Sanae Morihara

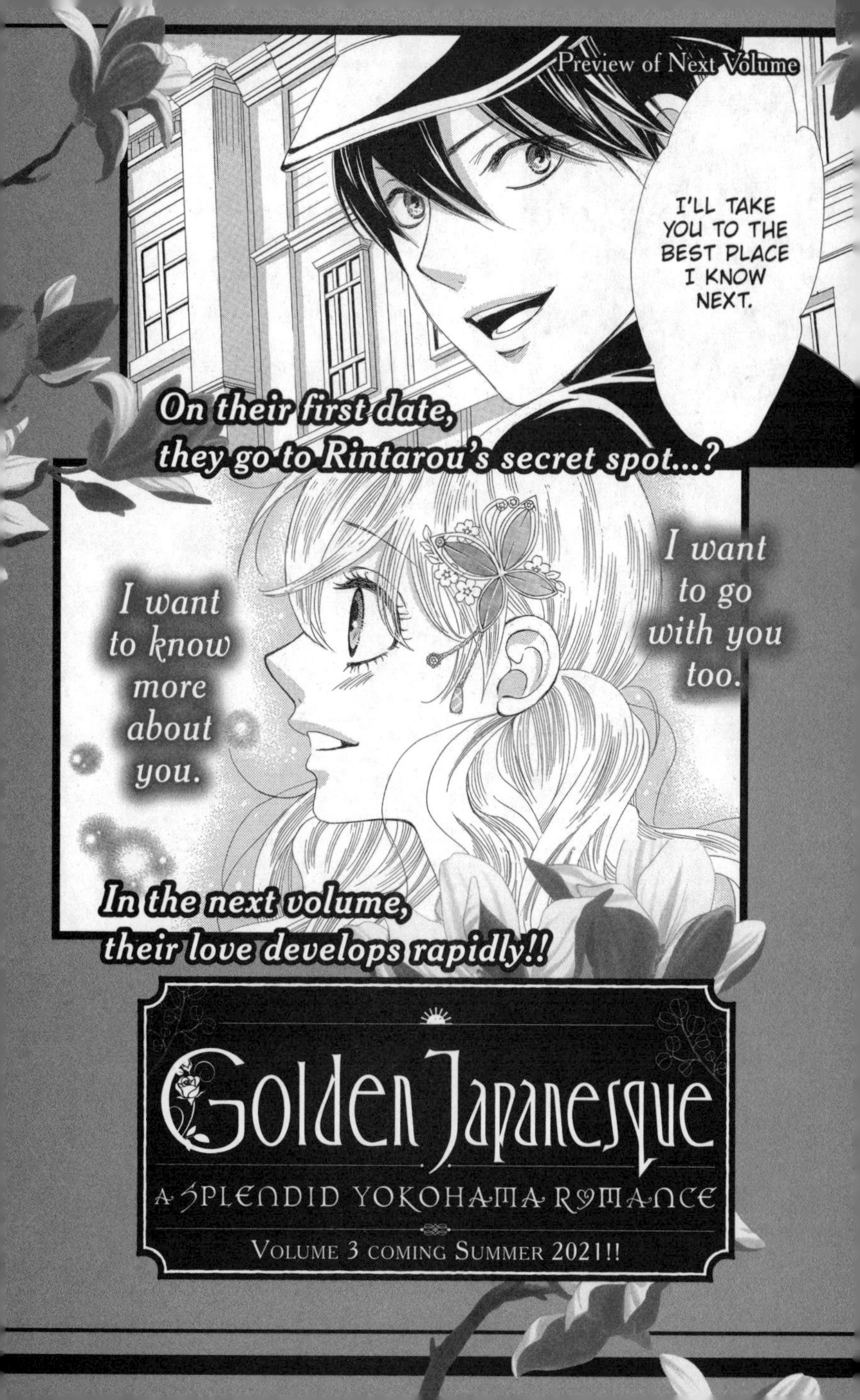
Preview of Next Volume
I'LL TAKE YOU TO THE BEST PLACE I KNOW NEXT.
On their first date, they go to Rintarou's secret spot...?
I want to go with you too.
I want to know more about you.
In the next volume, their love develops rapidly!!
Golden Japanesque
A Splendid Yokohama Romance
Volume 3 coming Summer 2021!!

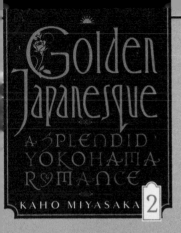

Golden Japanesque
A SPLENDID YOKOHAMA ROMANCE

KAHO MIYASAKA 2

Translation:
TAYLOR ENGEL

Lettering:
LYS BLAKESLEE

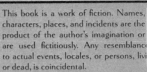

KINIRO JAPANESQUE
-YOKOHAMA KARENTAN- vol.2 by Kaho MIYASAKA
© 2019 Kaho MIYASAKA
All rights reserved.
Original Japanese edition published by SHOGAKUKAN.
English translation rights in the United States of America, Canada, the United Kingdom, Ireland, Australia and New Zealand arranged with SHOGAKUKAN through Tuttle-Mori Agency, Inc.

English translation © 2021 by Yen Press, LLC

Yen Press
150 West 30th Street, 19th Floor
New York, NY 10001

Visit us at yenpress.com
facebook.com/yenpress
twitter.com/yenpress
yenpress.tumblr.com
instagram.com/yenpress

First Yen Press Edition: April 2021

Yen Press is an imprint of Yen Press, LLC.
The Yen Press name and logo are trademarks of Yen Press, LLC.

The publisher is not responsible for websites (or their content) that are not owned by the publisher.

Library of Congress Control Number:
2020948881

ISBNs: 978-1-9753-1978-6 (print)
       978-1-9753-2416-2 (ebook)

10 9 8 7 6 5 4 3 2 1

BVG

Printed in the United States of America

CEYA